TWITTER AND ELECTIONS AROUND THE WORLD

Twitter already has become an important electoral communication tool between candidates, parties, and their specific constituencies. No serious candidate campaign ignores Twitter, while political party organizations utilize Twitter to communicate with partisans, reinforce supporters, and mobilize voters.

Whereas much scholarship to date has focused primarily on Twitter's political usage in the United States, there still remain many questions about the political uses and effects of Twitter in a global context. Does Twitter affect how reporters interact with candidates or even with each other? Does Twitter increase voter participation? Who is tweeting about elections? Why do people use Twitter in electoral contexts? Which type of candidate is more likely to use Twitter and why? Do parties differ in their use of Twitter, and why? Does Twitter increase candidate–voter interaction? Is Twitter shaping elections in various system contexts, and if so how? What is the influence of system context on Twitter use by parties, candidates, reporters, and voters?

Eloquently combining theory and practice, established and rising scholars in the field of political communication have been brought together to provide an essential overview of the influence of Twitter on elections in a comparative perspective. Readers of this book will not only learn everything there is to know about this specific influence of Twitter, but more broadly how to approach the study of various online tools in general.

Richard Davis is Professor of Political Science and Director of the Office of Civic Engagement at Brigham Young University, USA. His research concentrates on political communication, new media, and judicial communication.

Christina Holtz-Bacha is Professor of Communications at the University of Erlangen-Nürnberg, Germany. Her research and instruction focus on political communication and strategic communication as well as German and European media policy.

Marion R. Just is Professor of Political Science at Wellesley College, USA, and an associate of the Shorenstein Center on Media, Politics and Public Policy at Harvard's Kennedy School of Government, USA.

ROUTLEDGE STUDIES IN GLOBAL INFORMATION, POLITICS AND SOCIETY

Edited by Kenneth Rogerson, Duke University and Laura Roselle, Elon University

International communication encompasses everything from one-to-one cross-cultural interactions to the global reach of a broad range of information and communications technologies and processes. *Routledge Studies in Global Information, Politics and Society* celebrates – and embraces – this depth and breadth. To completely understand communication, it must be studied in concert with many factors, since, most often, it is the foundational principle on which other subjects rest. This series provides a publishing space for scholarship in the expansive, yet intersecting, categories of communication and information processes and other disciplines.

1. **Relational, Networked and Collaborative Approaches to Public Diplomacy**
   The Connective Mindshift
   Edited by R. S. Zaharna, Amelia Arsenault, and Ali Fisher

2. **Reporting at the Southern Borders**
   Journalism and Public Debates on Immigration in the US and the EU
   Edited by Giovanna Dell'Orto and Vicki L. Birchfield

3. **Strategic Narratives**
   Communication Power and the New World Order
   Alister Miskimmon, Ben O'Loughlin, and Laura Roselle

4. **Talk Show Campaigns**
   Presidential Candidates on Daytime and Late Night Television
   Michael Parkin

5. **The Networked Young Citizen**
   Social Media, Political Participation and Civic Engagement
   Edited by Brian D. Loader, Ariadne Vromen, and Michael Xenos

6. **Framing War**
   Public Opinion and Decision-Making in Comparative Perspective
   Francesco Olmastroni

7. **Political Communication and Leadership**
   Mimetisation, Hugo Chávez and the Construction of Power and Identity
   Elena Block

8. **The Power of Information Networks**
   New Directions for Agenda Setting
   Edited by Lei Guo and Maxwell McCombs

9. **Television News and Human Rights in the US & UK**
   The Violations Will Not Be Televised
   Shawna M. Brandle

10. **Beyond the Internet**
    Unplugging the Protest Movement Wave
    Edited by Rita Figueiras and Paula do Espírito Santo

11. **Twitter and Elections Around the World**
    Campaigning in 140 Characters or Less
    Edited by Richard Davis, Christina Holtz-Bacha, and Marion Just

12. **Political Communication in Real Time**
    Theoretical and Applied Research Approaches
    Edited by Dan Schill, Rita Kirk, and Amy Jasperson

TWITTER AND ELECTIONS AROUND THE WORLD

Campaigning in 140 Characters or Less

*Edited by Richard Davis,
Christina Holtz-Bacha, and Marion R. Just*

LONDON AND NEW YORK

First published 2017
by Routledge
711 Third Avenue, New York, NY 10017

and by Routledge
2 Park Square, Milton Park, Abingdon, Oxon, OX14 4RN

Routledge is an imprint of the Taylor & Francis Group, an informa business

© 2017 Taylor & Francis

The right of the editors to be identified as the authors of the editorial material, and of the authors for their individual chapters, has been asserted in accordance with sections 77 and 78 of the Copyright, Designs and Patents Act 1988.

All rights reserved. No part of this book may be reprinted or reproduced or utilised in any form or by any electronic, mechanical, or other means, now known or hereafter invented, including photocopying and recording, or in any information storage or retrieval system, without permission in writing from the publishers.

Trademark notice: Product or corporate names may be trademarks or registered trademarks, and are used only for identification and explanation without intent to infringe.

Library of Congress Cataloguing in Publication Data
Names: Davis, Richard, 1955- editor. | Holtz-Bacha, Christina, editor. | Just, Marion R., editor.
Title: Twitter and elections around the world : campaigning in 140 characters or less / edited by Richard Davis, Christina Holtz-Bacha, and Marion Just.
Description: New York, NY: Routledge is an imprint of the
Taylor & Francis Group, an Informa Business, [2016] |
Series: Routledge studies in global information, politics and society; 11 |
Includes bibliographical references and index.
Identifiers: LCCN 2016006523 | ISBN 9781138949348 (hbk) |
ISBN 9781138949355 (pbk)
Subjects: LCSH: Communication in politics–Technological innovations. |
Political campaigns–Technological innovations. |
Political campaigns–Press coverage–Technological innovations. |
Twitter–Political aspects. | Internet in political campaigns. |
Social media–Political aspects.
Classification: LCC JA85.T85 2016 | DDC 324.7/302854692–dc23
LC record available at https://lccn.loc.gov/2016006523

ISBN: 978-1-138-94934-8 (hbk)
ISBN: 978-1-138-94935-5 (pbk)
ISBN: 978-1-315-66911-3 (ebk)

Typeset in Bembo
by Out of House Publishing

Printed and bound in the United States of America by Publishers Graphics, LLC on sustainably sourced paper.

CONTENTS

List of Figures	*viii*
List of Tables	*ix*
Series Editor's Foreword	*xi*
About the Contributors	*xii*

Introduction   1
Marion R. Just and Christina Holtz-Bacha

PART I
Election Journalism   **11**

1   Did Twitter Kill the Boys on the Bus? A Report from
the Romney Campaign in 2012   13
Peter Hamby

2   Tweeting to the Press? Effects of Political Twitter Activity
on Offline Media in the 2013 German Election Campaign   27
Christina Holtz-Bacha and Reimar Zeh

3   US Political Journalists' Use of Twitter: Lessons from
2012 and a Look Ahead   43
Logan Molyneux, Rachel R. Mourão, and Mark Coddington

vi Contents

4 Media Coverage of an Election Campaign on Twitter: The Case of Belgium in the EU Elections 57
Evelien D'heer and Pieter Verdegem

PART II
The Audience 73

5 Communication with Constituents in 140 Characters: How Members of Congress Used Twitter to Get Out the Vote in 2014 75
Heather K. Evans

6 South Korean Citizens' Political Information-Sharing on Twitter During the 2012 General Election 90
Jisue Lee, Hohyon Ryu, Lorri Mon, and Sung Jae Park

PART III
Parties, Candidates, and Campaigns 109

7 Message Repetition in Social Media: Presidential Candidate Twitter Feeds in the 2012 US General Election 111
Kate Kenski and Bethany A. Conway

8 Campaigning on Twitter: The Use of Social Media in the 2014 European Elections in Italy 126
Sara Bentivegna and Rita Marchetti

9 Candidate Use of Twitter and the Intersection of Gender, Party, and Position in the Race: A Comparison of Competitive Male/Female Senate Races in 2012 and 2014 141
Marion R. Just, Ann N. Crigler, and Rose A. Owen

10 Who Gets to Say #AreYouBetterOff? Promoted Trends and Bashtagging in the 2012 US Presidential Election 159
Joel Penney

11 Parties, Leaders, and Online Personalization: Twitter in Canadian Electoral Politics 173
Tamara A. Small

Contents **vii**

12 Social Media Coming of Age: Developing Patterns of
Congressional Twitter Use, 2007–14   190
David S. Lassen and Leticia Bode

13 From a Tweet to a Seat: Twitter, Media Visibility, and
Electoral Support   207
Reimar Zeh

Conclusion   222
Richard Davis

Index   *229*

LIST OF FIGURES

2.1	Number of tweets of selected Twitter accounts over time	34
4.1	Spring-embedding representation of the relation between media sources and political candidates	67
6.1	Magnitude of entire retweeted messages	99
6.2	Magnitude of top 40 retweeted messages	99
6.3	Results from classification of types of messages	101
6.4	Clustering of supported and unsupported message types	102
6.5	Classification of messages for three classes	103
6.6	Results from sentiment identification	105
9.1	Sample tweet	149
9.2	Attacks by gender and position in the race	149
9.3	Gender by mention of economy versus jobs in candidate tweets	152
9.4	Mean favorites by candidate gender, party and position in the race	154
9.5	Mean favorites by candidate gender, party and position in the race	156

LIST OF TABLES

2.1 The Sample	31
2.2 Issues dealt with in the tweets	36
2.3 Determinants of favorites	37
2.4 Determinants of the retweet rate	39
2.5 Twitter activity and presence of parties in the media	40
4.1 Categories of media sources	64
5.1 CIRCLE's civic engagement indicators	77
5.2 US House average number of tweets regarding civic engagement, 2014	80
5.3 Average number and percent of tweets regarding civic engagement for the US House, 2014	80
5.4 Negative binomial regression results for the US House, 2014	81
5.5 US Senate average number of tweets regarding civic engagement, 2014	83
5.6 Average number and percent of tweets regarding civic engagement for the US House, 2014	84
5.7 Negative binomial regression results for the US Senate, 2014	85
6.1 Codebook of eight message types	96
6.2 Results of public opinion polls for six weeks	100
6.3 Pearson correlation between retweeted message and public opinion poll	100
6.4 Results from classification of message types for three keywords	104
6.5 Pearson correlations among types of message and public opinion	104
6.6 Results from sentiments identification	105
6.7 Pearson correlations among sentiments and public opinion	106
7.1 Candidate, campaign, and party tweeting activity between August 1 and November 6, 2012	118

x   List of Tables

7.2	Candidate, campaign, and party tweets between August 1 and September 30, 2012	119
7.3	Candidate, campaign, and party retweeting activity between August 1 and November 6, 2012	120
7.4	Duplication percentage of August 1 through November 6, 2012 tweets between sources (three-word matches)	121
7.5	Duplication percentages between August tweets and September tweets within sources (three words)	121
8.1	Active users, Twitter users and tweet productivity by political party	129
8.2	Types of tweet by party	130
8.3	Hashtag use by party	133
8.4	Functions of tweets by party	134
8.5	Tweeting style by party	136
8.6	Tweeting styles and year of account creation	137
8.7	Tweeting styles by number of followers acquired during the campaign	137
9.1	US Senate candidates for 2012 and 2014 elections	146
9.2A	US Senate candidates' use of Twitter during the 2012 general election (October 9-16, 2012 and October 31 to November 6, 2012)	147
9.2B	US Senate candidates' use of Twitter during the 2014 general election (September 1 to November 3, 2014)	148
9.3	Sample mean tweets, retweets, and favorites by gender and party of candidates in 2012 and 2014 (rounded to the nearest tweet)	148
9.4	Gender by focus of tweets, 2012 and 2014	151
9.5	Gender of candidates by mention of issues in candidates' tweets, 2012 and 2014	153
9.6	Party by race of people in candidates' Twitter images, 2012 and 2014	154
11.1	Tweeting in the 2011 federal election by account	179
11.2	Tweet personalization coding scheme	180
11.3	Twitter followers in the 2011 federal election	180
11.4	Twitter personalization in the 2011 federal election	182
12.1	Total tweets posted by year	198
12.2	Member users by year	198
12.3	Total tweets by member and year	199
12.4	Structural features of member tweets	200
12.5	Content features of member tweets	201
13.1	Election result and dataset	214
13.2	Twitter activity by party affiliation	214
13.3	Generalized linear model: Explaining electoral support for parliamentary candidates	215
13.4	Generalized linear model: Electoral support by parties	216
13.5	Generalized linear model: Electoral support through communicative styles	218

SERIES EDITOR'S FOREWORD

During elections in democratic polities, a candidate's main goal is to communicate with potential supporters, the holders of the votes needed to win an election. Over time, these messages have been targeted at diverse segments of society—from shady attempts to influence those who can "pad the ballot box" to opinion leading elites and workaday citizens. Where does Twitter fit into this spectrum of potential voter persuasion and candidate utilization?

Richard Davis, Christina Holtz-Bacha and Marion Just provide the answers to this question in the present edited volume. Twitter is influential, but there are caveats. Twitter is pervasive, but doesn't reach as large a population as other communications channels. The editors leave us with a very satisfying understanding of the global and cross-cultural role that this example of microblogging plays in political processes around the world. They not only deepen our knowledge but encourage us to question Twitter's uses and impact.

Ken Rogerson

ABOUT THE CONTRIBUTORS

Sara Bentivegna is a professor of political communication at the University of Rome "Sapienza." She is the author of several books on the web and politics in Italy including *A colpi di tweet* (*Shots of Tweets*, il Mulino, 2015), *La politica in 140 caratteri* (*Politics in 140 Characters*, FrancoAngeli, 2014), *Parlamento 2.0* (*Parliament 2.0*, FrancoAngeli, 2012), and *Disuguaglianze digitali* (*Digital Inequalities*, Laterza, 2009).

Leticia Bode is an assistant professor in the communication, culture, and technology Master's program at Georgetown University. She received her PhD in political science from the University of Wisconsin—Madison, and her Bachelor's degree from Trinity University. Her work lies at the intersection of communication, technology, and political behavior, emphasizing the role communication and information technologies may play in political information, political communication, and political mobilization. For more on Bode's work, see https://lbode. wordpress.com.

Mark Coddington is an assistant professor in the Department of Journalism and Mass Communications at Washington and Lee University, where he teaches and studies digital journalism and media sociology. A contributor to Harvard University's Nieman Journalism Lab and former newspaper reporter, he has been published in *Mass Communication and Society*, *Journalism & Mass Communication Quarterly*, and the *International Journal of Communication*.

Bethany A. Conway is an assistant professor of communication studies at California Polytechnic State University who specializes in political communication, persuasion, and social influence. Her research focuses on news coverage of and collective sense-making in politics. This includes the role of new media in political campaigns and its influence on journalistic outcomes, as well as the networks of sources that journalists turn to for information on elections and government policy. Her research has been published in the *American Behavioral Scientist*, *Journal of Computer-Mediated Communication*, and *International Journal of Public Opinion Research*.

Ann N. Crigler is professor of political science with appointments in the Price School of Public Policy and the Annenberg School for Communications at the University of Southern California. She has published numerous articles and essays on political communication, elections, emotions and political behavior as well as co-authored, edited, or co-edited five books. These include: *Common Knowledge: News and the Construction of Political Meaning* (University of Chicago Press, 1992); the award-winning *Crosstalk: Citizens, Candidates and the Media in a Presidential Campaign* (University of Chicago Press, 1996); *The Psychology of Political Communication* (University of Michigan Press, 1996); *Rethinking the Vote: The Politics and Prospects of American Election Reform* (Oxford University Press, 2004); and *The Affect Effect: Dynamics of Emotion in Political Thinking and Behavior* (University of Chicago Press, 2007). Her current research examines the role of social media in US Senate elections, emotions and political decision-making, and youth civic engagement. She and her students are currently working with elementary schools in Los Angeles to conduct research and increase children's civic skills, involvement, and community networks through the USC Penny Harvest.

Richard Davis is a professor of political science and director of the Office of Civic Engagement at Brigham Young University. He is the author or co-author of several books on media and politics including *New Media and American Politics* (Oxford University Press, 1998) with Diana Owen; *The Web of Politics* (Oxford University Press, 1999); and *Campaigning Online* (Oxford University Press, 2003) with Bruce Bimber. He is co-editor of *Making a Difference: A Comparative View of the Role of the Internet in Election Politics* (Lexington Books, 2008) with Stephen Ward, David Taras, and Diana Owen.

Evelien D'heer is PhD candidate in new media and information and communication technologies (iMinds) in the Department of Communication Sciences at Ghent University, Belgium. Her main research interests are in the role of social media in the public debate, and more specifically the altering relations between political actors, media, and citizens.

Heather K. Evans is an associate professor in the Department of Political Science at Sam Houston State University. Her primary research interests are political engagement, competitive Congressional elections, female representation in the discipline, social media (Twitter), and the effect of entertainment media on political attitudes.

xiv About the Contributors

Peter Hamby is head of news at Snapchat, running the mobile app's original news and politics content. Prior to joining Snapchat, Hamby covered five election cycles for CNN as a producer and national political reporter. Hamby was spring 2013 fellow at Harvard University's Shorenstein Center on Media, Politics, and Public Policy. A native of Richmond, Virginia, he is a graduate of Georgetown University and New York University's graduate school of journalism.

Christina Holtz-Bacha is professor of communications at the School of Business and Economics, University of Erlangen-Nürnberg, Germany. She studied communications, political science and sociology. She received her PhD at the University of Münster and her postdoctoral dissertation (Habilitation) in Hannover. Prior to her current position she has taught at the universities of Munich, Bochum, and Mainz. In 1986, she was a visiting scholar at the University of Minnesota in Minneapolis. In 1999, she was a research fellow at the Shorenstein Center, Harvard University. In 2011, she was a guest researcher at the University of Gothenburg, Sweden. She is a co-editor of the German journal *Publizistik* and a member of the editorial boards of several international journals. Her main research interests are in political communication, media systems, and (European) media policy.

Marion R. Just is a professor of political science at Wellesley College and an associate at the Shorenstein Center on Media, Politics, and Public Policy at Harvard's Kennedy School. Her research in political science focuses on elections, politics, and the media. She is a co-author of *Crosstalk: Citizens, Candidates and the Media in a Presidential Campaign* and *Common Knowledge: News and the Construction of Political Meaning*,

Kate Kenski is an associate professor of communication at the University of Arizona where she teaches political communication, public opinion, and research methods. Her book *The Obama Victory: How Media, Money, and Message Shaped the 2008 Election* (co-authored with Bruce W. Hardy and Kathleen Hall Jamieson; Oxford University Press, 2010) has won several awards including the 2011 ICA Outstanding Book Award, 2012 NCA Diamond Anniversary Book Award, and the 2012 NCA Political Communication Division Roderick P. Hart Outstanding Book Award. Kenski is also co-author of the book *Capturing Campaign Dynamics: The National Annenberg Election Survey* (Oxford University Press, 2004). Her current research focuses on social media and politics, incivility in online forums, and multimedia teaching strategies to mitigate cognitive biases.

David S. Lassen is a doctoral candidate in the Department of Political Science at the University of Wisconsin-Madison. His research centers on the nature and consequences of political communication in the modern, often conversational media environment. His current projects examine elite use of social media, the role of humor in American politics, mass political participation, and media coverage of government officials and institutions.

Jisue Lee is a doctoral candidate in the School of Information at Florida State University. Her research interests lie in how individuals engage in collaborative information behaviors with others for political communication, deliberation, decision-making, and collective actions toward social movements via ever-changing technologies. Her dissertation examines South Korean citizens' information-sharing behaviors on Twitter during 2014 Seoul mayoral election.

Rita Marchetti is a postdoctoral research fellow and lecturer in "Theory and Techniques of Digital Media" at the University of Perugia. Her research interests are social aspects of Web 2.0 applications, with particular attention to the introduction of social media in politics and in religion. She is the author of *La Chiesa in internet. La sfida dei media digitali* (*The Church in the Internet: The Challenge of Digital Media*, Carocci, 2015). Her publications have appeared in *European Journal of Communication* and *Journalism Practice*.

Logan Molyneux is an assistant professor of journalism at Temple University. His research focuses on digital media and mobile technology, specifically as they relate to journalistic practices and products. Recent work includes studies of learning from mobile news, how journalists use social media in political coverage, and personal branding among journalists.

Lorri Mon is an associate professor in the School of Information at Florida State University's College of Communication and Information. Her research examines online information services in e-government, online education, and digital libraries, particularly focusing on emerging digital technologies such as social media, chat, email, instant messaging, SMS text messaging mobile technologies, and virtual worlds. She is the co-author with Dr. Christie Koontz of the recently published book *Marketing & Social Media: A Guide for Libraries, Archives & Museums.*

Rachel R. Mourão (MA, University of Florida) is a doctoral candidate at the University of Texas at Austin. Her research focuses on political communication, protests, gender, new media, and Latin American studies. She is particularly interested in the relationship between government, media, and social movements when facing event-driven news. Her work has appeared in several journals, including *Journalism: Theory, Practice and Criticism, International Journal of Communication, Digital Journalism,* and *Journal of Information Technology & Politics.*

Rose A. Owen is a PhD student in Political Science at the University of Chicago. She is interested in feminist political theory and statistics.

xvi About the Contributors

Sung Jae Park is an assistant professor at Hansung University in Korea. Currently, he is interested in several public library issues and space concepts, in particular the social significance of libraries, connecting LIS with geography and sociology, in that social relationships among people in the library are studied in the context of geographical space. He has been awarded as the 2013 winner of the Jesse H. Shera Award for Distinguished Published Research for the article, "Measuring Public Library Accessibility: A Case Study Using GIS," by the Library Research Round Table (LRRT).

Joel Penney is an assistant professor in the School of Communication and Media at Montclair State University. His research focuses on symbolic political expression in online venues, with particular attention to processes of peer persuasion. His writing has appeared in journals such as *New Media & Society*, *Convergence*, and *The Journal of Computer-Mediated Communication*. He is currently at work on his first book, entitled *The Citizen-Marketer: Political Promotion and Participatory Media*, and also runs the blog *Viral Politics*.

Hohyon Ryu is a senior software engineer at Twitter. He has worked in the Language Engineering team and Search Quality team. He is the author of an open-source Korean processing library, Twitter-Korean-Text (https://github.com/twitter/twitter-korean-text).

Tamara A. Small is an associate professor in the Department of Political Science at the University of Guelph. Her research interests focus is digital politics: use and impact of the Internet by Canadian political actors. She is the co-author of *Fighting for Votes: Parties, the Media and Voters in an Ontario Election* (UBC Press) and the co-editor of *Political Communication in Canada: Meet the Press, Tweet the Rest* (UBC Press) and *Mind the Gaps: Canadian Perspectives on Gender and Politics* (Fernwood Press).

Pieter Verdegem is an assistant professor in new media and information and communication technologies in the Department of Communication Sciences at Ghent University, Belgium. His main research interests are in ICT and society, social media, new media and ICT policies and governance, including the political economy of the media.

Reimar Zeh is assistant professor in communication at the University of Erlangen-Nürnberg. His research interests are in political communication, environmental communication, and social media.

INTRODUCTION

Marion R. Just and Christina Holtz-Bacha

The microblogging platform Twitter was founded in 2006. By the second quarter of 2015, there were 304 million people around the world actively using this social media platform—a tenfold increase in five years. While Twitter use in the United States is leveling off, it is still increasing dramatically in other countries (Statista 2015a). Eighty percent of global users use cellphones to access Twitter. In the United States alone, there are 65 million users—a penetration of more than 15 percent.

Twitter has a fraction of the penetration of Facebook, which is nearly half of the US adult population (Statista 2015b). Nevertheless, Twitter still has growth potential in other areas of the world. The most significant growth area for it is in the South and East Asia, although China has limited Twitter in preference to its own (controlled) microblogging platform. The Western European penetration rate is about 10 percent, with lower rates in Latin America (mostly Argentina, Mexico, and Brazil), Eastern Europe, and the Middle East.

The potential to reach Twitter's audience has led many politicians to adopt Twitter accounts, especially since the 2008 US presidential campaign, when Barack Obama posted his first tweet:

Barack Obama
✓@BarackObama
Thinking we're only one signature away from ending the war in Iraq. Learn more
    at www.barackobama.com
3:04 PM–29 Apr 2007

Obama, as candidate and then president of the United States, remains the most "followed" political figure in the world on Twitter (with 62.5 million followers), with India's prime minister Narendra Modi second at 16.7 million followers. Even popes use Twitter. A year before the 2016 presidential election, large numbers of followers were drawn to candidates such as Donald Trump (4.7 million), Hillary Clinton (4.6 million), Bernie Sanders (800,000), and Marco Rubio (937,000). Down-ballot candidates around the world have embraced Twitter.

Twitter possesses certain advantages for candidates. First, it is a campaign tool that is easily controlled by candidates. The content is not filtered through traditional journalists. Politicians can tweet what they wish and as often as they wish. They also can create a sense of intimacy with voters, particularly if candidates themselves actually tweet. Like other social media, Twitter is not necessarily a tool for converting undecided voters. Rather, candidates mainly find it handy for communicating with activist followers and raising money.

Political journalists use Twitter differently from candidates but are no less active. They depend on Twitter to gauge public sentiment during campaigns, follow breaking news, and communicate with each other. The public—especially educated young people—is increasingly relying on Twitter as a daily source of news, and candidates go where the voters are. This volume compares the use of Twitter in election campaigns worldwide, focusing on these key political actors—the candidates, the media, and the public.

When Did Research Begin on Twitter?

The whole world anxiously followed the Iranian protests about the 2009 elections, often called the Twitter Revolution, although the Moldovan parliamentary election protests a few months before actually deserve to be known as the first. The first studies of the political uses of Twitter began almost as soon as it was founded, but the election studies really took off in 2010 (Google Scholar search for twitter/election).

Scholars have concentrated on the use of Twitter by candidates, parties, and legislators and books on the topic were published as early as 2011. Research has shown that candidates use Twitter mostly as a top-down rather than an interactive form of communication. The greatest use of Twitter is for campaign purposes rather than debating policy. Campaigning on Twitter is characterized by mobilizing and reinforcing activists and raising money. Interestingly, candidates rarely engage with other candidates or parties through Twitter, perhaps because their audiences are primarily supporters who are both self-motivated and fairly homogeneous (Borondo et al. 2012; Mirer and Bode 2015).

Candidates' Use of Twitter

A goal of candidates in using Twitter is to attract the attention of traditional media to their campaigns (Chadwick 2013; Solop 2010; Jungherr 2013a). Parties and candidates with built-in support (especially incumbents or major parties) are generally less interested in Twitter than candidates from minor parties or outside the establishment (Conway et al. 2013; Evans et al. 2014; Gainous and Wagner 2014; Kim and Park 2012).

Several researchers emphasize that candidates predominantly use Twitter for campaign purposes, to announce their campaigns, post campaign updates, and provide their followers with opportunities to volunteer and to get involved with the campaign (Abroms and Lefebvre 2009; Parmelee and Bichard 2012; Gainous and Wagner 2014). Drumming up cash as well as followers is another reason for Twitter use in the United States (Hong 2013; for a contrary view on organizing, see Graham et al. 2013).

Most candidates use Twitter as a broadcasting device (Elter 2013; Graham et al. 2013; Grusell and Nord 2012; Macnamara 2011). Parties use Twitter primarily in the broadcasting mode, especially in party- rather than candidate-oriented systems. Parties use Twitter to convey information to supporters and as another channel for political advertising (Jungherr 2012; Klinger 2013).

So far, politicians' Twitter usage is not very sophisticated. Many scholars who have studied the subject find not only that interaction with the public is sparse, but common Twitter communication devices, such as hashtags, @users, hot links, and images are underused in campaigning. Some researchers have made the tantalizing discovery, however, that using these dialogic conventions increases vote share (Gilmore 2011; Gainous and Wagner 2014).

One of the key findings in the study of Twitter use by politicians is that there are remarkable, and not always well-explained, differences between competing candidates and parties (Vergeer et al. 2013; Gainous and Wagner 2014; Ammann 2010; Evans et al. 2014; Bruns and Highfield 2013; Elter 2013; Graham et al. 2013; Lilleker and Jackson 2010). There are also cultural differences in the use of Twitter cross-nationally. For example, in South Korea politicians of the same party tend to follow each other as a matter of courtesy (Kim and Park 2012).

Journalists on Twitter

As with politicians, using Twitter in their reporting is "normal" for journalists. From a research standpoint, however, there is less study about how journalists use Twitter in following campaigns. We do know that along with celebrities, politicians, and business entities, journalists are among the largest group of "verified" Twitter users—25 percent overall (https://medium.com/@Haje/who-are-twitter-s-verified-users-af976fc1b032). Studies of journalists' use of Twitter are hampered because reporters rarely identify Twitter as a source for their stories about campaigns. They follow Twitter to track breaking news stories and to see what information other journalists have on a developing story. They share what they have found—in a sense, advertising themselves and their news outlet (Newman 2010). We know anecdotally that journalists follow politicians during elections in the hopes of finding a quotable remark that they can use in their coverage of the campaign. Using social media instead of having to physically follow candidates is cost-effective and efficient for journalists (Broersma and Graham 2012). To better understand journalists' behavior on Twitter, it will be necessary to conduct more research by interviewing and tracking journalists individually.

Public's Use of Twitter in Elections

The public uses Twitter throughout election campaigns, but there are notable spikes in activity around television events, especially party or candidate debates. In the United States, Twitter has actually sponsored several general election and primary debates. Other campaign events are also reflected in increased Twitter activity, with the highest peak on Election Day itself.

In all of the systems in which Twitter operates, there are only a small number of active users. Most active users are politicians, celebrities, and journalists. Active Twitter users, of those who are not using it in the course of their professions, are concentrated among the young and well-educated. A surprising number of young people depend on interactive Internet media for news, although Facebook surpasses Twitter for this purpose. A study of US Twitter users showed that people who used Twitter more than Facebook for news were younger, more educated, and more likely to access the platform on their cellphones (Mitchell and Guskin 2013).

The most active Twitter users are people who are most attentive to politics, which inevitably means, the most partisan users. As a result, the Twitterverse exhibits strong hemophilic behavior with clusters around parties or ideologies (Bekafigo and McBride 2013; Conover et al. 2012). When citizens tweet about the election, they generally comment about parties and candidates, rather than policies (unless the policy is about the Internet itself), but the tone of their assessments tend to be more negative than other forms of campaign communication (Dang-Xuan et al. 2013; Burgess and Bruns 2012). In one German study, there was no mistaking the sentiment because users identified their feelings with specific negative hashtags (Jungherr 2013b).

There is strong evidence of intermediation in the public's use of Twitter. When there are high-profile events such as political party conventions or debates, Twitter activity surges (Hanna et al. 2013; Larsson and Moe 2013). The phenomenon of "live tweeting" ongoing events, gives the public an opportunity to participate with the more professional media users. In general, the professional comments on the event are more likely to spread on the Internet than those by ordinary users, and most users interact with the professional users, rather than with other ordinary users (Hawthorne et al. 2013; Mascaro and Goggins 2012).

Network behavior of retweeting differs from user-to-user interaction. Retweeting reflects homophily, while user interactions reflect an attempt to convert opponents. Honing a tweet that is meant to be retweeted is somewhat of an art and there are programs to help people develop a tweeting style that results in retweets. The key to stimulating retweeting is to express emotions in tweets. Other research shows that tweets conveying emotions—negative or positive—were more likely to be retweeted. User-to-user tweeting may be useful for public deliberation, because the non-retweet networks are integrated across partisan and ideological lines (Stieglitz and Dang-Xuan 2012).

Using Twitter to Predict Election Outcomes

Whether the Twitter conversation can be useful in predicting election outcomes is open to debate. Some early analyses claimed that simply counting the number of mentions of a party would predict the election outcome (Tumasjan et al. 2010). Many journalists were thrilled with the idea that they could get a jump on polling simply by following Twitter, but considerable doubt was cast on the process by observing more election practices. The case of the German Pirate Party was especially useful in pouring cold water on the concept that more tweets would result in more votes. The Pirate Party was originally a party of young hackers and its strength was based on the Internet. The party surely had the most tweets, but it failed to meet the 5 percent threshold for parliamentary representation. Since then, researchers have stepped back to consider the circumstances in which Twitter activity might predict outcomes (Gayo-Avello 2013; Jungherr et al. 2012).

Recent Trends

Whatever its predictive power, Twitter attracts researchers because it lends itself to the simplest form of content analysis. Most research on Twitter has been carried out with at least partial hand-coding of tweets. Tabulating the number of tweets with certain characteristics may sound elementary, but like most content analysis, it is robust. Still results can be difficult to replicate across time and systems because the Twitter platform itself is undergoing constant change in a competitive environment. In the past few years, Twitter has added images, Moments (a compilation of popular tweets), "instant news," and direct tweeting networks. The demographics of the users change and the relative advantage of one party over another varies with the political context.

The emphasis in many contemporary studies has shifted to rhetorical devices on Twitter, such as the use of hashtags, @users, and keyword searches. Machine coding of sentiment is gaining in sophistication and popularity with researchers. Newer studies have used Big Data, namely the Twitter "Firehose," to conduct analysis of large volumes of tweets and to map user spaces. In order to carry out

6 Marion R. Just and Christina Holtz-Bacha

these studies, researchers require access to very large computers. Twitter depositories (such as the US Library of Congress) have made it possible to search historical collections of tweets as well as conduct real-time analysis. The prospects are exciting for more collaborative and international research using Twitter resources.

This Volume

This volume is the first to bring together scholars and practitioners to address the influence of Twitter on elections in a comparative perspective. The scholars gathered for this volume have explored Twitter's electoral role from a variety of facets as well as system contexts. In previous volumes, attention has been paid to Twitter's electoral role in the United States (Gainous and Wagner, 2014; Weller et al. 2013; Murthy 2013; Parmalee and Bichard 2012). Others have examined the role of Twitter in the politics and news reporting of social movements, such as the Arab Spring and European anti-austerity protests, but not elections (Trottier and Fuchs 2014; Bebawi and Bossio, 2014).

In this volume, three broad aspects of Twitter's electoral role are addressed. The first is Twitter's influence on news coverage of elections. In Chapter 1, former journalist Peter Hamby describes the effect of Twitter on contemporary journalists' coverage of elections. Similarly, in Chapter 3, Logan Molyneux, Rachel R. Mourão, and Mark Coddington content-analyzed journalistic tweets to determine how journalists are using Twitter to report presidential elections. The other chapters in Part I turn to news organizations generally and their use of Twitter for news coverage and agenda setting. Evelien D'heer and Pieter Verdegem (Chapter 4) undertook a study of how varying news organizations used Twitter to cover a European Parliament election in the divided media and political environment of Belgium. And Christina Holtz-Bacha and Reimar Zeh (Chapter 2) used the 2013 German election to analyze the effects of Twitter on media outlets' news agendas.

The second emphasis in this volume centers on the audience. In Chapter 5, Heather Evans's study of Twitter content by candidates in the 2014 US Congressional campaign examines how candidates sought to use tweets to foster civic engagement by their Twitter followers. Whether Twitter followers' retweets of political messages correspond to general public opinion about three presidential candidates was the subject of a study by Jisue Lee, Hohyon Ryu, Lorrie Mon, and Sung Jae Park in Chapter 6.

The third category of chapters addresses Twitter, candidate campaigns, and party organizations. How does Twitter impact campaigning? How are political parties and candidate campaign organizations adapting to Twitter as an electoral communication medium? These questions are addressed through varying approaches answering more specific questions. In Chapter 12, David Lassen and Leticia Bode seek to understand whether members of Congress are adopting

Twitter as a re-election tool, and in Chapter 11, Tamara Small uses a study of a Canadian national election to examine the extent to which personalization has affected party messages on Twitter. Marion Just, Ann Crigler, and Rose Owen (Chapter 9) appraise the role of gender in candidate use of Twitter, that is, do male and female candidates approach this new medium in significantly different ways? Kate Kenski and Bethany Conway (Chapter 7) concentrate on whether campaigns exercise message discipline in their Twitter presence. In Chapter 8, Sara Bentivegna and Rita Marchetti look at the level of interactivity in candidate tweeting during electoral campaigns, and in Chapter 10, Joel Penney analyzes the practice of bashtagging to determine how Twitter users seek to undermine a candidate's Twitter message.

A major question of media and elections research is the effect of media messages on electoral outcomes. This applies as well to Twitter. Reimar Zeh's study of national elections in Luxembourg examines the success of a political party that relied on Twitter for electoral communication rather than traditional media outlets (Chapter 13).

Overall, this volume's cutting-edge studies offer scholars a unique view of Twitter's global impact on the electoral process. We hope it will stimulate future studies by raising new questions about a dynamic electoral process impacted by this new political communications medium.

References

Abroms, L.C., and R.C. Lefebvre. 2009. Obama's Wired Campaign: Lessons for Public Health Communication. *Journal of Health Communication* 14(5): 415–23.

Ammann, S.L. 2010. *Why Do They Tweet? The Use of Twitter by US Senate Candidates in 2010.* Social Science Research Network. http://papers.ssrn.com/sol3/papers.cfm?abstract_id=1725477.

Bebawi, S., and D. Bossio. 2014. *Social Media and the Politics of Reportage: The "Arab Spring."* New York: Palgrave Macmillan.

Bekafigo, M.A. and A. McBride. 2013. Who Tweets about Politics? Political Participation of Twitter Users during the 2011 Gubernatorial Elections. *Social Science Computer Review* 31(5): 625–43.

Borondo, J., A.J. Morales, J.C. Losada, and R. M. Benito. 2012. Characterizing and Modeling an Electoral Campaign in the Context of Twitter: 2011 Spanish Presidential Election as a Case Study. *Chaos: An Interdisciplinary Journal of Nonlinear Science* 22(2).

Broersma, M. and T. Graham. 2012. Social Media as Beat: Tweets as a News Source during the 2010 British and Dutch Elections. *Journalism Practice* 6(3): 403–19.

Bruns, A. and T. Highfield. 2013. Political networks on Twitter: Tweeting the Queensland State Election. *Information, Communication & Society* 16(5): 667–91.

Burgess, J. and A. Bruns. 2012. (Not) the Twitter Election: The Dynamics of the #ausvotes Conversation in Relation to the Australian Media Ecology. *Journalism Practice* 6(3): 384–402.

Chadwick, A. 2013. *The Hybrid Media System: Politics and Power.* New York: Oxford University Press.

Conover, M.D., B. Gonçalves, A. Flammini, and F. Menczer. 2012. Partisan Asymmetries in Online Political Activity. *EPJ Data Science* 1(6): 1–19.

Conway, B.A., K. Kenski, and D. Wang. 2013. Twitter Use by Presidential Primary Candidates during the 2012 Campaign. *American Behavioral Scientist* 57(11): 1596–610.

Dang-Xuan, L., S. Stieglitz, J. Wladarsch, and C. Neuberger. 2013. An Investigation of Influentials and the Role of Sentiment in Political Communication on Twitter During Election Periods. *Information, Communication & Society* 16(5): 795–825.

Elter, A. 2013. Interaktion und Dialog? Eine quantitative Inhaltsanalyse der Aktivitäten deutscher Parteien bei Twitter und Facebook während der Landtagswahlkämpfe 2011. *Publizistik* 58(2): 201–20.

Evans, H.K., V. Cordova, and S. Sipole. 2014. Twitter Style: An Analysis of How House Candidates Used Twitter in Their 2012 Campaigns. *PS: Political Science & Politics* 47(2): 454–62.

Gainous, J. and K.W. Wagner. 2014. *Tweeting to Power: The Social Media Revolution in American Politics*. Oxford University Press.

Gayo-Avello, D. 2013. A Meta-Analysis of State-of-the-Art Electoral Prediction from Twitter Data. *Social Science Computer Review* 31(6): 649–79.

Gilmore, J. 2011. Ditching the Pack: Digital Media in the 2010 Brazilian Congressional Campaigns. *New Media & Society* 14(4): 617–33.

Graham, T., M. Broersma, and K. Hazelhoff. 2013. Closing the Gap: Twitter as an Instrument for Connected Representation. In R. Scullion, R. Gerodimos, D. Jackson, and D. Lilleker (eds.), *The Media, Political Participation and Empowerment*. London: Routledge, pp. 71–88.

Grusell, M. and L. Nord. 2012. Three Attitudes to 140 Characters: The Use and Views of Twitter in Political Party Communications in Sweden. *Public Communication Review* 2(2): 48–61.

Hanna, A., C. Wells, P. Maurer, D.V. Shah, L. Friedland, and J. Matthes. 2013. Partisan Alignments and Political Polarization Online: A Computational Approach to Understanding the French and US Presidential Elections. In I. Weber, A.-M. Popescu, and M. Pennacchiotti (eds.), *PLEAD 2013: Proceedings of the 2nd Workshop Politics, Elections and Data*. New York: ACM, pp. 15–21.

Hawthorne, J., J.B. Houston, and M.S. McKinney. 2013. Live-Tweeting a Presidential Primary Debate: Exploring New Political Conversations. *Social Science Computer Review* 31(5): 552–62.

Hong, S. 2013. Who Benefits From Twitter? Social Media and Political Competition in the US House of Representatives. *Government Information Quarterly* 30(4): 464–72.

Jungherr, A. 2012. Online Campaigning in Germany: The CDU Online Campaign for the General Election 2009 in Germany. *German Politics* 21 (3): 317–40.

Jungherr, A. 2013a. Schleppender Beginn: Deutsche Politiker entdecken Twitter nur zögerlich. *Internationale Politik* (March/April): 54–9.

Jungherr, A. 2013b. Tweets and Votes: A Special Relationship: The 2009 Federal Election in Germany. In I. Weber, A.-M. Popescu, and M. Pennacchiotti (eds.), *PLEAD 2013: Proceedings of the 2nd Workshop Politics, Elections and Data*. New York: ACM, pp. 5–14.

Jungherr, A., P. Jürgens, and H. Schoen. 2012. Why the Pirate Party Won the German Election of 2009 or the Trouble with Predictions: A Response to Tumasjan, A., Sprenger, Sander, P.G., and Welpe, "Predicting Elections with Twitter: What 140 characters Reveal about Political Sentiment." *Social Science Computer Review* 30(2): 229–34.

Kim, M. and H.W. Park. 2012. Measuring Twitter-based Political Participation and Deliberation in the South Korean Context by Using Social Network and Triple Helix Indicators. *Scientometrics* 90(1): 121–40.

Klinger, U. 2013. Mastering the Art of Social Media: Swiss Parties, the 2011 National Election and Digital Challenges. *Information, Communication & Society* 16(5): 717–36.

Larsson, A.O. and H. Moe. 2013. Twitter in Politics and Elections: Insights from Scandinavia. In K. Weller, A. Bruns, J. Burgess, M. Mahrt and C. Puschmann (eds.), *Twitter and Society*. New York: Peter Lang Publishing, pp. 139–330.

Lilleker, D.G. and N.A. Jackson. 2010. Towards a More Participatory Style of Election Campaigning: The Impact of Web 2.0 on the UK 2010 General Election. *Policy and Internet* 2(3): 69–98.

Macnamara, J. 2011. Pre and Post-Election 2010 online: What Happened to the Conversation? *Communication, Politics & Culture* 44(2): 18–36.

Mascaro, C. and S. Goggins. 2012. *Twitter as Virtual Town Square: Citizen Engagement during a Nationally Televised Republican Primary Debate.* Paper presented as the American Political Science Association 2012 Annual Meeting.

Mirer, M.L. and L. Bode. 2015. Tweeting in Defeat: How Candidates Concede and Claim Victory in 140 Characters. *New Media & Society* 17(3): 453–69.

Mitchell, A., and E. Guskin. 2013. *Twitter News Consumers: Young, Mobile and Educated.* Pew Research Journalism Project, www.journalism.org/2013/11/04/twitter-news-consumers-young-mobile-and-educated.

Murthy, D. 2013. *Twitter: Social Communication in the Twitter Age.* Cambridge: Polity Press.

Newman, Nic. 2010. *#UKelection 2010, Mainstream Media and the Role of the Internet: How Social and Digital Media Affected the Business of Politics and Journalism.* Working paper, Reuters Institute for the Study of Journalism.

Parmelee, J.H. and S.L. Bichard. 2012. *Politics and the Twitter Revolution: How Tweets Influence the Relationship between Political Leaders and the Public.* Lanham, MD: Lexington Books.

Solop, F.I. 2010. RT @Barack Obama We Just Made History: Twitter and the 2008 Presidential Election. In J.A. Hendricks and R.E. Denton, Jr. (eds.), *Communicator-in-Chief: How Barack Obama Used New Media Technology to Win the White House.* Plymouth: Lexington Books, pp. 37–49.

Statista. 2015a. The Number of Monthly Active Twitter Users, www.statista.com/statistics/282087/number-of-monthly-active-twitter-users.

Statista. 2015b. Facebook Penetration From 2013 to 2019, www.statista.com/statistics/183460/share-of-the-us-population-using-facebook.

Stieglitz, S., and L. Dang-Xuan. 2012. Political Communication and Influence through Microblogging—an Empirical Analysis of Sentiment in Twitter Messages and Retweet Behavior. In *System Science (HICSS)*, 2012 45th Hawaii International Conference, pp. 3500–9.

Trottier, D. and C. Fuchs (eds.) 2014. *Social Media, Politics and the State: Protests, Revolutions, Riots, Crime and Policing in the Age of Facebook, Twitter and YouTube.* New York: Routledge.

Tumasjan, A., T.O. Sprenger, P.G. Sandner, and I.M. Welpe. 2010. Predicting Elections with Twitter: What 140 Characters Reveal about Political Sentiment. *ICWSM* 10: 178–85.

Vergeer, M., L. Hermans, and S. Sams. 2013. Online Social Networks and Micro-blogging in Political Campaigning: The Exploration of a New Campaign Tool and a New Campaign Style. *Party Politics* 19(3): 477–501.

Weller, K., A. Bruns, and J. Burgess, 2013. *Twitter and Society.* Edited by M. Mahrt and C. Puschmann. New York: Peter Lang.

PART I
Election Journalism

1

DID TWITTER KILL THE BOYS ON THE BUS?

A Report from the Romney Campaign in 2012

Peter Hamby

The 2012 class of reporters made their 1988 forefathers look like Mötley Crüe. In 1988 reporters still only had to file stories once or—gasp!—twice a day, and sometimes for the Sunday edition of their papers. CNN was alive, but cable news was not the hungry beast it is today. Jack Dorsey, the co-founder and chairman of Twitter, was 11 years old.

Thanks to an evolutionary mish-mash of Drudge, blogs, cable, *Politico*, *BuzzFeed*, Twitter, and a general migration of journalism toward the web, campaign journalism in 2012 was a culture that rewarded hustle, impact, and "winning"—even when it came to the most incremental of stories. Plenty of cocktails were consumed, but work was the most intoxicating element of the trail.

Print reporters still had to file day stories for the next morning's paper, but the notion of a deadline was just that—notional. To cover a campaign in 2012, a reporter had to be always-on, tweeting with gusto, filing multiple blog posts per day and preparing for television live shots and "phoners," all the while fielding calls or emails from editors and desperate for nuggets of news in an environment that was often devoid of content. And if you embedded in one of the candidate's campaigns, you also had to shoot and transmit broadcast-quality video.

The campaign trail today attracts reporters with the kind of metabolism to thrive in this new world order. To the dismay of the Romney campaign—and their Obama counterparts in Chicago—that meant their press retinue was young and, in their eyes, ill-equipped to cover the most far-reaching and momentous story in the country.

Ashley Parker, one of two *New York Times* reporters assigned to cover Romney, was 29 for most of the campaign. Philip Rucker of *The Washington Post* was 28. Most of the television embeds were even younger. Many of the reporters in the

14 Peter Hamby

press pack were covering their first presidential campaign, but some had covered previous ones and most, including Parker and Rucker, had experience covering politics in other contexts.

Both the reporters on the bus and campaign they were covering would find themselves struggling throughout 2012 to adapt to a treacherous media obstacle course that incentivized speed, pettiness, and conflict, leaving little room for goodwill or great journalism—but plenty of tweets.

The Gathering Place

For campaign reporters on and off the plane, Twitter was usually the first iPhone app they opened bleary-eyed in the morning, and the last one they peeked at before falling asleep at night.

Everyone in politics, it seemed, was on Twitter: journalists, editors, pundits, campaign managers, television producers, bureau chiefs, flacks, pollsters, activists, lobbyists, donors, wives of donors, daughters of donors, hacky operatives, buffoonish down-ballot candidates, cousins of direct mail specialists, interns desperate for retweets. Even Dick Morris was on Twitter.

"I feel like for covering the campaign, [Twitter] was part of being part of the conversation and doing your job," said Ashley Parker of *The New York Times*. Parker and many of her colleagues on and off the campaign plane came to regret the way Twitter affected newsgathering and the tone of their coverage, but in the heat of the campaign, it would have been malpractice to ignore the social media service for more than a few hours.

When political news broke, Twitter was the place to find it. Top officials from the Obama and Romney campaigns would joust, publicly, via tweet. When news producers back in Washington or in New York were deciding what to put on their shows, many looked first to their Twitter feeds.

"Twitter is where that central conversation is taking place," said Ben Smith of *BuzzFeed*. "It's not that Twitter is where you're discussing the news. So much of it is actually happening on Twitter. It was just the central stream of the conversation for everyone."

Jonathan Martin of *The New York Times*, who uses the service to share news, tweet political trivia and swap food tips with other frequent travelers, agrees:

> It's the gathering spot, it's the filing center, it's the hotel bar, it's the press conference itself all in one. It's the central gathering place now for the political class during campaigns but even after campaigns. It's even more than that. It's become the real time political wire. That's where you see a lot of breaking news. That's where a lot of judgments are made about political events, good bad or otherwise.

Twitter consumed the political class, especially the media, throughout the campaign battles of 2011 and 2012. Among reporters, the pressure to join was immense, even if some of the reporters signing up eyed it warily.

"I think there is a feeling on the part of some folks that if I'm not tweeting, I'm not in the game, and my voice isn't being heard," said longtime *Washington Post* reporter Dan Balz—a Twitter user, but a cautious one. "So much of what we write never quite gets read. At least with tweeting you've got an inside audience."

Twitter launched in the summer of 2006 but took almost three years to reach critical mass in political circles as early users struggled to figure out the point of sending out 140-character bursts of information. Among the early adapters were a young class of web-savvy political operatives and activists, many of them in the conservative movement, who saw it as a way to connect and share information with like-minded people.

A handful of reporters began using Twitter in 2007, but its reach within the political class was limited, and so was its impact on the presidential race the following year. By the end of 2008, however, younger reporters in Washington were rushing to sign up, in part as a way to find news and information faster than their older colleagues in the business. The service also offered a means for up-and-coming reporters to push their stories and report into the Washington bloodstream, bypassing the traditional pathways up the Beltway media ladder and enhancing their "personal brands" on the way.

For talented journalists this was a blessing. Twitter was a meritocracy. Smart reporters who hustled and had a knack for breaking news or delivering incisive, informed analysis thrived on Twitter and were rewarded with promotions, TV bookings, or even columns at the stolid news organizations they once derided.

Twitter was also the great corrector. Bad reporting was, generally, mocked or debunked with great speed.

And for consumers exhausted by hackneyed Washington viewpoints and lazy reporting, the discovery of new voices, both in journalism and politics, was refreshing.

"Someone who's young but has an edge and a voice and an ability to cut through and be concise can absolutely break out, especially if they're funny," said Tommy Vietor, a former Obama White House spokesman. "It's good to cut through the roving, musical chairs game of people that go on *Meet the Press* or on those Sunday show political panels who have a perspective that is often entirely colored by the Clinton administration or the Bush administration or whatever their past experience was that isn't necessarily anchored in the reality of today."

Veteran journalists remained skeptical—a few still refuse to sign up—but by the time *Politico*'s Mike Allen slugged the February 19, 2009 edition of his morning "Playbook" note with the headline "Washington-a-Twitter," the service had already caught fire in the green rooms, lunch spots and U Street watering holes where political gossip was being shared.

"Social networking programs tend to tear through communities—high schools, upper levels of media—at exponential rates, and Twitter has now fully arrived in Washington's media scene," Smith, formerly of *Politico*, wrote that same week in a blog spot titled "Twitter solidifies grip on Beltway."

The Golden Era?

Twitter is here to stay. Whether this is good or bad for politics and political journalism depends very much on who you talk to—their ages, their affiliations, their experiences in the news business, or their roles in the political universe. The answer is most often a qualified one.

"Twitter is a really imperfect medium," said Maggie Haberman, a senior reporter for *Politico*. "I use it. We all use it. But the reality is that 140 characters is not ideal and I don't think that anybody would argue that it is."

There are plenty of skeptics and evangelists standing on both sides of the Twitter debate.

Tim Miller, a GOP operative and former spokesman for the Republican National Committee, remembers being a college student starved for updates about the 2000 presidential campaign, but with only limited resources to find them.

"The only information a 19-year-old political junkie like me could get on the campaign was from one random politics blog I stumbled upon, Judy Woodruff's TV show on CNN, stodgy newspaper coverage, or I'd have to go to the library to read a weeks-old copy of the *Weekly Standard*," he said.

Now, he argues, we are living in "the golden era of political news," where consumers have at their fingertips polling data, an array of viewpoints, behind-the-scenes reporting and the ability to follow a campaign minute-by-minute on Twitter. Miller, whose job is to sift through a digital avalanche of news to construct a narrative that he can peddle to the media, thrives on having as much information as possible.

"Our current political information environment is an unqualified benefit for voters and our democracy," Miller said. "To complain about the triviality of Twitter and glorify the golden era of journalism is ridiculous. For starters, there was no such thing. Letting a bunch of cranky old white men determine what they deigned worthy of the masses' ears only served them and the ruling elites who were in on the joke."

But reams of studies have shown that a byproduct of this free-flowing information, on social networks and other media platforms, is an increase in partisanship, as like-minded communities of people silo themselves in their preferred news bubbles. Conservatives are only listening to conservatives, and liberals to liberals.

And in Washington, political insiders are mostly just talking to political insiders.

Liz Sidoti, the national politics editor of the *Associated Press*, called Twitter "a great measure of what a narrow select band of people are talking about in this business." She added:

> In that sense, it's a good tip sheet, but one that has no standards and has a lot of opinion and snark. What it's done, it's created a groupthink, and the groupthink component of it is really kind of scary. It means we're all reporting the same thing, and only half of it might be right. We are thinking the same way. It's become the new conventional wisdom setter, and that conventional wisdom gets amplified as well, because you have editors sitting in bureaus watching this stuff. When everything is in 140 characters, it gives a skewed version of reality, and that impacts how editors think about what reporters should be covering, and it impacts what reporters think is important.

Flacking Twitter

During the 2010 midterms and by the beginning of 2011, when the Republican primary season was beginning, political operatives understood the potency of Twitter as a way to watch, and influence, how narratives were forming among journalists.

Romney adviser Eric Fehrnstrom said his campaign began to notice this phenomenon during the marathon GOP primary debate schedule:

> Every debate reinforced how important Twitter was to the coverage of the campaign and how it presaged the reporting you'd be seeing later that evening in TV or in the next day's newspapers. In every debate we would open up our laptops and would call up Tweetdeck, and we'd be able to search all the Romney mentions, whatever the debate hashtag happened to be for that debate. We would search all that, and be able to react in real time to what people were thinking and saying about the candidate. It became part of the rapid response. The most important element of the debate rapid response was reacting to Twitter.

Fehrnstrom said Twitter "made it easier to spin."
He added: "We knew if there was a favorable storyline that was developing on Twitter, we knew to take that and emphasize it in the spin room. If there was negative storyline that had developed during the debate we knew that that was going to be a talker in the spin room. And we would prepare a specific response to that."

The trend was most evident during the first general election debate between Obama and Romney in Denver. Even a casual observer watching Twitter during the debate could see that Obama, with his halting and uninspiring stage presence, was losing the spin war before the debate had even concluded.

Longtime *New York Times* political reporter Adam Nagourney, who took a pass on the 2012 campaign while spearheading a new general interest beat in California, observed how the debate consensus formed rapidly on Twitter. "It was kind of weird," he said. "Four years ago it would take little time for opinions to coalesce."

There were eye-rolls in the press file at the University of Denver when, just 40 minutes into the showdown, Ben Smith posted an item on *BuzzFeed* titled, "How Mitt Romney Won The First Debate." But Smith was only reporting what was obvious to any political junkie—Obama was stumbling badly and was quickly losing control of the narrative. Smith just didn't feel the need for the bell to ring before posting his story. The Twitter chorus had already rendered its verdict.

"We were clobbered in almost every way in the first debate," said David Axelrod, a top adviser to President Obama. "One thing was clear was that the Republican-oriented tweeters, and also their influence on what reporters were tweeting, was far more effective in the first debate than our efforts. And we really beefed up on those efforts in the second and third debates. These tweets tend to frame how people are reading this and how they are evaluating what they are seeing. Twitter was a big player in the debates. Twitter is a powerful force."

Throughout the campaign, reporters on and off the bus began to notice something startling: campaign operatives seemed to care more about their tweets than the stories they were actually writing or linking to.

"I could write a piece that was incredibly critical of either campaign and no one would care," said John Dickerson, the *CBS News* political director and *Slate* columnist. "And say one snarky thing on Twitter and you get phone calls and outraged emails from both campaigns."

This depended, of course, on the reporter's platform: the campaigns considered an *AP* story that might be published in thousands of local papers to be more consequential than, say, a blog post on ABCNews.com.

But it was true that Twitter became the first place that campaign press operatives went to engage with journalists, either to halt one storyline from developing or to peddle another. "I got more push-back from the campaign for tweets than for anything I ever wrote online or said on television, easily," said Garrett Haake of NBC News.

Strategists in the campaigns came to understand that the meta-narratives of a race were no longer being formed by a small group of ink-stained print reporters riding around on a bus in Ohio. For the operative class, this presented both danger and opportunity.

"The Boys on the Bus model, where a handful of people analyze and interpret a candidate for the entire country, those days are gone," said Ben LaBolt, the Obama campaign's national press secretary. "There's a lot of reasons for it: you can go online and watch candidates directly. The Twitter narrative, in some ways, allows anybody to be on the bus and to communicate their impressions. Their impressions of something might take off and lead to a new narrative. That's absolutely the case."

"A Link is a Link, Dude"

LaBolt, Obama's press secretary, said that back during the 2008 campaign, his press shop could safely assume that the producers of the network television morning shows would read, or at least scan, the front page of *The New York Times* before going to air each day. That was no longer the case in 2012.

The campaign correctly figured out that reporters, producers, anchors—and voters—are gathering information from an ever-expanding, complex patchwork of news and opinion sources beyond the front pages of the legacy newspapers. Twitter became the clearinghouse for that news.

"That's one of the reasons why any time we got a story placed, either a proactive push on the president or a contrast on Romney, we'd create a digital package to push out with that story to make sure that people actually saw it, because we couldn't assume that getting it in the paper was enough to get it on TV nationally, and certainly not regionally," he said.

The Romney campaign took similar steps.

The *Times* content that mattered to the people working on the campaigns was the their digital product—the stories seen by political insiders who woke up in the morning and immediately starting scanning the headlines on email and Twitter using their BlackBerrys or iPhones.

One Obama campaign press official said flatly that *BuzzFeed*, which thrived on Twitter, was a more reliable outlet to reach media elites than *CBS News*.

"I hate to use the word, but they're just buzzier in political circles," the Obama official said of *BuzzFeed*. "They contributed more to political opinion among the political class."

BuzzFeed could get campaign press operatives the link they needed—and quickly. "In today's media age, *BuzzFeed* is just as important as *The New York Times*, and the price of doing business is cheaper," said Mo Elleithee, a Democratic strategist who was Hillary Clinton's traveling press secretary in 2008. "All I need is the link. Matt Drudge taught us that. The Internet takes care of the rest."

While blogs and news websites had been serious players in past campaigns, it was only this cycle that many seasoned reporters realized their print content was going mostly unnoticed.

"I would get pushback from a campaign for a web story or a tweet, something that was happening more or less in real time," said Paul West. "I never got one single reaction, pushback, or comment for something that appeared in print. And that goes for the Obama campaign that was based in Chicago and was reading the *Chicago Tribune*."

Editors of iconic newspapers were also aware that the campaign information wars were mostly playing out online instead of in their thinning print editions.

Marcus Brauchli, the executive editor of *The Washington Post* during the election, beefed up what he called the paper's "intra-day" reporting staff, hiring more reporters to work under franchise bloggers such as Chris Cillizza and Ezra Klein, in order to feed the web monster.

"I don't think you can call us a newspaper anymore," Brauchli said. "Basically these are news organizations. We have one more big platform than some of our real-time rivals do, but we produce video and breaking news throughout the day."

The link-driven culture of 2012 meant that campaign operatives had a major advantage over previous cycles: they could increasingly sidestep the traditional print and television media filters of Washington and create news for the web on their own terms.

Campaigns produced their own content and pushed it out through their social media channels and watched as the rest of the media scrambled to chase it. Not that it was all good news: press shops repeatedly had to play whack-a-mole to knock down false or unflattering stories that popped up on Twitter by the minute.

But the campaigns could go to friendly outlets to generate a favorable story, and then push that link to other news organizations.

One Romney official pointed to Robert Costa, a talented Republican-friendly reporter for *The National Review*, as an example of how this process works. Costa was skilled at sniffing out and breaking his own news, but the Romney campaign also liked to go to him with scoops and inside information.

"No offense to CNN.com, there is a lot of traffic there, but I can go to Robert Costa and I can take his link off 'The Corner' on the *National Review* and I can generate as much news out of 'The Corner,' the official said. "Now with Twitter, you can make your own news and put it up on your Twitter feed."

The balance of power was tipping away from the press and toward campaigns, even though reporters and their news organizations in 2012 had more platforms to deliver news and opinion than at any point in the history of mankind.

Pew's Project for Excellence in Journalism documented this phenomenon during the campaign by studying the sources of the major narratives and assertions about Obama and Romney. The results were striking, and in some ways embarrassing, for the news media.

Political candidates and their allies—spokespeople, cable news surrogates, Super PACs and the like—were the source for about half of the prevailing narratives about the campaigns in the press, Pew found. The media was not setting the agenda: they generated only about a quarter of the national political conversation.

That's a remarkable shift from the presidential race of just 12 years ago, when reporters and pundits generated most of what was talked about during the campaign. In 2000, 50 percent of the "master narratives" and claims about the candidates emerged from media types. Just 37 percent of the discussion emerged from campaigns and their allies.

The Pew study determined that today, "journalists to an increasing degree are ceding control of what the public learns in elections to partisan voices … The press is acting more as an enabler or conduit and less as an autonomous reportorial source."

The erosion of sourcing standards in the press was a notable factor in this shifting power dynamic, Pew found.

"Interestingly, 41% of the time that these surrogates appeared, they were anonymous or on background, meaning a formal staffer was allowed to talk about a candidate without being named," Pew wrote. "That ratio is higher from what we have found in the past. In 2004, for instance, 33% of the assertions were from unnamed sources."

Partisan claims went unchallenged as reporters scraped for even the tiniest shred of news.

Campaign operatives, when they bothered to go through a mainstream media complex they no longer thought they needed, still fed national reporters a pellet of news here and there.

Most of the time, however, they were looking for other avenues to get their message out.

"We're just fishing where the fish are," said David Axelrod. "Our job as a campaign was to find out the viewing habits and the reading habits of the people who were going to be decisive in the campaign. And as it turns out, a lot of those people were low-information voters who were absolutely not reading *The New York Times* and likely weren't reading a newspaper at all. They weren't watching the *CBS* or *ABC* or *NBC Nightly News*. They weren't watching 'Morning Joe.' They were more likely to have been watching ESPN or re-runs of Star Trek."

@jakesuski #nobodycares RT @fivethirtyeight: We'll have a new SC forecast out in about 10 minutes.

In March of this year, the Pew Research Center released a study comparing Twitter reaction to public events to the public response as measured by polls.

The study examined big political moments, like President Obama's 2012 State of the Union address and the Supreme Court's decision to uphold the president's healthcare reform law. Pew found a startling disconnect between how Twitter users interpreted the events versus the reaction of the public at large. The explanation was fairly straightforward: "Twitter users are not representative of the public."

Only a "narrow sliver" of Americans—just 13 percent—were using Twitter during the fall campaign. Twitter users are younger and skew liberal. And only 3 percent of Twitter users "regularly or sometimes tweet or re-tweet news or news headlines on Twitter."

In other words, what political junkies were talking about on Twitter—the newswire that directly informed what influential reporters, editors, and show producers decided to write and talk about on a minute-by-minute basis—was mostly irrelevant to the American populace.

But the risk of bathing in a Twitter waterfall from dawn until dusk is that reporters become so consumed with the inside game that they lose sight of what Americans want to read about, said Dan Balz.

"Most people aren't on Twitter," Balz said. "It's just a fact of life. It's a very small percentage of people who are on Twitter. To some extent it just accentuates the gap between the media and ordinary folks. I think Twitter has an important place but it is not necessarily reflective of public opinion and shouldn't be mistaken as such."

Richard Stevenson, who presided over political coverage for *The New York Times* during the 2012 cycle, admitted that even the Grey Lady was guilty of occasionally lapsing into process coverage. He said the paper succeeded, however, in keeping a larger focus on basic themes such as the character of the candidates, their policies, and their visions for the country.

Stevenson frequently urged his reporters to step back from the kind of Twitter-driven story "that had a shelf life of like six hours before it gets overtaken by events." He continued:

> Things start blown out of proportion. Everything becomes tactical, everything is about not just winning the news cycle but winning the hour, winning each engagement, and defining the terms of the game before the game even begins. I think one of our jobs as journalists and certainly one of my jobs as an editor during this process was to try to detach from all of that and keep in mind that the vast, vast majority of our audience doesn't consume news that way and certainly doesn't want that kind of journalism.

Speed Freaks

Nearly every political hand I interviewed levied a similar complaint against today's web-driven reporter. The journalist's impulse, they argued, is to post a story as quickly as possible, blast it out on Twitter so he or she can be "first," and update the story later as needed.

The need for speed comes at the expense of reporting that is rigorous, thoughtful, and accurate, argues Mo Elleithee, a Democratic strategist: "There is less due diligence to check it out and less due diligence to contextualize it."

Elleithee admitted to peddling his fair share of negative research about opponents over the years. Doing so is an essential part of the campaign toolkit. But operatives today pass out "oppo" like Halloween candy, knowing that the endless hunger for content is a driving imperative for reporters and their editors. More and more in the Internet era, he and others argued, one-sided information is eagerly repackaged as news.

Axelrod said "the race to get impressions and reporting out before everybody else" in the Twitterverse conspires against thoughtful analysis. "Today, you have in most cases young embeds and less experienced reporters who are basically being fed by the campaigns, who rarely stray beyond the campaigns," he added. "I think it's deluded coverage. This has been a trend for some time. Cable also contributes to it. Everything that lends itself to the free flow of unfiltered, unreflective, unedited information has eroded the quality of political reporting."

In cases of factual errors, strategists often grouse that corrections are rarely added to stories—language is instead "tweaked" or "fixed" in digital copy. If stories are corrected outright, readers might never see the clean-up because narratives take off so quickly in the Twitter ecosystem.

The *Huffington Post*'s Jon Ward said there is a certain allure to breaking even the most incremental of stories. On Twitter, you can witness your scoop, or "scooplet," go viral in real time and collect congratulatory tweets from your colleagues in the process.

But Ward views that type of "ephemera" reporting as ultimately kind of pointless. "Even if I had an appetite for endless, 200-word posts or just tweeting all day—which I don't, I find it exhausting and boring—but even if I did, I wouldn't be able to sustain that for more than five years, faster than the 22-year-old who is coming up behind me who is also adapting to new technologies faster than I am," he says.

Retweet Journalism

Just as troubling to political professionals is the tendency of reporters to tweet or retweet news that they, or their parent organizations, have not confirmed to be accurate.

"The only thing worse than Twitter journalism is re-tweet journalism," said Elleithee. "It used to be journalists wouldn't even dare utter a word unless it's been sourced twice. Now they are broadcasting thoughts after its only been tweeted once, even if it's wrong, and with no ramifications."

Elleithee and others working in politics regularly grouse about reporters pretending that the commentary or content they share on Twitter "doesn't count" as real news, even though they sometimes have thousands of followers who follow them for news updates.

For Sidoti of the *Associated Press*, there is "responsibility that comes with the power to publish."

"To me, tweeting is publishing," Sidoti said. "Why is re-tweeting something any different from verifying something and putting it in our papers?"

New media cheerleaders might argue they're just pulling back the curtain on a "conversation" between reporters, editors and sources that was already happening before Twitter. But the common disclaimer "RTs do not equal endorsements"— the one that's posted on many a reporter's Twitter bio—is nothing more than a lame excuse to tweet anything and everything that flits across their screen without repercussions, said Tim Pearson, the Haley adviser.

Death to the Filter

In September 2012, Mitt Romney's press plane encountered some mechanical problems on a tarmac in Richmond, Virginia. Romney, his aides and the press were stranded in the plane for hours.

After another long day on the campaign, reporters in the back of the cabin passed the time by drinking and playing music—and sending out a flurry of sarcastic tweets about the broken plane:

@mckaycoppins I wonder if—at moments like this, when Romney's stranded on a tarmac & press is blasting Kanye on the plane—he questions his life choices.

@samyoungman Defense attorneys, doctors and chartered planes—three things you don't wanna cheap out on

@bkappCBS Romney charter turned power off+on twice now. reax in press section: that's what I do with my computer when it isn't working

"These guys were sitting in the back of the plane drinking their faces off and tweeting non-stop," said one Romney official present at the time. "Like three, four drinks deep, and tweeting non-stop about themselves. They were reporting about themselves. And then they were reporting about the plane, and there was this non-stop snark."

Although was late on a Saturday night, Romney aides in Boston were also watching the tweets with increasing alarm, and worriedly calling their co-workers on the plane in search of a solution to the broken plane.

"You don't want the *Today Show* the next morning being like, 'A sign of the state of the Romney campaign! The plane broke down!'" said one of Romney's top advisers.

Fehrnstrom called the reporting on the plane "petty." Stevens went so far as to compare the reporters to paparazzi. "Can you imagine if campaigns tweeted about reporters the way reporters tweet about campaigns now?" Stevens asked. "Like, I am going to tweet about what they are wearing? The snarky stuff. You don't think that occurs to us?"

A surprisingly large number of reporters who were asked to reflect on the campaign experience said they now regret how they used Twitter to fill their idle moments.

"In some ways, I wish Twitter hadn't existed," said Parker. No matter how responsible you try to be, you have moments where you're like, 'Maybe I shouldn't have tweeted that.'"

Sam Youngman, then of Reuters, says Twitter "enhanced the pettiness" that already existed in politics. It only corroded the already bitter relationship between reporters and the Romney team.

"Racing Toward Nothing"

"Do we have this?"

It's one of the most annoying emails a reporter can get. The answer, of course, is usually no.

But if an editor is sending you that question, you can be sure someone else has it—and your job is to go get it.

Political reporters have always been forced to chase news, but they say the impulse grew worse during the 2012 campaign because of Twitter. Editors and producers back home were following the campaign on Twitter, and when another news outlet broke a story, even one of dubious value to their readers or viewers, they felt obligated to confirm and report it.

Maybe it was a "major" endorsement from a no-name state legislator, or a flattering fundraising leak, or a thinly sourced story about a staff "shakeup"—if another news organizations had the story, their competitors wanted it as well.

"It started to feel like with Twitter you had to chase every little thing," the *Times'* Ashley Parker said. "Sometimes, all the editor sitting in front of the computer screen knows is that this tweet just came past their eyes and they want you to match that. And all your time is spent racing toward nothing."

Parker and other reporters on the bus said they began to internalize the pressure to confirm even the most fleeting of stories being tweeted about by their rivals sitting across the aisle from them on the bus.

"If you looked at the tweets, especially on the endorsements that don't matter, like some New Hampshire state delegate or something, it would be one tweet that goes out, normally from the *Union-Leader* or whoever the Romney campaign gave it to," said one reporter.

"There's not even a huge degree of journalism involved. And then you see the tweet from the NBC intern, saying 'NBC News can now confirm.' And then it's like '*Wall Street Journal* can now confirm,' '*New York Times* can now confirm' … It's almost like you were tweeting to prove that you got it, too, to the person sitting next to you who is about to get it in three seconds or just got it three seconds ago."

The context-free nature of the news being shared on Twitter also frustrated Axelrod and his compatriots back in Obama's Chicago headquarters (unless, of course, the news was damaging to Romney).

"If two kids with an abacus in Keokuk, Iowa put out a release that said we just did a poll, and that went out on Twitter there would be a lot of discussion in Washington and Twitter about the Keokuk poll," Axelrod said. "And completely indiscriminate. Nobody would know whether this was a good poll or a bad poll, whether the methodology was right. When you have 140 characters, there is not a lot of room to provide for disclaimers about the quality of the poll. And there is no doubt that assignment editors watch Twitter, so Twitter has had some impact in that regard."

To 2016, and Beyond

Technology, and its obvious potential to disrupt reporting techniques, makes it even harder to plan for 2016.

It's impossible to know what new advancements will be in play come 2016, how they will impact newsgathering values, and how candidates might react to them—especially on the bus. The iPhone did not exist when Barack Obama announced his candidacy in 2007, and Twitter was only a blip on the Washington media radar.

Richard Stevenson of *The New York Times* acknowledged the diminishing value of reporting from the bubble in the face of new technologies and guarded campaign operatives. He even suggested that concept of putting reporters on the plane or bus full-time might be dying off.

"I don't know how sustainable that model is in the future, but I am glad we were able to have the resources to do that for at least one more cycle," Stevenson said.

2

TWEETING TO THE PRESS?

Effects of Political Twitter Activity on Offline Media in the 2013 German Election Campaign

Christina Holtz-Bacha and Reimar Zeh

German parties and individual politicians have been present on the Internet since the 1990s. The first digital campaign occurred in 1998 but the Internet played a significant role only during the 2009 European election campaign, when parties opened accounts on social network sites (SNS). The 2013 parliamentary election in Germany finally saw a full integration of social media into the election campaign. Parties, their top candidates, and other political actors posted on Twitter or Facebook extensively. In just the last four weeks of the campaign, the six major parties released about 2,500 tweets. However, it turns out that the use of SNS by campaigners mostly remains a one-way street. Voters still do not regard SNS as a channel to look at for political let alone electoral information.

This study examines the use of the Twitter by politicians during the 2013 German parliamentary election campaign and whether they had any success in influencing the media's agenda. In the first step, this chapter will lay out background data on the reach and use of the Internet and SNS in the election year. This will be followed by a brief overview of previous research before presenting the findings on the role of Twitter during the campaign.

Online Communication in Germany

As in other countries, the use of the Internet has increased tremendously in Germany during recent years. In election year 2013, more than 54 million Germans (aged 14 years and over) were online, which provided a penetration rate of 77 percent. The overall average conceals a gap between female and male users, with women lagging more than 10 percent behind men. The increase in more recent years was mainly due to users in the 50+ age bracket making the Internet a communication channel for all age groups. Nevertheless, with only 43 percent, seniors (60+) still have a backlog that lowers the average and earns Germany a rank in the upper midrange on a worldwide scale (Van Eimeren and Frees 2014, p. 380).

The two most important applications on the Internet are the use of search engines (83 percent) and writing and receiving e-mails (79 percent). Ranking third (61 percent) in 2013 was the targeted search for specific information (Van Eimeren and Frees 2013, p. 369). In 2012, 59 percent of the Internet users looked for news online "frequently" or "occasionally," which represents a 13-point increase compared to 2004 (Van Eimeren and Frees 2013, p. 370). While this development seems to speak for a gradual replacement of the traditional news media, data show that people preferably turn to the traditional media's websites for news delivery and only a very small group looks for news online exclusively (e.g., Hölig and Hasebrink 2013). Thus, when it comes to news, they are just changing the channel but not the source.

Whereas the Internet more and more reaches all age groups, this is not yet true for SNS, which still remain attractive mostly for younger people. In 2013, 46 percent of the German online users (14+) also reported usage of SNS. With 87 percent who use SNS at least occasionally, the age bracket from 14 to 19 is the most active. They are followed by 80 percent in the age group from 20 to 29, whereas only 16 percent of the oldest age group (50+) were active on SNS in 2013. SNS, however, are overwhelmingly employed for personal contacts and staying in contact with friends and families. Among SNS users, 43 percent send personal mail or write posts on a daily basis, and 33 percent say they follow daily what happens in their network. SNS, however, are not a channel for political engagement. Only 6 percent of the users look for news on SNS every day. (See Busemann 2013)

In contrast to Facebook and Co., the networking and microblogging service Twitter is public but it still appears to be a niche medium that is mostly used by the political elite. In 2013, only 7 percent of the German Internet users (14+) had a Twitter account. Almost half of them were 29 years and younger (Busemann 2013, p. 398). So, Twitter could be used to address the young generation in particular. However, German politicians have not fully integrated Twitter into their campaign strategies. A study conducted in 2013 found that 60 percent of the members of the national parliament (Bundestag) employ the microblogging service at least "sometimes"; in comparison, only 40 percent of the members of state parliaments (Landtage) have taken up Twitter for speaking to the electorate (Institut für Medien- und Kommunikationsmanagement 2013, p. 58). According to an earlier study of different strategies in the use of Twitter during several state election campaigns, politicians mostly tweeted for advertising events, motivating voters for casting their vote and for negative campaigning (Thimm et al. 2012). Additionally, Twitter was employed for internal communication of the parties. These findings are in line with the experiences during election year 2009, when

Twitter was mostly used for drawing attention to website content and for information about recent or upcoming events (Albers 2009, p. 36).

Even though journalists more and more take information from the web, Twitter has not yet gained much importance for news media professionals (Neuberger et al. 2010, pp. 44, 54). Almost two-thirds of the editors said that Twitter was rather unimportant for their day-to-day work: In more than half of the editorial offices (57 percent), less than a quarter of the journalists use Twitter. Nevertheless, journalists do employ Twitter for searching for information from time to time, but editors concede that it is mostly the case for not even half of the editorial staff. If Twitter is used for journalistic research, it is mainly for getting a sentiment on current issues, observing Twitter as a phenomenon, following the response on their own reporting and getting tips on Internet sources or ideas for articles (Neuberger et al. 2010, p. 55). So, in Germany, the microblogging service does not seem to be very important for the reporting of the traditional media and for daily newspapers in particular.

Previous Research

Elsewhere, several studies assessed the role SNS play for journalists in their daily work and in particular how Twitter changed journalistic routines (e.g., Broersma and Graham 2012, 2013; Hermida 2010). Not much research, however, is available on their effectiveness in the sense of actually influencing the coverage of the media, what they report, and how they evaluate the issues. With political actors more and more relying on SNS for their routine press activities and their campaigning in particular, the question is whether these messages have an impact on the media by putting issues on their agenda and also suggesting how they are treated (first- and second-level agenda-building). If journalists indeed use Twitter for getting story ideas, politicians' tweets may be a welcome source. Since media act as agenda-setters for their audience, successful agenda-building by politicians may indirectly affect the public agenda.

Based on the findings of a content analysis of Dutch and British newspapers, Broersma and Graham (2013) concluded that Twitter enjoyed increasing popularity among journalists. In general, tweets overwhelmingly served as illustration but may also trigger news stories, in the popular press more often than in broadsheets. The British and Dutch newspapers showed major differences in the top four sources of the tweets used in their reporting. Whereas British newspapers drew much more on celebrities and somewhat more on citizens (vox pop), Dutch newspapers sourced more tweets by athletes and considerably more by politicians (Broersma and Graham 2013, p. 458). The latter was particularly true for elections (Broersma and Graham 2012, p. 412).

Parmelee (2014) conducted in-depth interviews with newspaper journalists in the US and found that "[l]eaders' tweets are: story idea generators, tip sheets,

30 Christina Holtz-Bacha and Reimar Zeh

sources of quotes and data, places to find diverse sources, resources for background information, and fact-checking tools" (2014, p. 446) and also concluded that leaders' tweets may impact on second-level agenda-building. Among the factors that the journalists mentioned as making the politicians' tweets useful were their breaking news character, information to be added to an existing news story, inside information and information that is clearly and quickly delivered (Parmelee 2014, p. 446).

In contrast to the earlier research, a study from Norway did not find evidence for agenda-setting between politicians' SNS activities and traditional news media during a local election campaign (Skogerbø and Krumsvik 2015). Findings from a survey of business and financial journalists in the US also did not indicate much use of SNS by this group of reporters and thus did not provide support for a successful agenda-building role of social media (Lariscy et al. 2009).

All in all, findings are mixed. These results may be due to the electoral or non-electoral settings, the methods employed for research and particularly to the diverse cultural backgrounds with differences in the use of social media by politicians and journalists and also in the relationship between political actors and the media.

Method

The research presented here is based on content analysis seeking to establish agenda-building effects between political tweets and newspapers during the 2013 parliamentary election campaign in Germany. This study[1] had two objectives, first to assess the Twitter activities of the parties and their top (lead) candidates during the campaign and, in the next step, to examine whether these had any influence on the reporting of the traditional media.

In July 2013, 556 out of 620 members of parliament had at least one account on SNS (Fuchs 2013). With an 83 percent registration rate, Facebook was the most popular SNS followed at some distance by Twitter where 53 percent of the MPs (n = 328) had an account. Due to the high amount of data that could be expected, not all Twitter accounts could be included in the analysis. Therefore, a sample was drawn according to a systematic multistage selection process. It was decided to consider two Twitter accounts of each party represented in the German national parliament at the time of the campaign, that is: the Christian Democrats (CDU) and their Bavarian sister party Christian Social Union (CSU), the Social Democrats (SPD), the Free Democratic Party (FDP), Alliance 90/Green Party and The Left (Die Linke). For each of them, their party's main Twitter account was chosen for analysis. In addition, the accounts of their lead candidates were included. If the parties lined up several top candidates, the choice fell on the person with the highest

TABLE 2.1 The sample

	Accession Twitter	Tweets during time of analysis 8/25–9/29/2013	Number of followers (cut-off date 9/29/2013)	Average favs	Average retweets
@RegSprecher	5-Jan-11	111	113,819	4	8
@cdu_news (now @cdu)	9-Feb-09	462	41,849	2	7
@groehe	3-Dec-09	43	8,615	4	10
@CSU	17-Feb-09	198	8,862	2	5
@MdLBeate-Merk	n/a	33	n/a	0	0
@spdde	25-Mar-09	700	45,641	8	13
@peersteinbrueck	1-Oct-13	201	59,746	19	25
@Die_Gruenen	27-Apr-08	945	73,108	5	12
@GoeringEckardt	4-Jul-12	303	14,038	5	12
@fdp_de (now @fdp)	12-May-09	128	17,107	2	4
@philipproesler	17-Sep-08	21	14,127	2	5
@dieLinke	2-Jun-09	347	22,916	8	12
@GregorGysi	18-Oct-12	78	21,103	27	38

Twitter activity (tweets per day, cut-off date June 23, 2013). This concerned the Greens who always nominate one female and one male top candidate. The account of Katrin Göring-Eckardt was chosen because she showed more Twitter activity than her male colleague Jürgen Trittin. The Left went into the campaign with seven top candidates. Due to his popularity, Gregor Gysi was included in the study. Because the CDU's chancellor candidate Angela Merkel did not have a personal Twitter account, the choice fell on the party's general secretary Hermann Gröhe. In the case of the CSU, neither top candidate Gerda Hasselfeldt nor party leader Horst Seehofer had a Twitter account. Therefore, the CSU's deputy party leader Beate Merk was included. However, her account was closed right after the election. The top candidate of the FDP was also not present on Twitter and he was replaced by party leader Philipp Rösler. For comparative reasons, the account of government spokesperson Steffen Seibert was analyzed in addition to the party and candidate accounts. Seibert took up Twitter in early 2011 and is by now the account most cited by the media. The government spokesperson, who also is the head of the Press and Information Office, is not allowed to engage in any party-related campaign activity. Table 2.1 gives an overview of the sample for this study.

The collection of the data was done through the aggregator *Twitonomy*—a service that uses Twitter's Streaming-API.[2] In addition to the tweets, *Twitonomy* reports the account names, the time and date of the tweets, the number of retweets and favorites. The observation period of the Twitter activities on the accounts listed in Table 2.1 was from August 25 to September 29, 2013. These were the last four weeks before Election Day, which is the so-called "hot phase" of the campaign, and one week after the election on September 22, 2013. This allowed for capturing any reactions on the election results. Altogether, 3,570 Tweets were recorded during this period.

Some of the variables included in the codebook were generated by the system itself or through searches of the contents of the tweets. Tweets that did not contain any political content were excluded from the analysis. Five trained coders were involved in the content analysis. The minimum reliability coefficient was 0.88 (according to Holsti's formula). Coding of the individual tweets was done according to ten categories. The content of the tweets was assigned to 19 policy areas such as "environment," "social policy," or "society." The variable "actor" identified the main actor of the tweets. This is not to be confused with the account holder who was the source of the tweet. The main actor is the person, group, or organization that is the focus of the tweets and who is centrally involved in or dominates the event or subject. Usually, the main actor plays an active role and is the most important source of the tweet. For instance, main actors tell about other actors, about their office or their subordinates. This variable includes 59 actors, grouped according to different political levels. The actor variable is always coded with reference to the hierarchy level that serves the geographical-political classification of the main actor: from the supranational to the local hierarchy. Thus, a mayor is, for example, coded as "head of government" and the hierarchy level "city." Furthermore, the political function of each actor was coded; for instance, whether they are part of the party leadership, a top candidate or have no special position in the party. Finally, it was coded whether a tweet presented facts, opinions, and positive or negative emotions.

In addition to the analysis of the politicians' Twitter activities, this study examined whether there were any interdependencies between the tweets and the traditional news media. In order to assess a possible influence of Twitter on newspaper reporting during the election campaign, a keyword search of newspapers available on LexisNexis was performed. The following newspapers were included: *Die Welt*, *die tageszeitung*, and *Frankfurter Rundschau*, which are national dailies.[3] Among the regional newspapers, which dominate Germany's newspaper market, the papers with the highest circulation were chosen: *Stuttgarter Zeitung*, *Rheinische Post*, *Nürnberger Nachrichten*, *Sächsische Zeitung*, *Mitteldeutsche Zeitung*, *Hamburger Abendblatt*, and *Berliner Zeitung*. In addition, the news website of the political magazine *Der Spiegel*, *Spiegel Online*, was included, which has the highest reach in Germany. Keyword searches were employed to identify matching articles within these publications. The names of the parties and politicians who stand behind the observed Twitter accounts as well as the central topics of the tweets served as keywords. The daily aggregates of the Twitter activity and newspaper coverage were merged into a single dataset to calculate cross-lagged correlations that would indicate agenda-setting effects by either news media.

Findings

The analysis of the Twitter activities of individual candidates yielded considerable differences. The number of tweets ranged from a total of 21 tweets by Philipp Rösler (FDP) up to 303 tweets by Katrin Göring-Eckardt (Greens) in the entire survey period. The same is true for the party accounts: With 128 tweets the FDP showed the lowest activity, compared to the maximum value of 945 tweets by the Greens (see Figure 2.1).

The daily total is calculated from the total number of 12 accounts.

No linear increase in the number of tweets was recorded during the hot campaign phase, neither on a daily nor on a weekly basis. However, there is a remarkable decrease right after Election Day: Whereas an average of 702 tweets per week (118 per day) were sent during the four weeks before the election, the number of tweets fell to just 138 tweets (20 per day) after Election Day. The accounts of the CSU, of FDP party leader Philipp Rösler and of SPD chancellor candidate Peer Steinbrück recorded not a single tweet during the week after the election (September 23–29), the account of the FDP only one and that of CDU general secretary Hermann Gröhe three. Only the party account of the Greens recorded a moderate activity, but this referred almost entirely to a party event on September 28, which was the day when the party held an internal discussion of the election results.

Also striking was the behavior of the Christian Democratic parties on the day of the Bavarian state election (September 15) and on Election Day one week later. While both CDU accounts were almost completely silent (three tweets) on the weekend of the election in Bavaria, the CSU remained similarly low-key on the weekend of the federal election (11 tweets). It is likely that this was the result of strategic considerations in order not to interfere with the other party's campaign finish.

As can be seen from Figure 2.1, Twitter activity peaked on three days: On September 1 and 2—the dates of the "TV duel" between chancellor candidates Angela Merkel and Peer Steinbrück and of the "TV triathlon" with the leaders of the smaller parties Rainer Brüderle, Gregor Gysi, and Jürgen Trittin—and September 21, one day before the election. Smaller account-specific peaks appear due to specific party events (September 3, SPD: Twitter Town Hall; September 7, Greens: Grüner Länderrat), the Bavarian TV debate (September 3, CSU, Greens, and SPD), or around television appearances on talk shows and election broadcasts (September 9, CDU: Angela Merkel in "ARD Wahlarena"; September 11,

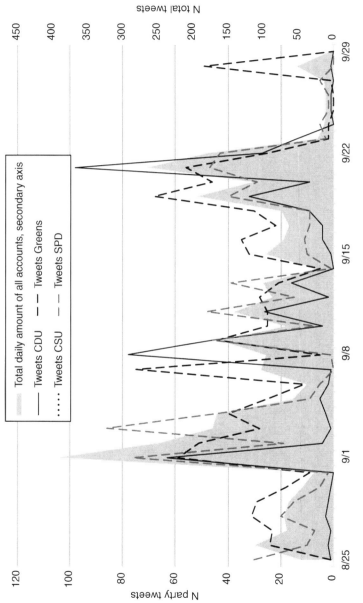

FIGURE 2.1 Number of tweets of selected Twitter accounts over time.

SPD: Peer Steinbrück in "ARD Wahlarena"; September 19, CDU, CSU, Greens, SPD: "Berliner Runde").

The assumption that politicians would use the weekend with low coverage of the traditional media to communicate on Twitter about political issues and views could not be confirmed with the data. In fact, tweets peaked over two weekends (August 31/September 1 and September 21/22), which was, however, related to major media events (TV duel and Election Day). On the other weekends, the number of tweets was close to the average. If only Sundays are considered, when comparatively few newspapers are published in Germany, Twitter activity was even lower: Only on the day of the TV debate with Merkel and Steinbrück (September 1) the number of tweets lay clearly above the weekly average (that is, by a factor of 3.5). These findings confirm that parties and candidates use Twitter primarily to publicize and comment on their own campaign events and appearances. If at all, references to other parties and candidates were included in tweets on campaign events. Thus, Twitter primarily represents just an additional advertising tool for campaigning with only few attempts to set the agenda.

The fact that Twitter was not employed much for campaigning, agenda-setting, or critical remarks on competitors can be illustrated by the following example: The much-commented-on impromptu song by then SPD secretary-general Andrea Nahles in front of the parliament (the theme song of "Pippi Longstocking") was mentioned on the accounts included here only once with a funny remark asking whether she would have to pay a copyright fee for her performance. The opportunity to use this anecdote for strategic purposes was not taken up by the other observed accounts of political parties and leading candidates. The rapid drop of activity after Election Day also underlines the function of Twitter as just another campaign tool.

Issues dealt with in the tweets were assigned to policy areas as they were also mentioned in the election manifestos such as work/social policy, environment/ energy, and taxes/economy. These three issues made up approximately 78 percent of all tweets with a policy issue. Since candidates did not differ significantly in their choice of issues from their parties they were merged in order to assess the topics addressed in the tweets.

Almost one-third of the tweets (31 percent) included one of the three issues labor/social policy, environment/energy, and taxes/economy. Another almost third (31 percent) accounted for tweets which focused on the campaign. This category was dominated by the two big parties (CDU: 49 percent; SPD: 39 percent), which can be explained by the prominent position and the media presence of the chancellor candidates who were also present in the Twitter campaign. The other tweets either dealt with policy issues that are not covered by the three subject areas mentioned (9 percent), referred to other topics (8 percent), were coded as trivial (13 percent), or were without any recognizable subject (8 percent). For clarity, the latter three variables are summarized as "other."

36 Christina Holtz-Bacha and Reimar Zeh

TABLE 2.2 Issues dealt with in the tweets

	Government spokesperson	CDU/ Gröhe	CSU/ Merk	FDP/ Rösler	SPD/ Steinbrück	Greens/ Göring-Eckardt	The Left/ Gysi
	%	%	%	%	%	%	%
Labor/social policy	16	13	21	11	21	17	15
Environment/ energy	6	1	5	4	2	14	1
Taxes/economy	6	6	14	28	7	7	4
Other policy issues	34	7	10	6	6	8	13
Campaign	8	49	32	26	39	26	20
Other	29	25	18	25	25	29	48
n =	111	500	231	149	901	1,248	425

Table 2.2 demonstrates that the political priorities of the parties coincided with what was mentioned on Twitter. For instance, environment/energy is a classical field of the Green Party and it is also a major topic in the tweets of the Greens and of Göring-Eckardt (14 percent to 6 percent). The same applies to the aggregate accounts FDP and Rösler (28 percent to 8 percent) and CSU and Merk (14 percent to 8 percent) with their issue taxes/economy. The distribution of labor/social policy is more balanced although it is usually very much associated with the Social Democrats. Social issues play a role in the tweets of all parties involved. However, they are slightly higher on the SPD and CSU accounts and slightly lower on the accounts of CDU and FDP. Apart from the FDP, labor/social policy has the largest share of all policy issues in the tweets of all parties, which also demonstrates that the SPD was not able to establish the issue as their own during the campaign.

What Contributes to the Success of Tweets?

A big advantage of Twitter aggregator tools is that a tweet is automatically associated with rudimentary impact indicators. For instance, it is possible to retrace for each tweet how often it was favorited by users. Another way to express agreement with a tweet lies in the possibility to retweet a message. By way of a retweet, a message will be received among friends or followers even if they do not follow the source of the original message.

With the assumption that the political actors use modern campaign tools, and Twitter in particular, to generate attention among the media, the resulting attention was measured on the basis of the favorited tweets (Table 2.3). Linear regression analysis was applied to assess which factors explain a greater amount of likes or retweets.

Tweeting to the Press? **37**

TABLE 2.3 Determinants of favorites

	1st block	2nd block	3rd block
Twitter accounts parties			
SPD (*reference category*)			
CDU	−0.27***	−0.27***	−0.29***
CSU	−0.23***	−0.23***	−0.21***
FDP	−0.14***	−0.14***	−0.12***
Alliance 90/The Green Party	−0.15***	−0.13***	−0.10***
The Left	n.s.	n.s.	n.s.
Issues mentioned in tweets			
Election campaign (*reference category*)			
Labor and social policy		−0.05*	−0.06**
Environment and energy		−0.06**	−0.06**
Taxes and economy		−0.05*	−0.06**
Other		−0.14***	−0.13***
Reference to candidates in tweets			
Angela Merkel			0.12***
Peer Steinbrück			0.13***
Change in R^2	0.11***	0.02***	0.03***
Adj. R^2	0.10***	0.12***	0.15***
n =			2,160

Table reports standardized beta coefficients from OLS regression analyses, and reports p-values as follows: * $p \le .05$; ** $p \le .01$; *** $p \le .001$.

Among the independent variables, the Twitter accounts were entered in the first step. To establish comparability, the analysis was limited to the official party accounts to eliminate personal effects. This reduced the sample size to 2,780 tweets but did not lead to a significant restriction compared to the 3,570 tweets originally captured.

The issues that the tweets dealt with were entered as the second block of independent variables. Again the simplified categorization in four issue areas was used. The resulting coefficients stand for the effect of the issue "campaign" on the dependent variables. In addition to the topics of the tweets, it was examined how the mention or reference to one of the two chancellor candidates Angela Merkel and Peer Steinbrück affected favoriting or retweeting of a tweet.

The account of the SPD serves as reference category in the regression. With the exception of The Left, the tweets of other parties were significantly less favorited than the SPD tweets (Table 2.3). That does not change significantly when the issues are entered into the model. Here, the issue "election campaign" is the reference category. If the campaign is mentioned in the tweets, it is more likely that users favorited the message. Both mentioning the chancellor and the challenger reinforced the positive assessment of the tweets, without substantially changing the influence of the variables entered before. In view of the coefficients for the variables entered in the first block, it seems likely, however, that the mentions of Steinbrück are primarily positive and those of Merkel primarily negative. This is also suggested by the fact that that SPD and Greens had significantly more followers than the conservative parties (Table 2.1).

Whether a tweet is retweeted depends on the source (Table 2.4). Tweets of the conservative parties are significantly less retweeted. The retweet rate was also slightly higher for The Left, which may be due to the fact that leftist groups are more active in the web in general. The earlier finding that tweets referring to the campaign were more popular than tweets with reference to policy areas is confirmed here. A reference to the chancellor or her challenger increased the chance of a tweet of being retweeted. Again, it can be assumed that these were mostly positive mentions of Steinbrück and negative statements on Merkel.

The regression analyses are partly the product of the user structure of Twitter. The left-wing and alternative parties have more supporters here and that is why SPD, The Left and Greens are more popular. Whether this mainly reflects the increased presence of party members in this social network or not cannot be concluded from the data. However, the positive influence of the topic "election campaign," which stands for announcements and comments of media events, corroborates the assumption.

Interaction with Media Reporting

The spreading of messages in the network represents a criterion of success, but it loses its value if it can be assumed that the messages circulate primarily among a party's own members. Twitter may also have some relevance as a source of information for journalists. Conclusions about the relationship between media coverage and Twitter activity can be drawn from time series analysis. To a limited extent, the method also allows the assessment of a causal relationship.

For this purpose, data from the national newspapers *Die Welt, die tageszeitung*, and *Frankfurter Rundschau*, the regional daily newspapers *Stuttgarter Zeitung, Rheinische Post, Nürnberger Nachrichten, Sächsische Zeitung, Mitteldeutsche Zeitung, Hamburger Abendblatt*, and *Berliner Zeitung*, as well as the news site *Spiegel Online* were used. For the period of the analysis, a frequency count of references to parties, candidates, and policy issues was done and a new file created. This was aggregated on a daily basis and connected with the daily aggregates of the examined Twitter accounts.[4] It can thus be determined by cross-correlation to what extent Twitter activity and press reporting lagged behind Twitter. The findings are an indicator of the relevance and the perception of Twitter in the traditional media. *Spiegel Online* holds a special position; as a daily Internet medium that is subject to other production routines than the printed press, it may take up network activities earlier than the newspapers.

In fact, only few significant cross-correlations were discovered. They are summarized in Table 2.5. Effects were found for the parties and for the account of

TABLE 2.4 Determinants of the retweet rate

	1st block	2nd block	3rd block
Twitter accounts parties			
SPD (*reference category*)			
CDU	−0.10★★★	−0.10★★★	−0.11★★★
CSU	−0.18★★★	−0.19★★★	−0.17★★★
FDP	−0.15★★★	−0.16★★★	−0.13★★★
Alliance 90/The Green Party	n.s.	n.s.	0.06★★★
The Left	0.06★★	0.07★★	0.08★★★
Issues mentioned in tweets			
Election campaign (*reference category*)			
Labor and social policy		n.s.	n.s.
Environment and energy		n.s.	n.s.
Taxes and economy		0.04★	n.s.
Other		−0.13★★★	−0.13★★★
Reference to candidates in tweets			
Angela Merkel			0.16★★★
Peer Steinbrück			0.14★★★
Change in R^2	0.07★★★	0.03★★★	0.04★★★
Adj. R^2	0.07★★★	0.09★★★	0.13★★★
n =			2,492

Table reports standardized beta coefficients from OLS regression analyses, and reports p-values as follows:★ $p \le .05$; ★★ $p \le .01$; ★★★ $p \le .001$.

Peer Steinbrück with media reporting always following Twitter activities. In other words, Twitter activity preceded press reporting on the account holder. In this case, Twitter activity was two days ahead of press reporting but also the supposedly faster online news site *Spiegel Online* followed with a delay. Correlations were found more often for the regional than for the daily press.

However, these findings cannot necessarily be interpreted as an agenda-setting effect. A significant part of the parties' Twitter activities consisted of event announcements and comments on campaign events. Among others, they included television appearances by top politicians. The press as well as *Spiegel Online* responded to the same events one or two days later due to production constraints. In addition, not a single significant correlation was revealed for the issues, which speaks against a causal interpretation. The reporting of issues by the media and on Twitter by the parties seems to be mostly independent.

Conclusion

The descriptive analysis as well as time series and regression analyses show that political actors use Twitter mainly as an instrument to draw attention

40 Christina Holtz-Bacha and Reimar Zeh

TABLE 2.5 Twitter activity and presence of parties in the media

				Lead: Twitter activity of the parties (days)				
Lag: Media	Number of cross-correlations	−3	−2	−1	0	1	2	3
National dailies	21	—	—	—	—	—	2	—
Regional dailies	49	—	—	—	—	—	6	2
Spiegel Online	7					2	2	

Reading example: For two of the six parties an increase in Twitter activity is followed by an increased presence on *Spiegel Online* after two days.

to the campaign and specific events. Tweets mostly referred to the campaign and mentioned other policy areas only to a minor extent. This is also illustrated by the analysis of the Twitter activities over time. The highest number of tweets appeared around the major campaign events such as the TV debate and the election weekend. The parties and candidates did not try to capitalize on the reduced weekend media coverage of the traditional media by increasing their social media activities. Subsequent analyses can be interpreted accordingly. For the accounts of CDU, SPD, and the Greens, and for the account of Peer Steinbrück, time series analysis revealed significant lags for the reporting of the traditional media. However, a causal interpretation of these findings is difficult. Even if we assume a causal relationship, it fails to materialize for the small parties.

The regression analysis has shown that tweets yield attention particularly with campaign content and only find low resonance with party or policy-specific content, which is also consistent with the results presented so far. For the initial research question, how and with what success political actors in Germany used Twitter during the election campaign, this study reveals an ambiguous picture. In comparison with the US and the campaign of Barack Obama, German parties chose an entirely different approach. Whereas the US campaign was regarded as a prime example of a well-organized Internet campaign (e.g., Trankovits 2010, p. 13), a consistent strategy could not be observed in Germany. This stems in large part from the addressable target audience. In the online campaign and especially on Twitter, Obama explicitly tried to reach the voters directly, to mobilize and to draw attention to specific content or fundraisers.

This is not the case in Germany. First, the user structure of Twitter in Germany is heavily distorted in terms of socio-economic status and, second, the absolute numbers are too low. Twitter is actively used especially by journalists, bloggers and other politicians, which makes direct communication between politicians and the electorate difficult and does not hold nearly the same mobilization potential as in the United States. The user structure of Twitter in Germany also presents opportunities for political actors to distribute their content and goals. Journalists represent classic gatekeepers when it comes to disseminating information as widely as possible. Therefore, Twitter could be used during the election campaign to post political proposals especially in poor news periods, so as to direct the media reporting, as has already been described by Albers (2009). The results of this study do not show any such strategy. Actually they show the opposite: Twitter activity is high during classic media events.

Therefore, the question of the success of online campaigning via Twitter must remain unanswered for the time being. The fact that the new media are taking an increasingly important role in the election campaign is evident. Research will show whether they can be employed successfully in the future. Yet, no systematic imprint of social media on traditional media coverage was found, but occasional use of social media as a source or an inspiration for campaign stories cannot be ruled out.

Notes

1   The authors acknowledge the contributions of Andreas Dusch, Stefan Gerbig, Mario Lake, Sabrina Lorenz, Fabian Pfaffenberger and Urs Schulze (Universität Erlangen-Nürnberg).
2   Due to technical reasons, only the last 3,200 Tweets of an account can be retrieved. However, this number was not achieved by any account during the observation period.
3   Germany's national dailies with the highest circulation, *Frankfurter Allgemeine Zeitung* and *Süddeutsche Zeitung*, were not included in this study because they are not available on LexisNexis.
4   ARIMA correction was not necessary for the time series, because no autocorrelation was detected.

References

Albers, H. 2009. Onlinewahlkampf 2009. *Aus Politik und Zeitgeschichte* 52: 33–8.
Broersma, M. and T. Graham. 2012. Social Media as Beat: Tweets as a News Source during the 2010 British and Dutch Elections. *Journalism Practice* 6: 403–19.
Broersma, M. and T. Graham. 2013. Twitter as a News Source: How Dutch and British Newspapers Used Tweets in Their Coverage, 2007–2011. *Journalism Practice* 7: 446–64.
Busemann, K. 2013. Wer nutzt was im Social Web? Ergebnisse der ARD/ZDF-Onlinestudie 2013. *Media Perspektiven* 7(8): 391–9.
Fuchs, M. 2013. Social Media in der Politik: 90 Prozent der Bundestagsabgeordneten nutzen soziale Netzwerke. *Hamburger Wahlbeobachter*, www.hamburger-wahlbeobachter. de/2013/07/social-media-in-der-politik-90-prozent.html.
Hermida, A. 2010. Twittering the News: The Emergence of Ambient Journalism. *Journalism Practice* 4(3): 297–308.
Hölig, S. and U. Hasebrink. 2013. Nachrichtennutzung in konvergierenden Medienumgebungen. International vergleichende Befunde auf Basis des Reuters Institute Digital News Survey 2013. *Media Perspektiven* 11: 522–36.

Institut für Medien- und Kommunikationsmanagement. 2013. *Politiker im Netz. Treiber und Hürden der Social Media-Nutzung unter Bundes- und Landtagsabgeordneten.* St. Gallen: Institut für Medien- und Kommunikationsmanagement.

Lariscy, R.W., E.J. Avery, K.D. Sweetser, and P. Howes. 2009. An Examination of the Role of Online Media in Journalists' Source Mix. *Public Relations Review* 35: 314–16.

Neuberger, C., H.J. vom Hofe, and C. Nuernbergk. 2010. *Twitter und Journalismus. Der Einfluss des "Social Web" auf die Nachrichten*, 2nd edn. Düsseldorf: Landesanstalt für Medien Nordrhein-Westfalen (LfM).

Parmelee, J. H. 2014. The Agenda-building Function of Political Tweets. *New Media & Society* 16: 434–50.

Skogerbø, E. and A.H. Krumsvik. 2015. Newspapers, Facebook and Twitter: Intermedial Agenda Setting in Local Election Campaigns. *Journalism Practice* 9: 350–66.

Thimm, C., J. Einspänner and M. Dang-Anh. 2012. Twitter als Wahlkampfmedium: Modellierung und Analyse politischer Social-Media-Nutzung. *Publizistik* 57: 293–313.

Trankovits, L. 2010. *Die Obama-Methode.* Frankfurt am Main: FAZ.

Van Eimeren, B. and B. Frees. 2013. Rasanter Anstieg des Internetkonsums—Onliner fast drei Stunden täglich im Netz. Ergebnisse der ARD/ZDF-Onlinestudie 2013. *Media Perspektiven* 7–8: 358–72.

Van Eimeren, B. and B. Frees. 2014. 79 Prozent der Deutschen online—Zuwachs bei mobiler Internetnutzung und Bewegtbild. Ergebnisse der ARD/ZDF-Onlinestudie 2014. *Media Perspektiven* 7–8: 378–96.

3

US POLITICAL JOURNALISTS' USE OF TWITTER

Lessons from 2012 and a Look Ahead

Logan Molyneux, Rachel R. Mourão,
and Mark Coddington

"The Twitter Election"

Early in 2012, Twitter CEO Dick Costello predicted that 2012 would be "the Twitter election" (Milian 2012). While it may be difficult to quantify the effect of the platform on the presidential election, the campaign was certainly a hit on Twitter. Election topics were frequently trending, and Election Day set a record for the most-tweeted event with as many as 327,000 tweets per minute (Hockenson 2013). The two US presidential elections in the platform's short history have been major drivers of Twitter activity, causing jumps in subscriptions (Snyder 2008). By the end of 2012, Twitter reported 288 million monthly active users (Holt 2013) who posted nearly 400 million tweets per day (Tsukayama 2013).

Before the election began, a team of researchers at the University of Texas at Austin set up a system to collect tweets from hundreds of political journalists in order to study how they used the microblogging platform to gather and disseminate information about the election. The system collected more than 600,000 tweets from these journalists and almost 2 million more tweets from other users interacting with them. Unsurprisingly, activity was heightened around political events such as the conventions—typically seen as the official kickoff of the presidential campaigns—the presidential debates, and Election Day. The data offered clear pictures of challenges to journalistic norms, shifts in gatekeeping, and the ways in which journalists interact with each other and the general public.

This chapter collects and reflects upon findings from a series of studies using the data, both qualitative and quantitative, examining how political journalists used Twitter during the 2012 election (Coddington et al. 2014; Lawrence et al. 2014; Molyneux 2014; Mourão 2014; Mourão et al. 2015). A discussion of the relationship between Twitter and journalism is followed by an overview of research methods used. Main findings across the studies are then presented, providing a broad view of political journalism on Twitter in 2012. This chapter concludes with a discussion of what has changed since 2012 and Twitter's potential role in future elections.

Twitter and Journalism

Twitter is a microblogging service of many potential uses. Although it was not intended as a journalistic tool, journalists have appropriated it as such. Journalists frequently read Twitter as the "new AP wire" (Lawrence 2012), checking what others are saying in order to keep a finger on the political world's pulse. Twitter is thus frequently considered one of many "inputs" from which journalists draw tips and raw information as they report. This chapter, however, focuses on journalistic output on Twitter. Journalists create narratives and establish their professional identity and journalistic authority through producing a new type of news output characterized by smaller or "atomized" units of information—the tweet—that travel across timelines and networks.

Twitter, therefore, is a locus for "collective interpretation of key public events" (Zelizer 1993, p. 219), strengthening ties of identity and interpretive community. In other words, journalists use Twitter as a channel for informal networking, negotiating narratives about themselves and their work, and engaging in discourses that define what it means to be a political reporter on the campaign trail. Thus, how journalists use Twitter has more to do with the profession of journalism than with the public's access to news.

Political journalists acting together in an insular community is not a new idea (Crouse 1973). The novelty is that the audience can now observe these interpretive and discursive processes that were previously invisible to the public eye, potentially affecting what has been called journalists' primary currency: credibility. Yet, the content produced by journalists on Twitter does not constitute total access to the backstage of campaign reporting, but rather another type of news output, produced while news is being gathered, processed, and prepared for distribution in a polished news product. Tweets from the campaign trail display real-time "atomized" content; that is, simple blocks of stenography, minor commentary, snark, and self-promotion that can be shared, discussed, and reorganized in different ways across multiple timelines (Cohn 2013; Papacharissi and de Fatima Oliveira 2012; Papacharissi 2014).

The studies presented here treat Twitter as an important nexus of journalistic activity, one where journalists produce a different type of news product than what appears on television, in papers, or elsewhere online. A survey of journalists suggests that microblogs like Twitter are used by a majority of US journalists and are journalists' most commonly used social media (Willnat and Weaver 2014).

Scholarly work surrounding journalistic adoption of social media in general had focused on normalization, or the process by which journalists adopt some new norms along with the new technology while adapting its use to fit other existing norms (Lasorsa et al. 2012; Singer 2005). Our studies revolved around two overarching research questions about how political journalists used Twitter while covering the 2012 presidential election. These research questions focused on two key areas of the normalization process as journalists adopt Twitter. The first broad research question was, "How did political journalists' use of Twitter affect norms of objectivity?" Twitter was not subject to the same editorial oversight and publishing standards as other modes of journalism, so the goal of this research question was to examine whether traditional standards of objectivity remained in place or whether a new standard emerged for the social media space. The second general research question was, "How did political journalists' use of Twitter affect their relationship with the audience?" Twitter is potentially a space in which journalists and their publics may interact and be co-creators of news, and these studies provided insight into how some of those interactions occur.

Research Methods

Data was collected and analyzed through a combination of automated and manual techniques, similar to methods advocated by Lewis, Zamith, and Hermida (2013). First, a purposive sample of political journalists was selected. The sample included campaign reporters working for prominent national news outlets and those working for 76 other outlets located in key swing states: Ohio, Florida, North Carolina, Colorado, Iowa, Virginia, Nevada, and Pennsylvania. These were the top eight states in campaign advertising spending through July 2012 (when the sample was drawn; see Associated Press 2012; Parlapiano 2012). The sample was selected to include a broad array of political reporters, including those working for print media, broadcast television, cable, radio, wire services, and online outlets such as *Politico* and *BuzzFeed*. Individual journalists were chosen using a database curated by Cision, a media contact and marketing service. Both reporters and commentators were included, but editors were excluded. The final list of 430 political reporters and commentators with active Twitter accounts included 74 identified as "analyst," "columnist," "commentator," or "contributor" (17 percent)—in other words, journalists more likely to produce opinion-oriented work.

A custom-built software program was used to monitor all 430 of these Twitter feeds for updates and save new tweets to an archive. The program used Twitter's application programming interface (API) to communicate with Twitter every 15 minutes from the day before conventions started, August 26, 2012, to November 18, 2012, shortly after Election Day. The first study conducted a content analysis of tweets sent during the conventions (Lawrence et al. 2014). Two more studies conducted qualitative analyses of the tweets—one focusing on retweets during

46 Logan Molyneux, Rachel R. Mourão, and Mark Coddington

the conventions (Molyneux 2014) and another focusing on tweets during the first presidential debate (Mourão 2014). Two other studies conducted content analyses of tweets from the presidential debates—one focusing on fact-checking (Coddington et al. 2014) and another focusing on humor (Mourão et al. 2015). This chapter integrates findings from these five studies, identifying and discussing key themes that emerged across the analyses.

Findings

Our analyses suggest that journalists partially adapted to the new medium in an effort to self-brand and gain attention online, with behaviors that slightly challenged objectivity. Among these, we found that minor commentary, job talk, and humor were the most prevalent. Journalists also used Twitter as a way to gain attention and build a personal brand. And while the public may now be able to observe these "goings on," they are still primarily relegated to the sidelines as journalists interact with each other.

Challenges to Objectivity

The first research question referred to the challenges posed by the new medium to the norm of objectivity. In the 2012 presidential election coverage, journalists negotiated the boundaries of objectivity, often mixing their reporting with humor and commentary. However, we argue that this is part of a strategic goal to get attention online and these discourses rarely provided major opinion, thoughtful critiques, or meaningful challenges to the political players involved in the election.

One of the bedrocks of American journalism, the norm of objectivity states that journalists are supposed to report the facts, without being influenced by their own values and opinions (Kovach and Rosenstiel 2007; Schudson 2001). In practice, objectivity usually translates into "balancing" stories by quoting two sides of a dispute, and letting the audience decide who is right and wrong based on the presented facts. Tuchman (1978) contends that this type of objectivity serves as a ritualistic performance that protects journalism as a profession.

The journalists in our sample attempted to maintain this form of "professional" objectivity in the competitive landscape of social media (Coddington et al. 2014). But rather than pass judgments about who's right or wrong, political journalists chose to engage in less subversive types of opinion, most notably minor commentary. This type of opinion-sharing was present in almost a third of political reporters' tweets at the conventions (Lawrence et al. 2014). The reporters analyzed opted to offer their commentary on candidates' traits, the political parties and campaign management, focusing on the "horse race" and strategy. These are familiar aspects of political campaign reporting (see Aalberg et al. 2011 for a review), but on Twitter this reporting is injected with commentary and personal takes.

Another form of objectivity derives from the scientific method and takes shape through the practice of "fact-checking." In this mode, journalists build independence through verifying information and weighing evidence rather than from listening to the "two sides of the story." While Twitter could provide the space for real-time collaborative fact-checking, our results show that stenography—providing a simple record of candidates' statements—was a much more common use of Twitter than fact-checking involving evidence or judgments on the veracity of statements (Coddington et al. 2014). This echoes journalists' preference for "professional" objectivity, or the prevailing "he said/she said" type of reporting. In fact, less than 10 percent of all the tweets collected during the presidential debates dealt with factual claims at all. Instead, findings from all the papers in our research project suggest the bulk of the content produced by journalists on Twitter is a mix of humor, job talk, and minor opinion and commentary.

Retweets: Tweeting at Arm's Length

The findings are similar when considering Twitter's retweet function. Journalists have used it in attempting to strike the balance between objectivity and the type of discourse that is rewarded in social media. Using retweets, journalists pass along messages from others wholesale or (when quoting a tweet) append their own commentary to the original message. The key is that credit (and, importantly, blame) for the content of the message is given to the author of the original message rather than the journalist. In this way, journalists signal that the message should not be considered their own opinion, despite their role in curating it.

Perhaps not so surprisingly, our findings reveal that the retweet function was not predominantly used to spread news and information relevant to the election, but instead to send along bits of opinion and humor. This suggests that retweets had a role that was different from quoting speakers in a news story. Instead, retweets contained information that is not commonly part of finished news products at all. Journalists preferred to retweet messages that contained subtle commentary rather than strong editorial positions. While they were willing to use the function to share messages about themselves and their work, minor commentary, and humorous messages, reporters in our sample steered clear of retweeting controversial messages (Molyneux 2014; Mourão et al. 2015).

A Tweet and a Laugh

Another development related to shifts in objectivity norms is the fact that humor takes up a large part of political journalists' Twitter chatter. Humor has always had a place in US politics, from the earliest political cartoons, but it is particularly common on Twitter, where political journalists must blend with celebrities and myriad other social connections. Jokes were one of the most common forms of retweets (Molyneux 2014). Snark, a portmanteau of "snide" and "remark," was particularly popular in connection with candidate claims during speeches and debates. Humorous narratives, such as "Big Bird," "binders full of women," and "horses and bayonets" became driving forces of journalistic discourse online, reverberating between timelines for hours. However, our findings suggest that humor only partially challenged objectivity, with journalists employing critical humor mostly to target the media themselves, and resorting to the retweet function to pass along biting satire (Mourão et al. 2015).

Overall, about one-fifth of the tweets from all types of journalists working for all types of media outlets contained an attempt at humor. This suggests a growing acceptance of the rhetorical device on Twitter and journalists' willingness to depart from objectivity through tweeting and retweeting jokes. The preferred targets were the political actors, in particular Mitt Romney, but also included the political process and the media itself (Mourão et al. 2015).

Yet a deeper look at the type of humor employed revealed that professional journalists were reluctant to employ the more sophisticated form of satire, especially when targeting political actors. Only 11 percent of all the humorous tweets were satirical; that is, including elements of aggression, play, laughter, and judgment (Caufield 2008). When employing satire, journalists targeted the moderator and the media themselves, avoiding political criticism toward candidates and campaigns (Mourão et al. 2015).

Humor was also more prevalent on retweets than original tweets, and the difference was bigger for satirical pieces: satire was twice as likely to come in the form of a retweet as in an original post. Once again, we speculate that the retweet function allowed reporters to distance themselves from the critical jokes, retaining the appearance of objectivity.

While it is unclear if the format of Twitter is too short to be conducive to satire, we did observe that the sophisticated form of humor was used in self-deprecatory jokes about the role of the media in covering campaigns. As such, we suspect that journalists have mastered the format, but have opted to stay away from major controversies, using humor and minor opinion as a way to gain attention without really challenging entrenched norms of campaign reporting.

To summarize our studies' findings related to the first research question, about Twitter's influence on traditional norms of objectivity, it is clear that political journalists push the boundaries of objectivity on Twitter but do not entirely redraw them. When engaging in commentary, journalists chose to stay away from opinions that could be perceived as partisan. When engaging in humor, they avoided the more sophisticated form of critical satire. When fact-checking, they resorted to stenography more often than they offered judgments on the veracity of claims. Together, this suggests that rather than a major challenge to journalistic norms, Twitter serves as a place for minor disruptions.[1] In the next sections, we argue that these disruptions are part of a performative strategy and that journalists have attempted to find balance between professional objectivity and the type of openness rewarded in social media.

Tweeting as Personal Branding

The second broad research question asked what effect political journalists' use of Twitter had on journalists' relationship with their audience. Our findings add to those of Marwick and boyd (2011) on micro-celebrities on Twitter who adapt content to an imagined audience through strategic self-commodification—that is, deliberately appealing to followers in a way to publicize oneself as a good or service being offered. Self-commodification becomes more evident by the way journalists, especially those working for national news outlets, have tried to distance themselves from news organizations. Through self-referential tweets and retweets, the reporters in our sample invested in their personal brand through an openness about their lives that is not traditionally permissible in main media outlets.

The process of personal branding took shape in two particular ways: direct self-promotion and through the retweet function. When engaging in direct self-promotion, journalists frequently tweeted links to stories produced by themselves. When using the retweet function, journalists shared with their followers selected messages about themselves, which included not only praise, but also hate mail. This process of curating and sharing messages about themselves with the public represents an attempt to develop a personal brand, breaking the "fourth wall" between media practitioners and their audiences (Molyneux 2014). This finding has inspired other studies, which have confirmed that journalists consciously work to create a personal brand by engaging their audiences and building relationships (Molyneux and Holton 2015).

Keeping Twitter's Gates

Even though great potential exists for journalists and the public to use Twitter as a shared space in which to collaboratively collect and distribute news and information, our research suggests that this potential was not reached during the 2012 election. Journalists retweeted other journalists and political insiders more than 80 percent of the time, giving very little attention to members of the general public. A qualitative look at retweets found that journalists rarely incorporated audiences' comments and opinions into their output on Twitter, allowing other journalists and political actors to dominate their retweets (Molyneux 2014). Additionally, less than 2 percent of the tweets in the conventions sample were calls for information or crowdsourcing, another potential way to involve the public (Lawrence et al. 2014). So while the public may have been engaging with the news about the conventions on Twitter, political journalists reserved the spotlight for themselves.

This suggests that gatekeeping still plays an important role on Twitter, at least in the political arena. While it may be that, with an abundance of online information sources, the value of any one of them is diminished (Williams and Delli Carpini 2000), individual journalists still make gatekeeping decisions about what to pass on to others. Some suggest that the locus of journalistic gatekeeping has now shifted to social media (Zeller and Hermida 2015) because journalists are seizing the opportunity to connect with their audiences directly, cultivating followings and relationships (Molyneux and Holton 2015). This positions journalists as curators or guides in a sea of digital information. Many journalists in our samples seemed happy to fill this role, highlighting and commenting on key moments of the conventions and debates. But it's worth repeating that the majority of what came through political journalists' Twitter feeds was not what would normally be considered news for the purposes of filling a newspaper, television broadcast, or website.

Tweeting's Thin Transparency

Because tweets are public by default, Journalists' discourse on Twitter holds potential for a more transparent form of news production and political communication. Journalists' increased use of opinion in their one-liners as they live-tweet political events—and their retweets of similarly opinionated comments by others (Mclyneux 2014; Mourão et al. 2015)—help reveal to the public the attitudes and beliefs that lie behind the comparatively poker-faced political coverage of their main professional output. And their real-time tweeting of disputed factual claims and counterclaims helps render the contested process of fact-checking more visible to audiences (Coddington et al. 2014). In our study of journalists' tweeting from the 2012 conventions, we found that 15 percent of their political tweets contained information or comments on the daily work of journalism itself; the journalists at the conventions talked about their own work more often than policy, the candidates' characteristics, or political strategy (Lawrence et al. 2014). Through Twitter, political journalists are giving a segment of the public a window into some of the processes and attitudes that affect their production of news. Compared to a decade or two ago, audiences—at least those who follow these journalists on Twitter—are getting much more of a glimpse into the worlds of the journalists who produce their political news.

But the window that journalists on Twitter provide their audiences into their work is just that—a window. The transparency they provide is a thin version of the concept, one devoid of significant interaction and tending heavily toward the frivolous and minute rather than the substantial and insightful. The 2012 conventions study found that tweets in which journalists commented on their work weren't connected with substantial issues but were instead negatively correlated with mentions of policy, candidate characteristics, and political strategy (Lawrence et al. 2014). The information journalists offered in their tweets consisted more of superficial details of their work conditions, such as the weather or the movements of the media pack, than of the organizational or epistemological processes by which their news reports were produced. Self-disclosure on Twitter can toe a fine line between transparency and narcissism, and political journalists often appeared to fall on the latter side.

Media sociologist Michael Karlsson (2010) breaks the concept of journalistic transparency into disclosure transparency, through which journalists are open about how they produce news, and participatory transparency, which aims to involve the audience in the news production process itself. If political journalists' Twitter discourse displays little in the way of substantial disclosure transparency, it holds even less participatory transparency. Audiences may be able to vaguely see what is happening within journalists' bubble on Twitter, but they cannot puncture it in any substantial way. The transparency political journalists offer on Twitter is primarily performative, a way of broadcasting a highly selective view of their work to present themselves to their colleagues and audiences as savvy, witty observers of the political process. It is not meant to open the process of political journalism to a larger group of people in a truly transparent sense.

Looking to Twitter's Future in Political Journalism

By now, the novelty of Twitter has worn off. Supervisors at news organizations are beginning to clamp down and impose regulations regarding use and conduct (Holton and Molyneux 2015). Standard practices are beginning to be widely adopted. In other words, Twitter has become incorporated as part of the news ecosystem, and journalists' tweets constitute a news product. In upcoming elections, we expect to see less experimentation and more homogeneity in style and approach. There are a few important developments to watch, however, including changes to Twitter that emphasize images and video. In addition, Twitter now interacts with other media in ways that separate its role from that of other social media.

Changes in the Platform

Twitter has been in existence for nearly a decade, which may seem like a lifetime in social media years, but is in fact quite a short period for a technological platform to be considered stable and settled. Indeed, the technological affordances of Twitter are undergoing significant changes almost monthly, especially as the company aims to keep its user base and revenue continually growing to please its public shareholders. These changes are sure to affect the way journalists, politicians, and their various publics interact on this network in ways scholars have not previously examined. One major change that could prove a particularly fruitful arena for researchers has been the rise of images posted on Twitter, as the company has moved to more deeply integrate images into users' timelines. Since the 2012 election, Twitter has put image previews and auto-playing videos in users' timelines (Sippey 2013b; Vranica 2015); launched the six-second video app Vine, whose videos have shown remarkably fast propagation within large and dense networks (Sippey 2013a; Zhang et al. 2014); and bought and launched the live-streaming video app Periscope (Koh and Rusli 2015). In addition, it is also now common for people wishing to post longer blocks of text to Twitter to take a screenshot of text written in a notes app. The practice, called "screenshorting," is particularly common among celebrities (Williams 2015).

While social media images and memes have received significant scholarly attention (e.g., Bayerl and Stoynov 2014; Kharroub and Bas 2015; Peck 2014), the images and videos posted by politicians and journalists, particularly on Twitter and within a campaign context, have received relatively little scrutiny. Images and videos are playing a growing role in how campaign news and messages are being framed on Twitter, and scholars studying political communication through Twitter and other social networks would do well to examine the images posted there as thoroughly as they have the texts. However, we must be careful not to overstate the influence of social media images on political outcomes. For instance, some suggested that Periscope, which allows users to stream live video to their followers, would transform the campaign media, a claim of which we remain skeptical (Calderone 2015; Moody 2015; Nielsen 2015). Even so, social media images are an increasingly important part of online political discourse that must be attended to.

Differentiating between Twitter and Facebook

As Twitter matures, we have also begun to see more specialized uses for it, particularly in relation to politics. While Facebook and Twitter can be associated together as the two major US social media companies of the moment, they serve distinct purposes within the online political information environment. Facebook continues to be a major driver of web traffic to news sites and other political content, and the largest single online location for political discussion and sharing of news content. Twitter is much smaller by comparison and not as significant a traffic source, but serves more as a forum for chatter among journalists, politicos, and highly engaged users, as well as journalistic tool for gathering information and opinions from those users. Thus Twitter may be shifting toward a place where journalists, political actors, and heavily invested users can interact and compete to set campaign frames, while Facebook is more of a mass network in which those frames stabilize and spread more widely. This top-down flow is a characteristic of Twitter's network that was identified relatively early in its history (Kwak et al. 2010), but researchers should be closely attuned to how Twitter and Facebook, as well as other social network sites, are crystallizing in those distinct purposes as those scholars seek to contextualize their work.

Conclusion

Interestingly, Twitter's growth has slowed somewhat. The company reported 287 million monthly active users at the end of 2014, growing by between 1 and 5 percent each quarter since then, except for in the final quarter of 2015, when growth was flat. The company reported the same number of users—320 million—at the end of 2015 as it had in the third quarter of that year (Twitter 2016). Upcoming elections offer a host of opportunities to answer questions about political journalism in a digital, mobile age. Will Twitter continue to be a hub of news and political activity? Will the conversation continue to be dominated by elite political journalists? Will journalists be participating using images and video alongside text tweets? Now that the normalization process is largely complete, have there been any changes in behavior? If journalists primarily commune with other journalists on Twitter, how will campaigns tailor their messages there?

Whatever changes await for Twitter, journalism and campaigns, the findings presented here from 2012 provide a firm foundation to address these questions in future elections. Our research suggests there have been minor disruptions to objectivity, mainly characterized by superficial job talk, attempts to humor, and the injection of opinion. Political journalists use Twitter as a tool for personal branding and community-building. And while all these activities are conducted in plain view of the public, participation in the conversation is mainly restricted to other journalists and political elites. Thus, even as journalists and the public mingle on Twitter, journalists have reserved for themselves a gatekeeping position.

Note

1 It is important to note that national journalists, especially those working for newspapers and online outlets, were more likely to use humor and invest in self-branding than local reporters. Overall, local journalists shared less opinion, less personal content, and less backstage information.

References

Aalberg, T., J. Strömbäck, and C.H. De Vreese. 2011. The Framing of Politics as Strategy and Game: A Review of Concepts, Operationalizations and Key Findings. *Journalism* 13(2): 162–78.

Associated Press. 2012. Presidential Campaign Ad Spending Focused on 9 States. *Fox News*, www.foxnews.com/politics/2012/08/06/presidential-campaign-ad-spending-focused-on-states.

Bayerl, P.S. and L. Stoynov. 2014. Revenge by Photoshop: Memefying Police Acts in the Public Dialogue about Injustice. *New Media & Society*. Published online before print.

Calderone, M. 2015. The 2016 Election Will Be Live-Streamed: "We're All C-SPAN Now." *The Huffington Post*, www.huffingtonpost.com/2015/04/01/2016-live-stream-coverage_n_6972428.html.

Caufield, R.P. 2008. The Influence of "Infoenterpropagainment": Exploring the Power of Political Satire as a Distinct Form of Political Humor. In J. Baumgartner and J. S. Morris (eds.), *Laughing Matters: Humor and American Politics in the Media Age*. New York: Routledge, pp. 117–30.

Coddington, M., Molyneux, L., & Lawrence, R. G. 2014. Fact checking the campaign how political reporters use Twitter to set the record straight (or not). *The International Journal of Press/Politics*, 19: 391–409.

Cohn, D. 2013. The Unit of News We All Already Use. *Circa* (blog), https://blog.cir.ca/2013/07/25/the-unit-of-news-we-all-already-use.

Crouse, T. 1973. *The Boys on the Bus*. New York: Ballantine Books.

Hockenson, L. 2013. The Most-Tweeted Events on Record. *Gigaom*, https://gigaom.com/2013/07/08/the-most-tweeted-events-on-record.

Holt, R. 2013. Half a Billion People Sign Up for Twitter. *The Telegraph*, www.telegraph.co.uk/technology/9837525/Half-a-billion-people-sign-up-for-Twitter.html.

Holton, A.E. and L. Molyneux. 2015. *Identity Lost? The Personal Impact of Brand Journalism*. Journalism, published online before print November 3, 2015. doi:10.1177/1464884915608816.

Karlsson, M. 2010. Rituals of Transparency: Evaluating Online News Outlets' Uses of Transparency Rituals in the United States, United Kingdom and Sweden. *Journalism Studies* 11: 535–45.

Kharroub, T. and O. Bas. 2015. Social Media and Protests: An Examination of Twitter Images of the 2011 Egyptian Revolution. *New Media & Society*. Published online before print.

Koh, Y., and E.M. Rusli. 2015. Twitter Acquires Live-Video Streaming Startup Periscope. *The Wall Street Journal*, www.wsj.com/articles/twitter-acquires-live-video-streaming-startup-periscope-1425938498.

Kovach, B. and T. Rosenstiel. 2007. *The Elements of Journalism: What Newspeople Should Know and the Public Should Expect*. New York: Crown.

Kwak, H., C. Lee, H. Park, and S. Moon. 2010. What Is Twitter, a Social Network or a News Media? In *Proceedings of the 19th International Conference on World Wide Web (WWW '10)*. ACM, New York, pp. 591–600.

Lascrsa, D.L., S.C. Lewis, and A.E. Holton. 2012. Normalizing Twitter: Journalism Practice in an Emerging Communication Space. *Journalism Studies* 13: 19–36.

Lawrence, R.G. 2012. *Campaign News in the Time of Twitter: An Observational Study*. Paper prepared for presentation at the 2012 meeting of the American Political Science Association.

Lawrence, R.G., L. Molyneux, M. Coddington, and A. Holton. 2014. Tweeting Conventions: Political Journalists' Use of Twitter to Cover the 2012 Presidential Campaign. *Journalism Studies* 15: 789–806.

Lewis, S.C., R. Zamith, and A. Hermida. 2013. Content Analysis in an Era of Big Data: A Hybrid Approach to Computational and Manual Methods. *Journal of Broadcasting & Electronic Media* 57: 34–52.

Marwick, A.E. and d. boyd. 2011. I Tweet Honestly, I Tweet Passionately: Twitter Users, Context Collapse, and the Imagined Audience. *New Media & Society*, 13(1): 114–33.

Milian, M. 2012. Twitter CEO: "You Don't Pull the Batteries Out of the Microphone." *CNN*, www.cnn.com/2012/01/31/tech/social-media/twitter-ceo-political/index.html.

Molyneux, L. 2015. What journalists retweet: Opinion, humor, and brand development on Twitter. *Journalism*, 16: 920–935.

Molyneux, L., and A. Holton. 2015. Branding (Health) Journalism: Perceptions, Practices, and Emerging Norms. *Digital Journalism* 3: 225–42.

Moody, C. 2015. How Live-Streaming Will Change Campaigning. *CNN*, www.cnn.com/2015/03/26/politics/election-2016-live-streaming-campaigns.

Mourão, R. R. 2015. The boys on the timeline: Political journalists' use of Twitter for building interpretive communities. *Journalism*, 16: 1107–23.

Mourão, R., Diehl, T., & Vasudevan, K. 2015. I Love Big Bird: How journalists tweeted humor during the 2012 presidential debates. *Digital Journalism*, 4: 211–28.

Nielsen, R.K. 2015. No, This Won't Be the "Meerkat Election." Or the "Periscope Election." It's Digital Politics As Usual. *rasmuskleisnielsen.net* (blog), http://rasmuskleisnielsen.net/2015/03/31/no-this-wont-be-the-meerkat-election-or-the-periscope-election.

Papacharissi, Z. 2014. *Affective Publics: Sentiment, Technology, and Politics*. New York: Oxford University Press.

Papacharissi, Z. and M. de Fatima Oliveira. 2012. Affective News and Networked Publics: The Rhythms of News Storytelling on #Egypt. *Journal of Communication* 62: 266–82.

Parlapiano, A. 2012. The Ad Advantage in Battleground States. *The New York Times*, www.nytimes.com/interactive/2012/08/25/us/election-news/The-Ad-Advantage-in-Battleground-States.html.

Peck, A.M. 2014. A Laugh Riot: Photoshopping as Discursive Vernacular Practice. *International Journal of Communication*: 8:1638–62.

Schudson, M. 2001. The Objectivity Norm in American Journalism. *Journalism* 2: 149–70.

Singer, J.B. 2005. The Political J-Blogger: "Normalizing" a New Media Form to Fit Old Norms and Practices. *Journalism* 6(2), 173–98.

Sippey, M. 2013a. Vine: A New Way to Share Video. *Twitter Blog*, https://blog.twitter.com/2013/vine-a-new-way-to-share-video.

Sippey, M. 2013b. Picture This: More Visual Tweets. *Twitter Blog*, https://blog.twitter.com/2013/picture-this-more-visual-tweets.

Snyder, C. 2008. Another Election Result: Twitter Comes Through. *Wired*, www.wired.com/business/2008/11/twitter-survive.

Tsukayama, H. 2013. Twitter Turns 7: Users Send Over 400 Million Tweets Per Day. *The Washington Post*, www.washingtonpost.com/business/technology/twitter-turns-7-users-send-over-400-million-tweets-per-day/2013/03/21/2925ef60-9222-11e2-bdea-e32ad90da239_story.html.

Tuchman, G. 1978. *Making News: A Study in the Construction of Reality*. New York: Free Press.

Twitter. 2016. *Twitter Q4 and Fiscal Year 2015 Shareholder Letter*, https://investor.twitterinc.com.

Vranica, S. 2015. Twitter Finally Rolls Out Auto-Play Video. *The Wall Street Journal*, http://blogs.wsj.com/cmo/2015/06/16/twitter-finally-rolls-out-auto-play-video.

Williams, B.A. and M.X. Delli Carpini. 2000. Unchained Reaction: The Collapse of Media Gatekeeping and the Clinton-Lewinsky Scandal. *Journalism* 1: 61–85.

Williams, O. 2015. RIP Blogging, Killed by Screenshorts. *The Next Web*, http://thenextweb.com/opinion/2015/04/14/r-i-p-blogging-killed-by-screenshorts.

Willnat, L. and D.H. Weaver. 2014. *The American Journalist in the Digital Age: Key Findings*. Bloomington: Indiana University.

Zelizer, B. (1993). Journalists as interpretive communities. *Critical Studies in Media Communication* 10(3): 219–37.

Zeller, F. and A. Hermida. (2015). When Tradition meets Immediacy and Interaction. The Integration of Social Media in Journalists' Everyday Practices. *Sur le journalisme About journalism Sobre jornalismo* 4(1): 106–19.

Zhang, L., F. Wang, and J. Liu. 2014. Understand Instant Video Clip Sharing on Mobile Platforms: Twitter's Vine as a Case Study. In *NOSSDAV '14: Proceedings of Network and Operating System Support on Digital Audio and Video Workshop*. New York: ACM, pp. 85–90.

4

MEDIA COVERAGE OF AN ELECTION CAMPAIGN ON TWITTER

The Case of Belgium in the EU Elections

Evelien D'heer and Pieter Verdegem

Introduction

In our contemporary "network" society (Castells 2007), communication takes decisively new forms. The internet, and social media in particular, allow for multidirectional, non-linear and decentralized communication. Concerning the political sphere in particular, these technologies can potentially alter the relationship between politicians, the media, and the public. The European elections are a particularly interesting context to study the opportunities and tensions these transformations bring forth, as they "are both national and European at the same time" (Strömbäck et al. 2011, p. 5). Not only do political parties and candidates increase their efforts to communicate with voters, but also the media devote greater attention to politics during election campaigns. Whereas public opinion formation and media systems still predominantly exist at the national level, the internet and social media in particular allow for what is more broadly labeled as the "Europeanization" (Olsen 2002) of political communication. Media play a signification role in development of Europe as a so-called "imagined community" (Anderson 1991). Media coverage on European affairs can contribute to the formation of a European public opinion and in extension a general feeling of belonging to a European political and cultural entity. Then again, national media refract what Europe is and how it operates, potentially enhancing as well as traducing its status (Papathanassopoulos and Negrine 2011). In addition, the different member states are characterized by different media and political systems. More specifically, Hallin and Mancini (2004) distinguish between the polarized pluralist model (e.g., Spain), the democratic corporatist model (e.g., Belgium), and the liberal model (e.g., Britain). In this respect, the rise of the internet and social media in particular potentially alter the conduct and nature of political communication, or, as Papathanassopoulos and Negrine (2011, p. 146) argue, "a multiplicity of networks of information can open up discussions beyond what is made available through elites or traditional media outlets."

Based on the Twitter debate about the 2014 European elections in Belgium, we aim to define and understand the nature of European political communication. In other words, to what extent does Twitter election coverage reveal the Europeanization of political campaigns by transcending national boundaries? Twitter is part of the political news cycle, in which mainstream news media, politicians, but also non-elites have their place (Chadwick 2013). Drawing on the coverage of the EU elections on the microblogging service Twitter, we define and categorize the dominant media sources covering the Belgian candidates running for the European elections. In particular, we distinguish between mainstream media and non-established, alternative information sources, focusing on the possibilities of the latter to open up the discussion. In addition, we define to what extent media sources cross national borders and political levels. Concerning mainstream media sources, for example, we refer to the Flemish public broadcaster VRT. Non-mainstream media sources include web-based news initiatives, such as the European media source *Europe Decides* (i.e., http://europedecides.eu), which focused on the European Parliament elections in particular.

This chapter starts by scrutinizing related work on the role of Twitter in the political debate, followed by a contextual outline of the European elections in Belgium. The Belgian case is particularly relevant, as Belgium comprises two separate political and cultural "spaces"—Flanders and Wallonia—each having their "own" media and consequently their "own" public spheres. The presentation of the research goals and methodology is followed by the description of the findings and overarching reflections.

Twitter, Political Communication, and the European Elections

Within Europe, we notice a general evolution towards "hypermedia" campaigning, whereby politicians integrate both old and new media to communicate with voters (Lilleker et al. 2015). Although mainstream media, such as television and newspapers, are still deemed important, social media are now embedded in election campaign strategies across Europe. The advent of new, social media platforms has increased the opportunities for direct communication with the electorate. The usage of Twitter by politicians and campaigners has received considerable attention by researchers (for an extensive literature review see Jungherr 2014). These studies are inspired by social media's potential to transform politicians' relationship with the public, although strong empirical evidence for a two-way flow is still missing. We examine studies that identify and compare activity of multiple actor types on Twitter, or interactions between politicians as well as traditional media/journalists and citizens (e.g., Ausserhofer and Maireder 2013; D'heer and Verdegem 2014; Larsson and Moe 2012). These studies show that the debate is indeed open to participation of non-elites, but equally point to the centrality of elite actors in the debate—prominent politicians and journalists. Rather than functioning as an alternative platform, Twitter seems to be strongly intertwined with traditional media. It functions as a "backchannel" (Kalsnes et al. 2014), as the volume and content of Twitter messages follow media events, and televised debates in particular. Simultaneously, political journalists incorporate Twitter in their daily routines (Parmelee 2013; Rogstad 2014). In sum, research shows Twitter is reflective of the existing social structures, as the dominant actors in the debate reflect "established actors" in society (e.g., journalists and/or prominent politicians).

The Twitter studies discussed above are executed on a national level, characterized by established media systems. For analyzing the elections in Europe, this is not the case, as there are no European media available across all member states (Papathanassopoulos and Negrine 2011). In this respect, the Twitter debate about the European elections potentially shows the prominence of alternative, pan-European media sources that cover news *across* countries (e.g., news websites available in different languages) to fill this void. Additionally, another complexity is the variety and different traditions of how democracy is organized in the different EU member states (cf. classification of Hallin and Mancini 2004). Below we discuss existing Twitter research on the 2014 European elections, providing insight in the media sources that take central positions in the debate.

Compared to 2009, the year of the previous European elections, the 2014 European elections generated fairly substantial debate on the web and Twitter in particular. Although more academic work on Twitter and European elections is yet to be done, we found studies reporting more than 1 million tweets were sent in the period preceding the elections (Maireder and Schlögl 2014; Matsa and Jurkowitz 2014), with around 346,000 tweets sent during the election period (May 25–27) (Smyrnaios 2014).

The work of Maireder and Schlögl (2014) and Smyrnaios (2014) concentrate on the hashtag debate across Europe (based on #EP2014 and related hashtags). Although Maireder and Schlögl focus on users' followers and Smyrnaios focuses on interaction patterns (retweets and mentions), the results are very similar. In sum, the Twitter networks show clusters on the basis of national affinities, which are structured around a smaller, central cluster. The central cluster in the network contains international news media (such as the BBC), several MEPs (such as Martin Schulz, German politician and president of the European Parliament since 2014) and European institutions, such as the European Commission and the European Parliament. The presence of the latter shows the "institutionalization" of Twitter (Smyrnaios 2014). This refers to the adoption of Twitter by Europe's central institutions and the presentation of Twitter analytics about the elections on their websites. In addition, this central cluster is indicative of an online European public sphere, albeit at an early stage of development.

60 Evelien D'heer and Pieter Verdegem

Situated around the network core, we find large clusters primarily defined by language and nationality, such as Spanish, Dutch, or British communities of media institutions, journalists, bloggers, and political actors. Aside from the central cluster, the European "Twittersphere" very much represents the different nation-states and, by extension, Europe as a collection of nations. Notwithstanding the decentralization or the "deterritorialization" of networked forms of interaction, communication still takes place within a specific socio-spatial context, which co-defines its structure. Now we discuss the context of the European elections in Belgium, followed by an explanation of our research objectives and methodology.

The European Elections in "Bi-national" Belgium

The country under investigation in this chapter is the Western European country of Belgium. Based on the models of media and politics that Hallin and Mancini (2004) distinguish, Belgium represents a democratic corporatist model. Without extensive elaboration upon all its dimensions, it signifies media autonomy and journalistic professionalization, early development of the mass-circulation press and a strong tradition of public service broadcasting. The electoral context in Belgium is characterized by a multiparty system, whereby parties compete against one another but must work with each other to form a government coalition. Voting is mandatory and is based on candidate lists, organized per electoral district. This implies that, per party, citizens can vote for the list (and agree to the sequence of the candidates) or vote for specific candidates on the list (and potentially alter the sequence of the candidates).

Belgian society is divided into a Dutch-speaking part, Flanders, and a French-speaking part, Wallonia, with the bilingual Brussels as the capital in-between. Public life, including traditional media and political debates are constructed along these linguistic lines. On the political level, responsibilities about policy domains are divided across the federal level (e.g., the juridical system) and the regional levels (e.g., media and education). In this respect, Belgium's democracy is "bi-national" (Van Parijs 2013), containing separate media as well as political spaces. There are no countrywide political parties, and elections take the form of two separate contests for separate electorates.[1] In this respect, the Belgian case provides an interesting opportunity to detect differences in media coverage between French-speaking and Dutch-speaking candidates.

The European elections in Belgium coincided with the federal and regional elections. On Election Day, May 25, 2014, Belgian citizens had to vote for the three elections on the same day. Research has shown that European elections are of lesser importance to the media and voters. Therefore, they attract less attention than domestic ones (Papathanassopoulos and Negrine 2011). Reif and Schmitt (1980) were the first to distinguish between "first-order" and "second-order" elections, whereby European elections were considered as second-order national elections. Research on the 2009 European elections shows the European elections are still treated as second-order national elections (Raycheva and Róka 2011).

Research Objectives

Our study uses the Twitter platform to define and describe media sources covering the Belgian candidates running for the European elections. Employing Twitter as a digital tool, we study "culture and society with the internet" (Rogers 2009, p. 29). News organizations use Twitter to attract people to visit their website (Armstrong and Gao 2010). Likewise, non-mainstream users, organizations, and bloggers can add URLs to their profile and Twitter messages, linking to external content. Following this, the first question we put forth is self-evident but important:

> RQ1: What media sources cover the Belgian candidates running for the European elections and how can they be categorized?

In particular, we categorize mainstream, institutional media organizations as well as non-mainstream sources. In addition, we account for the nation from which they operate and the language in which they address their audiences. Since we do not focus on politicians' usage of Twitter as an election platform, we excluded all political party-related information channels (e.g., party websites). Communication coming from European institutions and related organizations, such as the European Commission, is included and defined as non-mainstream media sources.

Second, as a network medium, Twitter connects users, in this case media sources and political candidates. Both candidates' and media's attributes allow us to understand the relations we find on Twitter. Media's attributes are outlined above and concerning politicians we take into account the Belgian regions they represent—either Flanders or Wallonia. Building upon the findings of Maireder and Schlögl (2014) and Smyrnaios (2014), we question to what extent we find clusters centered around Dutch-speaking candidates on the one hand and French-speaking candidates on the other. Based on these studies, we expect to find media sources that are embedded in national clusters (in this case Flanders and Wallonia) and outlets that cross both nations. Therefore, we characterize whether media sources operate from Flanders, Wallonia, Belgium, or Europe. In addition, we distinguish mainstream and non-mainstream media sources. The former include news agencies, newspapers, magazines, and radio and television broadcasters whereas the latter are web-based initiatives. In this study, the definition of non-mainstream media sources is predominantly routed in the possibilities that digital technologies offer to set up alternative outlets. The discussion of the results provides specific examples of both mainstream and non-mainstream media sources found in this study.

Following our first research question, we propose a second set of research questions:

RQ2a: What characterizes media sources covering Dutch-speaking candidates and French-speaking candidates?
RQ2b: What characterizes media sources covering candidates originating from both Belgian regions—Flanders and Wallonia?

Methodological Approach: Research Design

The detection and definition of media sources covering Belgian candidates departs from Twitter users that mention Belgian candidates running for the EU elections. The most active users (identified as the top 10 percent in the number of messages sent about Belgian candidates) were analyzed to define media sources. Then, we elaborate on the selection and coding of the media sources.

Twitter data collection took place during the election campaign, a four-week period preceding Election Day (May 25, 2014). The Twitter Application Program Interface (API) allows us to capture tweets containing a certain keyword using the open-source tool yourTwapperkeeper (yTK) (Bruns 2012). Following this procedure, we collected all Twitter messages containing references to Belgian politicians' Twitter handles (e.g., @GuyVerhofstadt). More specifically, we take into account messages that contain addressivity markers (Papacharissi and de Fatima Oliveira 2012), that is, tweets including @-signs in the form of replies (tweets that start with "@name") and mentions (tweets with "@name" in the text). In total, we found 9,056 unique users tweeting about the Belgian candidates. As mentioned above, the 10 percent most active users (totaling 906 users) were selected for further analysis.

Not all Belgian candidates running for the European elections have a Twitter account. In total, 25 percent of the Dutch-speaking candidates (34 candidates) and 14 percent of the French-speaking candidates (22 candidates) have a Twitter account. Hence, our study is limited to the political candidates that are present on Twitter. In accordance with a cross-national EU study on campaign communication (Lilleker et al. 2015), traditional modes of communication (such as television or newspapers) are still important for politicians and concerning new media, Facebook is considered to be the dominant platform. In this respect, the importance of Twitter as an election tool is relative. Not surprising, only seven out of the 21 elected Belgian MEPs do not have a Twitter account. Twitter adoption among the Belgian population is fairly limited as well; about 20 percent of the population has an active account, compared to 70 percent for Facebook (iMinds-iLab.o 2014). This explains Facebook's appeal as a tool to communicate with voters, since Twitter reflects a rather limited selection of the population in which predominantly media and political elites have their place.

As mentioned above, we focus on a sample of 906 users to define media sources. We rely on users' profile information to do so (e.g., user description, followers/friends, listed count, location, language, and the profile URL). Hence, coding is based on the users' visible associations with media sources. As stated earlier, party-owned websites or politicians' websites/blogs are not taken into account. We focus on media institutions (e.g., broadcasters, news agencies, and newspaper companies) as well as non-mainstream media sources, such as blogs or information websites (including official communication coming from Europe's institutions such as the European Commission). In total, we found 114 users (or 13 percent out of 906 users) that qualify as media sources.

The results section starts with a definition and categorization of the media sources we detected in our dataset. Following that, we relate our typology of media sources to the coverage of the Belgian candidates running for the 2014 European elections. We use the Social Network Analysis (SNA) software UCINET (Borgatti et al. 2002) to analyze the relation between media sources and Belgian candidates. More specifically, we constructed a bipartite graph that combines two types of data, media sources and political candidates. We use UCINET's visualization tool NetDraw to demonstrate the connections between media and politicians. In addition, general network statistics allow us to define the positions media sources and candidates take within the network.

Media Coverage of the Belgian Candidates in the EU Elections

Defining Media Sources Covering Belgian Candidates

In line with our first research question, Table 4.1 shows the categorization of media sources. In the first instance, we categorize along national lines: Europe, Belgium, Flanders, Wallonia, and other countries. The table shows political communication is situated at the European level as well as the national level. Second, we distinguish between mainstream and non-mainstream media. Below, we discuss the different categories and subcategories. The discussion focuses on the actual media sources, rather than the Twitter users representing them. In addition, we provide specific examples, which are illustrative of the respective categories and subcategories.

Since there are no European media available across all EU member states (Papathanassopoulos and Negrine 2011), the number of mainstream media sources is rare. We found three transnational mainstream media organizations, Agence Europe, Euronews, and Euranet. Agence Europe or the European Union press agency is an international news agency publishing about Europe and its institutions on a daily basis. The European-wide TV news channel Euronews and radio network Euranet cover news and current affairs from a European perspective in multiple languages and across a variety of countries.

64 Evelien D'heer and Pieter Verdegem

TABLE 4.1 Categories of media sources

Sources	Count
European media sources	37
Mainstream media	*4*
Non-mainstream media	*33*
Belgian media sources	5
Mainstream media	*2*
Non-mainstream media	*3*
Flemish media sources	25
Mainstream media	*16*
Non-mainstream media	*9*
Wallonian media sources	12
Mainstream media	*11*
Non-mainstream media	*1*
Foreign media sources	35
Mainstream media	*25*
Non-mainstream media	*10*

Note: N = 114.

In addition, we found a number of web-based news initiatives, operating across European countries. For example, EurActive.com provides online news in 12 languages and is targeted at policy professionals. Europolitics.info is a newspaper and web publication on European affairs, situated in Brussels and available in French and English. Examples of other digital-only formats are Europedecides.com (a project in collaboration with the European Parliament), Europeanpublicaffairs. eu (a blog-like website of alumni of the European Public Affairs program at Maastricht University, a university in the Netherlands) and EUwatch.eu (a curator of tweets, posts, and articles about Europe). In addition, this category includes European institutions such as the website on the European Parliament in Belgium, Europarl.be, providing the latest news from the Press Service of the European parliament in Dutch and French, the two principal languages in Belgium.

In Belgium, we found two Twitter accounts referring to the Belgian news agency Belga, which were classified as mainstream media. Concerning non-mainstream media, we found the Belgian initiative beuvote2014.eu (available in Dutch and French), dedicated to the 2014 elections (but no longer accessible to date).

The largest number of media sources was counted for Flanders and Wallonia. More specifically, we notice the prominence of mainstream media since these are organized along regional lines in Belgium, Flanders, or Wallonia. Concerning

Media Coverage of an Election Campaign **65**

Flemish mainstream media, we found references to daily newspapers (e.g., Standaard.be) as well as the public service broadcaster VRT. In addition, we identified news websites operating as alternative news sources to commercial, mainstream media, such as doorbraak.be and mo.be. In addition, we found a Twitter account employing Twitter as a news medium, Twitter messages as updates, both with and without references to external news websites (@nieuws_anker).

Compared to Flanders, the total number of media sources situated in the French-speaking part is much smaller. Concerning mainstream media, we found references to the Public Service Broadcaster RTBF and daily newspapers such as Lesoir.be. In addition, we count one Twitter account referring to a personal blog, written in French (blog.marcelsel.com). This web blog functions as a non-mainstream news website (containing blog posts covering the EU). Related, and as we discuss in detail below, we found a smaller number of French-speaking politicians in our dataset, 13 (compared to 26 Dutch-speaking politicians).

Last, we found a number of Twitter users that are linked to media sources situated in other countries. For example, we discovered journalists working for the UK broadcaster the BBC and the Portuguese online newspaper Observador.pt. Examples of non-mainstream media are the Italian online magazine affarinternazionali.it, which focuses on politics, strategy and economics as well as the Spanish blog website devueltayvuelta.com. The presence of foreign news sources in our dataset is linked to one Flemish political candidate, Guy Verhofstadt (elected MEP for the liberal–centrist political group of the European Parliament ALDE). Compared to the other candidates, he is internationally present and acknowledged. Moreover, he is the only Belgian politician taking a central position in the overall election debate (Maireder and Schlögl 2014; Smyrnaios 2014). Guy Verhofstadt was the ALDE nominate running for EU Commission president.

To summarize, a large part of the media sources is situated at the European level. These news sources are specialized in European affairs and often operate across Europe, addressing citizens in multiple languages. Concerning Belgium, we found the large majority of the sources is related to either Flanders or Wallonia. This connects to Maireder and Schlögl's (2014) network analysis, showing national clusters of political and mainstream media actors.

As mentioned above, Belgium consists of a Dutch-speaking and French-speaking communities and accompanying public spheres. Consequently, we have both Dutch-speaking and French-speaking candidates running for the EU elections. Building upon our typology outlined above, we question what media sources cover (1) Dutch-speaking candidates, (2) French-speaking candidates, or (3) both.

Comparing Media Sources Covering Dutch-Speaking and French-Speaking Candidates

Before we discuss the network of media sources and politicians, we describe the differences between the Dutch and French-speaking candidates' Twitter presence.

As mentioned above, 34 Flemish candidates have a Twitter account, of which 26 (76.47 percent) are discussed on Twitter. Of the French-speaking candidates, 22 are present on Twitter and 13 of them (59.09 percent) are covered on Twitter. Moreover, there are large differences among politicians' coverage. For example, Guy Verhofstadt (elected MEP, ALDE) receives a total of 1,408 references (mentions/replies), whereas a group of nine lesser-known candidates are mentioned only once.

As the limited presence of French-speaking candidates already indicates, the number of media sources reporting about the French-speaking candidates is much smaller compared to the Dutch-speaking ones. In total, we found 18 media sources covering the French-speaking candidates, of which half (nine) are situated in Wallonia, five are based in Europe, three in Belgium, and one in France. Hence, no Flanders-based media report about the French-speaking candidates. Wallonia-based media sources are almost exclusively mainstream media, followed by European and Belgian web-based initiatives focusing on European affairs and the pan-European radio network Euranet. Last, the French press agency Agence News Press (newspress.fr) was found in our dataset as well.

The Dutch-speaking candidates are covered by 108 media sources. The strong profile of MEP Guy Verhofstadt (ALDE) explains this large number, and more specifically the large number of foreign media sources (see Table 4.1). Guy Verhofstadt is the only Belgian candidate among the top politicians mentioned in the Twitter debate (Maireder and Schlögl 2014). Since he is very distinct from all other Belgian candidates in our dataset, his presence confounds the comparisons we aim to make. In this respect, we exclude Guy Verhofstadt for the construction of the network of media and politicians and further analysis of the data. This results in a decrease in media sources covering Flemish candidates, with 40 sources remaining.

We elaborate on these 40 sources to understand the coverage of the Dutch-speaking candidates and make the comparison with the media sources covering the French-speaking candidates. Flemish media mainly cover Flemish candidates (26 out of 40), followed by European (five), Belgian (four), foreign (three), and Wallonian (two) media sources. Concerning Flemish media, we found a number of mainstream outlets, a current affairs program, and journalists. In addition, non-mainstream news websites were discovered as well. On the European level, we found the European press agency Agence Europe as well as web-based initiatives such as cosmopublic.eu. In addition, we found journalists working for foreign news media. Last, for Wallonia, we found the French commercial radio network RTL and a blogger (@marcelsel), writing in French.

In Figure 4.1, we visualize coverage of the Dutch-speaking and French-speaking candidates. The presentation of the network shows the distinctions in coverage between the two types of candidates. Both the number of media sources covering the respective candidates as well as the type of media sources, seem to differ. Flemish media and politicians are situated in the lighter grey area in the upper

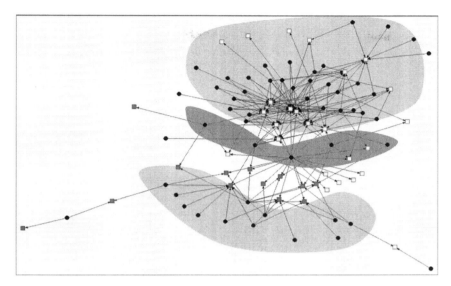

FIGURE 4.1 Spring-embedding representation of the relation between media sources and political candidates. *Legend*: Dots: media sources; dark squares: French-speaking candidates; light squares: Dutch-speaking candidates (excluding Guy Verhofstadt).

part of Figure 4.1, whereas Wallonian media and politicians are situated in the lighter grey area in the lower part. In the middle darker gray area, we find media sources reporting about Dutch-speaking as well as French-speaking candidates. As Figure 4.1 shows, a limited number of media sources cover candidates from both regions.

As visible in the figure, Flemish politicians are more closely linked to one another as media coverage is more exclusively linked to Flemish candidates. French-speaking candidates receive less overall media coverage. Moreover, media attention is more often shared with Flemish politicians. This is confirmed by the external/internal ratio analysis, or E-I index, which defines to what extent the overall network is characterized by out-group as opposed to in-group relations (Krackhardt and Stern 1988). Data was converted from two-mode (media–politicians) to one-mode (politicians–politicians) to calculate the E-I indices and compare Dutch-speaking and French-speaking candidates. Concerning connections between Dutch-speaking politicians we find an index of −0.246, whereas for the French-speaking politicians, the index is positive, 0.338. E-I indices range from −1 (all ties internal) to +1 (all ties external), and indicate what is already visible and aforementioned.

Although we excluded Guy Verhofstadt from the dataset, large differences between the candidates remain. The most covered politicians in the network are Dutch-speaking. Johan Van Overtveldt (elected MEP for the European

68 Evelien D'heer and Pieter Verdegem

Conservatives and Reformists Group; ECR), Gerolf Annemans (elected MEP, non-attached), Bart Staes (elected MEP for the Greens/European Free Alliance; Greens-EFA), Marianne Thyssen (elected MEP for the European People's Party; EPP), and Kathleen Van Brempt (elected MEP for the Progressive Alliance of Socialists and Democrats; S&D) are covered by 25 percent or more media sources.

Based on our categorization of media sources, we describe the six media sources that cover both Dutch-speaking and French-speaking candidates. They are distinct in terms of location (operating from Wallonia, Belgium, and Europe), but nearly all of them (five out of six) are labeled as non-mainstream media sources. Taking a closer look at these Twitter users, we found two "temporary initiatives," of which one is situated at European level, (@2014Europarl). This account no longer exists to date. It made no reference to a specific website, and hence employed Twitter as a news medium. Its description stated "Tweets are not the official position of the EP." Second, the Belgian account @bEUvote2014, communicates in Belgian's principal languages Dutch and French. Here again, the corresponding website is no longer accessible to date.

Third, @EP_Belgium is the information channel of the European Parliament tailored to Belgium, containing a reference to the website Europarl.be. Again, this account communicates in Dutch and French. The fourth initiative is called @EUWatchers, described as a European Citizen Information Network Hub curating EU info, blogs, critical opinions and a profile URL that links to EUwatch.eu. The last two accounts refer to individuals, of which one is a journalist working for the French broadcaster *RTL* (@ASolim) and the other is a blogger (@marcelsel) writing in French and linking to a personal blog written in French (blog.marcelsel.com).

Three of our six "bridging actors" are also the most central media sources in the network. Network centrality reflects the relative amount of users a media source reaches. The Twitter account @bEUvote2014 covers 61 percent of the political candidates, followed by @EP_Belgium, covering 26 percent of the candidates, and @marcelsel, covering 21 percent of the politicians in the network. Other central actors in the network are the European Press Agency @agence-newspress and two Flemish mainstream media accounts, the current affairs debate program @terzaketv and a newspaper journalist @PaulGoossens2. Their respective degree centrality scores are 24 percent, 21 percent, and 18 percent, reflecting the relative count of politicians they cover. However, these users exclusively cover Dutch-speaking candidates.

Conclusion

This study analyzed Twitter in order to get a broader understanding of the media sources covering the European elections. It focused on Belgium and its peculiar "bi-national" structure, reflecting two political and cultural spaces. In general, coverage about the respective candidates is strongly related to the regions in which

Media Coverage of an Election Campaign **69**

politicians are elected, in this case Flanders and Wallonia. The limited number of media sources that do cover both Dutch-speaking and French-speaking candidates are almost exclusively defined as non-mainstream media sources, the European Parliament, and EU-dedicated media with an international reach. These findings are indicative of the potential of the web to contribute to the "Europeanization" (Olsen 2002) of political communication.

In general, our results relate to the work of Maireder and Schlögl (2014) and Smyrnaios (2014), although they departed from a different approach (hashtags/keywords) to identify clusters in the network. National clusters of media and politicians are structured around a central collection of actors, with European institutions, Britain-based, and international news media being the most prominent. Compared to these existing studies, we took a "small sample" approach, combining the structure of the interactions with an in-depth focus on the actors included. In addition we highlight bridging actors, rather than focusing exclusively on the most central actors in the debate. In this respect, we defined actors that were not discussed in Maireder and Schlögl's (2014) and Smyrnaios' (2014) studies. Simultaneously, a number of actors that have central positions in the hashtag debate were not found in our sample (e.g., *The Guardian* and *The Economist*). These media organizations are internationally oriented, which is not the case for Flemish and Wallonian mainstream media. They represent smaller nations and communicate in less common languages (e.g., Dutch), hence, they reach smaller audiences. They do play a central role in the coverage of the Belgian candidates, which is not counterintuitive since elections of the European candidates are held in Belgium's respective regions of Flanders and Wallonia.

Our empirical work could be extended taking into account the total sample of users reporting about the Belgian candidates rather than the 10 percent most active users on which we focused. In addition, as mentioned in our research design, a fairly large part of the candidates do not have a Twitter account, hence not all Belgian candidates were taken into consideration. In addition, it is equally relevant to define and describe the media that were *not* found in our dataset, which requires a different approach. Last, our preliminary findings would benefit from the inclusion of other European countries, as "these [European] election campaigns offer an excellent opportunity for cross-national, comparative research" (Strömbäck 2011, p. 5). This would allow detecting the extent to which new communication tools allow to cross nations and their respective media and political systems. In addition, Twitter allows for a systematic comparison for a fairly large number of countries due to its comparable data structure.

Note

1 Since the 1960s and 1970s, political parties of Belgium split up into Flemish and French-speaking parties. The small Workers' Party is an exception here, as it operates as a single Belgian party (PVDA in Dutch and PTB in French). In addition, the growing

References

Anderson, C. 1991. *Imagined Communities: Reflections on the Origin and Spread of Nationalism.* London: Verso.

Armstrong, C.L. and F. Gao. 2010. Now Tweet This: How News Organizations Use Twitter. *Electronic News* 4(4): 218–35.

Ausserhofer, J. and A. Maireder. 2013. National Politics on Twitter: Structures and Topics of a Networked Public Sphere. *Information, Communication & Society* 16(3): 291–314.

Borgatti, S.P., M.G. Everett, and L.C. Freeman. 2002. *Ucinet for Windows: Software for Social Network Analysis.* Harvard, MA: Analytic Technologies.

Bruns, A. 2012. How Long Is a Tweet? Mapping Dynamic Conversation Networks on Twitter Using Gawk and Gephi. *Information, Communication & Society* 15(9): 1323–51.

Castells, M. 2007. Power and Counter-Power in the Network Society. *International Journal of Communication* 1: 238–66.

Chadwick, A. 2013. *The Hybrid Media System: Politics and Power.* Oxford University Press.

D'heer, E. and P. Verdegem. 2014. Conversations about the Elections on Twitter: Towards a Structural Understanding of Twitter's Relation with the Political and the Media Field. *European Journal of Communication* 29(6):720–34.

Hallin, D.C. and Mancini, P. 2004. *Comparing Media Systems: Three Models of Media and Politics.* Cambridge University Press.

iMinds-iLab.o. 2014. *Digimeter: Adoption and Usage of Media & ICT in Flanders. Wave 7.* Ghent: iMinds-iLab.o.

Jungherr, A. 2014. *Twitter in Politics: A Comprehensive Literature Review.* Rochester, NY: Social Science Research Network.

Kalsnes, B., A.H. Krumsvik, and T. Storsul. 2014. Social Media as a Political Backchannel: Twitter Use During Televised Election Debates in Norway. *Aslib Journal of Information Management* 66(3): 313–28.

Krackhardt, D. and R. Stern. 1988. Informal Networks and Organizational Crises: An Experimental Simulation. *Social Psychology Quarterly* 15(2): 123–40.

Larsson, A.O. and H. Moe. 2012. Studying Political Microblogging: Twitter Users in the 2010 Swedish Election Campaign. *New Media & Society* 14(5): 729–47.

Lilleker, D.G., J. Tenscher, and V. Štětka. 2015. Towards Hypermedia Campaigning? Perceptions of New Media's Importance for Campaigning by Party Strategists in Comparative Perspective. *Information, Communication & Society* 18(7): 747–65.

Maireder, A. and S. Schlögl. 2014. The European Political Twittersphere: Network of Top Users Discussing the 2014 European Elections, www.gfk.com/Documents/whitepaper/EuroTwittersphere_FINAL.pdf.

Matsa, K.E. and M. Jurkowitz. 2014. The EU Elections on Twitter. Mixed Views about the EU and Little Passion for the Candidates. *Pew Research Center Journalism & Media*, www.journalism.org/2014/05/22/the-eu-elections-on-twitter.

Olsen, P.J. 2002. The Many Faces of Europeanization. *Journal of Common Market Studies* 40(5): 921–52.

Papacharissi, Z. and M. de Fatima Oliveira. 2012. Affective News and Networked Publics: The Rhythms of News Storytelling on #Egypt. *Journal of Communication* 62(2): 266–82.

Papathanassopoulos, S. and R.M. Negrine. 2011. *European Media.* Cambridge: Polity Press.

Parmelee, J.H. 2013. Political Journalists and Twitter: Influences on Norms and Practices. *Journal of Media Practice* 14(4): 291–305.

Raycheva, L. and J. Róka. 2011. Similarities and Differences in Transformational Democracies: EP Campaigns in Bulgaria and Hungary. In M. Maier (ed.), *Political Communication in European Parliamentary Elections*. Aldershot: Ashgate, pp. 61–74.

Reif, K. and H. Schmitt. 1980. Nine Second-Order National Elections: A Conceptual Framework for the Analysis of European Election Results. *European Journal of Political Research* 8: 3–44.

Rogers, R. 2009. *The End of the Virtual: Digital Methods*. Amsterdam: Vossiuspers UvA.

Rogstad, I.D. 2014. Political News Journalists in Social Media. *Journalism Practice* 8(6): 688–703.

Smyrnaios, N. 2014. The European Elections through the Lens of Twitter. *Journées détudes Réseaux et TIC; réseaux et innovation Labex SMS, Toulouse*, www.academia.edu/11434548/The_European_Elections_through_the_lens_of_Twitter.

Strömbäck, J., M. Maier, and L.L. Kaid. 2011. Political Communication and Election Campaigns for the European Parliament. In M. Maier (ed.), *Political Communication in European Parliamentary Elections*. Aldershot: Ashgate, pp. 3–16.

Van Parijs, P. 2013. Is a Bi-National Democracy Viable? The Case of Belgium. In A. Shapira (ed.), *Nationalism and Binationalism: The Perils of Perfect Structures*. Brighton and Jerusalem: Sussex Academic Press and the Israel Democracy Institute, pp. 61–70.

PART II
The Audience

5

COMMUNICATION WITH CONSTITUENTS IN 140 CHARACTERS

How Members of Congress Used Twitter to Get Out the Vote in 2014

Heather K. Evans

Over the past few years, political scientists have turned to social media networks to examine how politicians campaign and to project winners of upcoming elections (Tumasjan et al. 2010). Recent research has shown that members of Congress use Twitter to announce where they have been, votes they have taken, and where they are going; to directly communicate with their followers; and to ask their followers to get engaged with the political process (Evans et al. 2014; Evans 2015; Golbeck et al. 2010; Glassman et al. 2013; Hemphill et al. 2013; Gainous and Wagner 2014). Instead of posting non-campaign related-materials, like pictures of food they had eaten that day, candidates for the US House in 2012 primarily sent tweets regarding their candidacy during the two months leading up to the election (Evans 2013).

In some recent work, researchers have suggested that what politicians say on Twitter can affect civic engagement. For instance, Greenberger (2012) shows that the average Twitter user is significantly more likely to visit a campaign donation page if they were directed to it from Twitter. This finding should not surprise us as others have found that citizens can be affected by mobilization efforts by individuals within institutions (Green and Gerber 2008). As I have suggested in earlier work (Evans 2015), if representatives were to spend more time discussing civic engagement on Twitter, followers may be more likely to engage in those activities.

Previously, I found that during the 2012 election and the following summer months, some members of Congress encouraged their Twitter followers to get engaged by volunteering, registering, and contacting their political officials. This chapter serves as a follow-up to that research by examining the ways in which candidates for the US House and the US Senate encouraged their followers to become civically engaged during the 2014 election on Twitter. This

76 Heather K. Evans

chapter presents the results of a content analysis of every tweet sent by candidates during the last two months of the campaign. Specifically, I showed that (1) civic engagement was discussed on Twitter by US House candidates during the 2012 election; (2) candidates didn't discuss civic engagement that often (3.4 percent of their total tweets were about civic engagement); and (3) partisanship was a predictor of civic engagement tweets (Democrats sent significantly more tweets about civic engagement). Even with that analysis, there are still unanswered questions. First, I only examined those running for the US House. Do individuals running for the US House spend more time focused on civic engagement activities than those running for the Senate? We might expect this is the case since constitutionally the US House was set up to be the "people's branch" due to the smaller, more personal, constituency. Second, my previous research examines many aspects of "civic engagement" as defined by the Center for Information and Research on Civic Learning and Engagement (CIRCLE), but does not examine the number of tweets sent specifically about voting. I found that very little time is spent by members of Congress on Twitter discussing civic engagement, but this may be because I do not examine whether candidates discuss voting. Finally, my previous work also does not examine all of the candidates for the US House and instead focuses on the winners only.

In this follow up, I conduct a content analysis of each tweet sent by all candidates for the US House and US Senate in 2014 (House n = 1,137; Senate n = 140). I re-examine the exact categories given in my previous research as well as one not included, i.e., vote. Examining both electoral and non-electoral aspects of civic engagement will give us a more robust picture regarding whether politicians encourage their followers to participate.

What is Civic Engagement?

One of the most difficult concepts to define is "civic engagement." CIRCLE conducted a series of focus groups with young people from around the country and developed indicators for identifying civic engagement activities.[1] CIRCLE divides civic engagement into civic activities, electoral activities, and political activities. The indicators are listed in Table 5.1.

In the analysis that follows, I focus on these forms of civic engagement, particularly voting, registering, volunteering, contacting, and joining a political group.

Members of Congress and Civic Engagement

Former representative Lee Hamilton (Republican, Indiana) published a commentary at the Center on Congress at Indiana University and had this to say about discussing civic engagement with his constituents: "civic life is best lived in the neighborhood, and that they could perform no better service than finding

TABLE 5.1 CIRCLE's civic engagement indicators

Civic	Electoral	Political voice
Community problem-solving	Voting	Contacting officials
Volunteering	Persuading others	Contacting the media
Membership in a group	Displaying buttons, signs, stickers	Protesting
Fundraising run/walk/ride	Campaign contributions	Petitioning
	Volunteering	Boycotting
		Buycotting
		Canvassing

a problem within their community, and doing something about it." Instead of giving advice on how to contact representatives in Congress or looking up their representatives' voting records, he writes that he believes "civic engagement is the greatest antidote for cynicism."[2] Do other current members of Congress share his feelings on this topic? Do members of Congress focus on encouraging their constituents to engage in the political and civic process?

As Mayhew notes in his book *The Electoral Connection* (1974), members of Congress care most about three activities: re-election, public policy, and influence. The only way that members can achieve each of those activities is through election. In this manner then, it is safe to assume that members of Congress care about voting. We see this especially as the election approaches, in television ads and social media postings.

Members of Congress, therefore, care about the electoral aspects of civic engagement. What about the non-electoral aspects of civic engagement, like Lee Hamilton paid reference to in his commentary? As Fenno (1978) details, legislators spend much time in their districts cultivating a "home style" of communicating with their constituents. This has evolved in today's electronic age to writing daily Facebook posts and emailing with constituents (Williams and Gulati 2008; Lawless 2011; Friedman et al. 2015). Representatives spend a great deal of time trying to engage with their followers and providing information on how they can get involved in Congressional issues. As my previous research demonstrates, representatives tried to engage their followers in the political process during the 2012 election (and seven months later), but they do so in a limited fashion (Evans 2015). Only 3.4 percent of their total tweets during the last two months of the election were dedicated to any civic engagement activities, as defined by CIRCLE.

As one might expect, my previous work shows that there was a partisan bias to the likelihood of a candidate tweeting about civic engagement. Democrats were significantly more likely to tweet about almost all of the civic engagement activities. As I argued, we should expect a difference between the candidates based on party depending on which party has a majority in the House. At the time of my study, Republicans held a majority in the US House, which meant that the Democrats were the out-party. We should, therefore, expect that Democrats would send more tweets aimed at increasing engagement in the political and civic process. My previous findings confirm this hypothesis. For instance, Democrats sent 21 times more tweets about registration than Republicans in the last two months of the 2012 election (Evans 2015).

In the results that follow, I examine incumbency and all of the candidates for the US House and Senate. This is an important extension to my previous work on the winners of the 2012 election. As Evans, Cordova, and Sipole (2014) show, incumbents and challengers tweet very differently. Incumbents were less likely to tweet about mobilization activities in 2012, and so we should expect that they will be less likely to tweet about civic engagement in 2014 as well.

Hypotheses

There are various reasons to expect that some individuals should tweet more about civic engagement than others. The "out-party innovation thesis," advanced by David Karpf (2014), suggests that the party in the minority will do whatever necessary to gain an advantage over their competition during an election, especially on social media. Since Democrats were the "out-party" in the US House, I expect that they will tweet more about civic engagement. In the Senate, they were positioned to possibly lose the majority. For this reason, they may tweet more than Republicans about civic engagement. At the same time, however, Republicans may tweet more in the Senate about these activities since they were in the "out-party" before the 2014 election.

I also expect that women, challengers, and those in competitive elections will tweet more often about these civic engagement activities than men, incumbents, and those in safe races. Female candidates are themselves an "out-party" since there are so few serving in Congress. Other research has also shown that women are more active in civic engagement than men (Kawashima-Ginsberg and Thomas 2013). Challengers should also tweet more about these activities because they should be spending a majority of their time trying to increase their chances in the election, and those in competitive elections should tweet more about civic engagement since in those races each vote matters more.

Since the US House was set up to be the "people's branch," I also expect those candidates to spend more time discussing civic engagement than candidates in the Senate.

Method

To investigate these hypotheses, I coded each tweet from the campaign Twitter pages for the candidates for the US House and Senate during the last two months of their campaign (September 1 through Election Day). Using a keyword search, I coded whether or not the candidates discussed the key words and phrases used in my previous research based on the Center for Information and Research on Civic Learning and Engagement's (CIRCLE) definition of civic engagement as well as voting. The list of phrases that I keyword-searched for are the following: vote, register, volunteer, encourage, join, contact, democracy, boycott.[3]

I also coded for gender, party, incumbency, and whether the race was considered competitive by the Cook Political Report two months before the end of the election. In the models that follow, female, Democrat, and Republican are coded as dummy variables (1 for female, 0 for male; 1 for Democrat, 0 for other; 1 for Republican, 0 for other). Competitiveness is also a dummy variable and is coded one if any race was deemed a "toss-up" or "leaning Republican" or "leaning Democrat" on September 12, 2014 for the US House elections, and on September 5, 2014 for the Senate elections.[4] Incumbency is also included as a dummy variable (1 for incumbent, 0 for challenger).[5]

Results for the US House

For the US House, 1,137 people were running in the general election. Out of those individuals, most had Twitter accounts. Only 290 had no Twitter presence at all. Two individuals tweeted more than 3,000 times from September 1 to Election Day, and when those individuals were dropped from the analysis, the average number of tweets sent by all candidates was 116.2. When we compare that average to the results from the 2012 election (Evans et al. 2014), we may be tempted to claim that Twitter use by candidates for the US House increased in 2014, but the average for 2014 includes retweets. When retweets are removed from the analysis, the averages are very similar (88 for 2012, 85 for 2014).

The tweet data show that 91 percent of the House candidates who tweeted sent at least one tweet about civic engagement. Table 5.2 gives the average number of tweets sent regarding each of the types of engagement. Out of those eight key words, tweets about voting were used most often, and account for 15.4 percent of the total tweets sent. The next most often used word was "join" which accounted for 3.73 percent of the total tweets sent. Civic engagement tweets make up 22.29 percent of the total dataset. This is a significant increase from the 2012 study, which shows that only 3.4 percent of the total tweets were specifically about civic engagement. When I drop mentions of voting from the 2014 House data, I find that the average number of tweets sent about civic engagement was 6.02 (5.12 percent).

In the 2012 election, Democrats spent significantly more time discussing civic engagement than Republicans (Evans 2015). To see if there were any predictors of tweeting about civic engagement in 2014, I first calculated overall tweet means as well as the average number of times Republicans, Democrats, women, men,

TABLE 5.2 US House average number of tweets regarding civic engagement, 2014

	Average number of tweets	Percentage of total tweets
Vote	17.90	15.40%
Register	1.11	0.95%
Volunteer	1.71	1.47%
Encourage	0.24	0.21%
Contact	0.24	0.21%
Join	4.34	3.73%
Democracy	0.37	0.32%
Boycott	0.02	0.00%

TABLE 5.3 Average number and percent of tweets regarding civic engagement for the US House, 2014

	Average number of tweets sent	Average number of tweets sent about civic engagement	Percentage of total percent of total tweets re civic engagement
Democrats	120.99	33.17	27.42%
Republicans	113.82	20.44	17.98%
Third party	108.47	18.23	16.81%
Women	147.94	37.21	25.15%
Men	108.50	23.20	21.38%
Incumbents	95.99	19.90	20.73%
Challengers	132.40	30.76	23.23%
Competitive	185.95	48.79	26.24%
Non-competitive	109.01	23.57	21.62%

incumbents, challengers, those in competitive races, and those in non-competitive districts sent any tweets regarding civic engagement. The results are reported in Table 5.3.

The results in Table 5.3 demonstrate that Democrats, women, challengers, and those in competitive races sent more tweets about civic engagement than Republicans, men, incumbents, and those in non-competitive districts. The largest difference between groups is due to partisanship. Approximately 27 percent of the tweets sent by Democrats referenced civic engagement, while only 18 percent of the tweets sent by Republicans and 17 percent of tweets by third-party candidates paid any reference to these activities.

To see whether there were specific types of engagement discussed more by any of these groups, I calculated negative binomial regression models for each type

TABLE 5.4 Negative binomial regression results for the US House, 2014

	Vote	Register	Volunteer	Encourage	Contact	Join	Democracy	Boycott
Republican	0.26	0.54 ★	1.16 ★★	0.99 ★★	0.83 ★	0.78 ★★	−1.83 ★★	−1.64 +
	(0.16)	(0.24)	(0.27)	(0.38)	(0.40)	(0.18)	(0.29)	(0.84)
Democrat	0.70 ★★	1.47 ★★	1.36 ★★	0.97 ★★	0.55	1.22 ★★	−0.42 +	−0.84
	(0.16)	(0.23)	(0.27)	(0.37)	(0.40)	(0.18)	(0.25)	(0.71)
Female	0.30 ★	0.22	−0.04	0.53 ★	−0.12	0.36 ★★	0.05	−1.57
	(0.12)	(0.16)	(0.19)	(0.21)	(0.30)	(0.13)	(0.21)	(1.14)
Incumbent	−0.82 ★★	−0.37 ★★	−0.24	−0.22	−0.91 ★★	0.36 ★★	0.29	−1.32
	(0.10)	(0.14)	(0.16)	(0.19)	(0.26)	(0.11)	(0.19)	(0.85)
Competitive	0.68 ★★	0.09	1.26 ★★	0.11	0.53	0.70 ★★	−0.17	0.43
	(0.16)	(0.22)	(0.25)	(0.30)	(0.37)	(0.17)	(0.30)	(0.88)
Constant	2.57 ★★	−0.82 ★★	−0.75 ★★	−2.39 ★★	−1.78 ★★	0.16	−0.38 +	−2.54 ★★
	(0.13)	(0.21)	(0.24)	(0.34)	(0.34)	(0.16)	(0.20)	(0.55)
Pseudo R^2	0.02	0.03	0.02	0.02	0.02	0.02	0.04	0.08

Note: Standard errors are reported in parentheses. ★★ $p \leq 0.01$, ★ $p \leq 0.05$, + $p \leq 0.1$, n= 845.

82 Heather K. Evans

of tweet used. My results are reported in Table 5.4. Partisanship is a significant predictor of each type of tweet. Gender, incumbency, and competitiveness are significant for particular types of tweets.

First, when it comes to tweeting about voting, all of the independent variables are significant. Democrats sent 23 tweets on average about voting, while Republicans sent 14 and third-party candidates sent 15. Women sent 35 percent more tweets about voting than men. Challengers also sent about 50 percent more tweets regarding voting. Those in competitive races sent almost twice as many tweets about voting as those in safe districts. The person who tweeted the most about voting was Rose Izzo (Republican, Delaware), who tweeted 449 times. Overall, 85 percent of the House candidates sent at least one tweet about voting.[6]

Only 40 percent of the House candidates tweeted about registration. Out of those who did, most of them were Democrats or challengers. Democrats sent four times as many tweets about registration as third-party candidates, while they sent 2.72 times as many as Republicans. Challengers sent 30 percent more tweets than incumbents. Elan Carr, a Republican running for California's 33rd district, sent the most tweets about registration (28).

Partisanship and competitiveness are also significant predictors of tweets about volunteering. Democrats and Republicans sent significantly more tweets than third-party candidates about volunteering (Democrats sent 3.91 times as many while Republicans sent 3.18 as many). Those in competitive races sent 3.52 times as many as those in non-competitive races. About 38 percent of the candidates sent at least one tweet about volunteerism, and the person who sent the most was Charles Djou (Republican, Hawaii's 1st district).[7]

When it comes to tweeting about joining some political cause, 69 percent of the candidates sent at least one tweet. The candidate that sent the most tweets about joining was Frederica Wilson (Democrat, Florida's 24th district), who tweeted about joining 273 times. Incident rate ratios reveal that Democrats sent 3.38 times as many tweets as third-party candidates, while Republicans sent 2.17 times as many. Women and incumbents sent 43 percent more tweets about joining than men and challengers, and those in competitive races sent twice as many tweets about joining than those in non-competitive races.

The other words (contact, encourage, democracy, and boycott) were used by at most 20 percent of the candidates. Major party candidates were more than 2.6 times as likely to mention "encourage" in their tweets than third-party candidates. Women were 1.71 times more likely to tweet about "encourage" than men.[8] Republicans were more likely to encourage their followers to "contact" someone, while challengers sent 60 percent more tweets about "contact" than incumbents. Major party candidates were less likely to use the word "democracy" than third-party candidates, and Republicans were also less likely to use the word "boycott" than third-party candidates. The term "boycott" was only used by 14 candidates.

TABLE 5.5 US Senate average number of tweets regarding civic engagement, 2014

	Average number of tweets	Percentage of total tweets
Vote	58.87	20.05%
Register	3.42	1.19%
Volunteer	5.80	2.02%
Encourage`	1.20	0.42%
Contact	0.77	0.27%
Join	10.20	3.55%
Democracy	0.80	0.28%
Boycott	0.01	0.00%

Results for the US Senate

There were 140 candidates running for the US Senate in 2014. Out of those candidates, 26 were incumbents seeking to be returned to office. More than two-thirds of the candidates had Twitter accounts and used the site regularly throughout the last two months of the campaign (41 did not have a Twitter account). Those running for the Senate seats tweeted more than those running for the House seats. On average, Senate candidates who had Twitter accounts tweeted approximately 371.68 times. One candidate, Steve Carlson from Minnesota, tweeted in excess of 8,649 times. Once he is removed from the dataset, the average number of tweets sent by Senate candidates is 287.21. When retweets are removed from the analysis, candidates sent an average of 216 tweets in the two months leading up to Election Day. In the analysis that follows, those without a Twitter account and Steve Carlson are dropped from the models.

When it comes to discussing civic engagement on Twitter, most candidates sent at least one tweet about those activities. Over 94 percent of the Senate candidates with Twitter accounts sent at least one tweet about civic engagement, with the average number of tweets about these activities being 81.

Like candidates for the US House, candidates for the Senate were also most likely to tweet about voting or joining. As shown in Table 5.5, Senate candidates on average sent about 59 tweets about voting (20.05 percent of total tweets), while they sent 10 tweets about joining some political cause (3.55 percent of total tweets).[9] All of these words make up 21.79 percent of the entire Senate Twitter data. Those in the US House elections tweeted a little more about these activities (22.29 percent), but the difference is not significant.[10] When voting is removed from the analysis, Senate candidates tweeted 15.85 times about civic engagement in general (4.26 percent).

To see whether partisanship, gender, incumbency, and competitiveness mattered for the way candidates tweeted, I calculated the average number of overall

84 Heather K. Evans

TABLE 5.6 Average number and percent of tweets regarding civic engagement for the US Senate, 2014

	Average number of tweets sent	*Average number of tweets sent about civic engagement*	*Percentage of total tweets sent re civic engagement*
Democrats	428.46	146.72	34.24%
Republicans	302.17	66.51	22.01%
Third party	124.52	29.74	23.88%
Women	331.52	112.83	34.03%
Men	281.36	73.01	25.95%
Incumbents	482.96	128.08	26.52%
Challengers	220.18	64.97	29.51%
Competitive	385.89	125.76	32.59%
Non-competitive	224.72	52.76	23.48%

tweets as well as the average number of tweets sent about civic engagement. The results are displayed in Table 5.6. As the results show, Democrats sent a higher percentage of tweets about civic engagement than Republicans or third-party candidates, who tweeted a similar percentage about these activities. Women, challengers, and those in competitive races also sent more tweets on average about civic engagement than men, incumbents, and those in safe races.

I calculated a negative binomial regression model for each type of civic engagement tweet sent to determine whether the differences are significant when other controls are included. Those results are displayed in Table 5.7.

When it comes to tweets about voting, 95 percent of candidates sent at least one tweet about it. Democrats tweet about the vote 3.86 times as often as third-party candidates, and 2.24 times as often as Republicans. Those in competitive races also tweet about voting 2.65 times as often as those in safe races.[11] Bruce Braley (Democrat, Iowa), tweeted the most about voting and sent 445 tweets about the activity, accounting for 38 percent of his total tweets.

About 50 percent of the candidates for the Senate seats tweeted about registration. Democrats and those in competitive races were also more likely to tweet about registration. Democrats sent 5.82 times as many tweets about registration than third-party candidates and 7.2 times as many when compared to Republicans, while those in competitive races sent 4.6 times as many as those in safe races. Mary Landrieu (Democrat, Louisiana) sent the most tweets about this activity (63).

While 60 percent of candidates tweeted about volunteerism, partisanship was also an important predictor of those tweets. Democrats and Republicans out-tweeted third-party candidates. On average, Democrats sent 11 tweets about volunteerism, Republicans sent 6, and third-party candidates sent 1.[12] Mary Nunn (Democrat, Georgia) tweeted the most about this activity (51 tweets).

TABLE 5.7 Negative binomial regression results for the US Senate, 2014

	Vote	Register	Volunteer	Encourage	Contact	Join	Democracy
Republican	0.39	0.21	1.96 ★★	1.50 ★	0.44	1.41 ★★	−1.90 +
	(0.33)	(0.52)	(0.42)	(0.68)	(0.78)	(0.32)	(1.04)
Democrat	1.35 ★★	1.76 ★★	2.66 ★★	2.76 ★★	0.57	1.62 ★★	0.22
	(0.38)	(0.56)	(0.52)	(0.75)	(1.10)	(0.37)	(1.02)
Female	−0.41	−0.09	−0.18	−1.03	0.67	−0.05	0.83
	(0.37)	(0.53)	(0.43)	(0.66)	(1.10)	(0.33)	(1.06)
Incumbent	0.09	0.21	−0.18	0.93 +	−0.82	0.71 ★	0.49
	(0.33)	(0.42)	(0.41)	(0.50)	(0.90)	(0.31)	(1.00)
Competitive	0.94 ★★	1.53 ★★	0.42	0.85 +	−1.12	0.99 ★★	−0.89
	(0.27)	(0.43)	(0.34)	(0.51)	(0.78)	(0.26)	(0.76)
Constant	2.93 ★★	−0.66	−0.36	−2.40 ★★	0.22	0.30	−0.12
	(0.24)	(0.44)	(0.34)	(0.65)	(0.59)	(0.26)	(0.66)
Pseudo R^2	0.03	0.08	0.06	0.01	0.01	0.07	0.06

Note: Standard errors are reported in parentheses.★★ $p \leq .01$, ★ $p \leq .05$, + $p \leq .10$, $n = 97$.

86 Heather K. Evans

Only 38 percent of the Senate candidates sent any tweets with the word "encourage." Partisanship, competitiveness, and incumbency are significant predictors of the use of the term. Democrats sent 12 times as many tweets about "encourage" as third-party candidates, while Republicans sent 4.5 times as many. Incumbents and those in competitive races sent more than twice as many tweets as challengers and those in safe races.[13] Cory Booker (Democrat, New Jersey) sent the most tweets about "encourage" (55).

"Join" was tweeted by 71 percent of the Senate candidates. Partisanship, incumbency, and competitiveness were again significant predictors of the use of this term. On average, Democrats sent 17.31 tweets about joining some political cause, compared to 11 for Republicans and 1.97 for third-party candidates. Incumbents and those in competitive races also tweeted more than twice as often regarding joining some political cause as challengers and those in safe races.[14] Mary Landrieu also sent the most tweets out of all Senate candidates about this activity (79).

The final two terms were used infrequently by any of the Senate candidates. Only 21 percent of the Senate candidates sent any tweets regarding contacting someone, while only 18 percent sent any tweets about democracy. None of the independent variables were significant predictors of tweeting about contact, while partisanship was a mildly significant predictor of tweeting about democracy.[15]

Discussion and Conclusion

As the above analysis shows, Senate and House candidates did tweet about civic engagement during the 2014 election, especially voting. Out of all the tweets sent in the House and Senate races, about 22 percent included CIRCLE's indicators of civic engagement.

When it comes to the independent variables included in this analysis, partisanship continues to be an important predictor of tweeting about civic engagement. Democrats sent significantly more tweets about most forms of civic engagement than Republicans and third-party candidates. Third-party candidates sent the fewest tweets about civic engagement, except for the terms "democracy" (Senate and House) and "boycott" (House).

Women sent significantly more tweets than men with the words "vote," "encourage," and "join" in the US House races. When it comes to each of those types of tweets, women sent 35 percent more tweets about voting; 71 percent more tweets about encouraging their followers to get involved in some way; and 43 percent more tweets asking their followers to join in doing some activity than male candidates.

Those in competitive race were also more likely to send tweets about voting, volunteering (House), registering (Senate), encourage (Senate), and joining some cause than candidates in non-competitive races. They sent

Communication with Constituents in 140 Characters **87**

twice as many tweets about voting and joining in both the House and Senate races, 3.52 times more tweets about volunteering, 4.65 times more tweets about registering, and twice as many tweets about "encourage" than those in non-competitive races.

Finally, incumbency was also significant in four of the models in the House and two in the Senate. Incumbents sent significantly *fewer* tweets regarding voting, registration, and contacting than challengers, while they sent significantly more tweets asking their followers to join some political cause and encouraging them to do something.

Overall, these results show that the context of the race greatly affects the style of tweeting the candidates engage in. Challengers and those in competitive races were generally more likely to tweet about these civic engagement activities.

This study also shows there are differences regarding Twitter use between the chambers. Those running for the Senate tweets sent more tweets in general, but those in the House sent more specifically about civic engagement. This finding is very different than early research on how members in each chamber tweeted (Glassman et al. 2010). Women also made more calls for civic engagement in the House, but that may be due to the low numbers of females running for office in the Senate (n = 17).

Partisanship continues to be the strongest predictor of what types of tweets were sent. Finding that Democrats continue to out-tweet Republicans (and third-party candidates) when it comes to civic engagement parallels some of the recent voting reform laws enacted by Republican state legislatures. Whether Republicans want to discourage voter engagement is not the topic of this chapter, but these results show that they do not spend quite the amount of time Democrats do discussing these activities on Twitter.

Overall, these results show that candidates do use Twitter to ask their followers to engage in the political process, even though they sent very few tweets focused on these activities other than voting. Since other research shows that asking someone to do something on Twitter can affect their likelihood of engaging in that activity, if representatives were to spend more time asking people to get involved in the civic process on Twitter, their followers might be more likely to engage in their communities.

Notes

1   See www.civicyouth.org/practitioners/Core_Indicators_Page.htm#1.
2   www.centeroncongress.org/the-merits-civic-engagement.
3   To accurately perform a content analysis of all tweets, first I converted all tweets to lowercase. Then I did a keyword search for the term "vot" to capture all mentions of voting, vote, and voter. For volunteering, volunteer, and volunteered, I did a search for the term "volunteer." I also searched for "regist" to capture all mentions of registration, registered, register. I also searched for the terms "civic engagement" and "buycott," but no one had sent tweets that included those words and phrases.

4 This is an improvement over other studies examining competitiveness. Earlier work has used margin of victory as a proxy. This measure was taken at the beginning of the coding cycle. By using this measure, I am able to see if a candidate will tweet differently if the media views their race as competitive two months before the end of their campaigns.

5 In Evans (2015), age of the representative is also included. Age is not included here due to lack of information regarding the age of third-party candidates.

6 Incident rate ratios: Democrat = 2.01; Republican = 1.3; female = 1.35; incumbent = 0.44; competitive = 1.98.

7 Differences were calculated as incident rate ratios. Djou sent 46 tweets about volunteering.

8 Incident rate ratio estimates.

9 Only one Senate candidate tweeted about boycotting: Dick Durbin, Democrat, Illinois, linked up a story about his boycott of Burger King on September 9, 2014.

10 Difference of means t-test.

11 Incident rate ratio estimates.

12 Means: Democrats = 10.94; Republicans = 5.57; third party = 0.74

13 Incidence rate ratios: Democrat = 15.88; Republican = 4.50; competitive = 2.34; incumbent = 2.54.

14 Incident rate ratios: Democrat = 5.04; Republican = 4.08; incumbent = 2.02; competitive = 2.68.

15 Republicans sent significantly fewer tweets about democracy. On average, Republicans sent 0.14 tweets about democracy, compared to 0.61 for third-party candidates and 1.69 for Democrats.

References

Evans, H.K. 2013. What Do Members of Congress Tweet About? http://themonkeycage. org/2013/03/what-do-members-of-congress-tweet-about.

Evans, H.K. 2015. Encouraging Civic Participation through Twitter during (and after) the 2012 Election. In M.T. Rogers and D. Gooch (eds.), *Civic Education in the 21st Century: A Multidimensional Inquiry*. Lanham, MD: Lexington Books, pp. 145–60.

Evans, H.K., V. Cordova, and S. Sipole. 2014. Twitter-Style: An Analysis of How House Candidates Used Twitter in Their 2012 Campaigns. *PS: Political Science and Politics* 47(2): 454–61.

Fenno, R.F. Jr. 1978. *Home Style: House Members in Their Districts*. New York: Little, Brown.

Friedman, S., J.L. Aubin, and R. Spice. 2015. The Role of Congressional Outreach in Civic Engagement: An Examination of Legislator Websites. In M.T. Rogers and D. Gooch (eds.), *Civic Education in the 21st Century: A Multidimensional Inquiry*. Lanham, MD: Lexington Books, pp. 115–44.

Gainous, J. and K.M. Wagner. 2014. *Tweeting to Power: The Social Media Revolution in American Politics*. New York: Oxford University Press.

Glassman, M.E., J.R. Straus, and C.J. Shogan. 2010. *Social Networking and Constituent Communications: Member Use of Twitter during a Two-Month Period in the 111th Congress*. Washington, DC: Congressional Research Service.

Glassman, M.E., J.R. Straus, and C.J. Shogan. 2013. *Social Networking and Constituent Communications: Member Use of Twitter during a Two-Month Period in the 112th Congress*. Washington, DC: Congressional Research Service.

Golbeck, J., J.M. Grimes, and A. Rogers. 2010. Twitter Use by the US Congress. *Journal of the American Society for Information Science and Technology* 61(8): 1612–21.

Green, D.P. and A.S. Gerber. 2008. *Get Out the Vote: How to Increase Voter Turnout.* Washington, DC: The Brookings Institute.

Greenberger, P. 2012. How Tweets Influence Political Donations: New Twitter Study with Compete. *The Twitter Advertising Blog*, https://blog.twitter.com/2012/how-tweets-influence-political-donations-new-twitter-study-with-compete.

Hemphill, L., J. Otterbacher, and M.A. Shapiro. 2013. What's Congress Doing on Twitter? In *Proceedings of the 2013 Conference on Computer Supported Cooperative Work.* New York: ACM, pp. 877–86.

Karpf, D. 2014. *The MoveOn Effect: The Unexpected Transformation of American Political Advocacy.* New York: Oxford University Press.

Kawashima-Ginsberg, K. and N. Thomas. (2013) *Civic Engagement and Political Leadership among Women: A Call for Solutions.* The Center for Information & Research on Civic Learning and Engagement, www.civicyouth.org/wp-content/uploads/2013/05/Gender-and-Political-Leadership-Fact-Sheet-3.pdf.

Lawless, J.L. 2011. Twitter and Facebook: New Ways to Send the Same Old Message? In R.L. Fox and J. Ramos, *iPolitics.* New York: Cambridge University Press, pp. 206–32.

Mayhew, D.R. 1974. *Congress: The Electoral Connection.* New Haven, CT: Yale University Press.

Tumasjan, A., T.O. Sprenger, P.G. Sandner, and I.M. Welpe. 2010. Predicting Elections with Twitter: What 140 Characters Reveal about Political Sentiment. *Proceedings of the Fourth International AAAI Conference on Weblogs and Social Media*: 178–185.

Williams, C.B. and G.J. Gulati. 2008. The Political Impact of Facebook: Evidence from the 2006 Midterm Elections and 2008 Nomination Contest. *Politics & Technology Review* (March): 11–21.

6

SOUTH KOREAN CITIZENS' POLITICAL INFORMATION-SHARING ON TWITTER DURING 2012 GENERAL ELECTION[1]

Jisue Lee, Hohyon Ryu, Lorri Mon, and Sung Jae Park

Social media tools such as Twitter, Facebook, and YouTube are now considered as politically transformative communication technologies as radio and television. There are predictions that social networking sites (SNSs) such as Facebook and Twitter will transform democracy, allowing citizens and politicians to communicate, connect, and interact in ways never before thought possible (Grant et al. 2010). In Barack Obama's presidential campaigns in 2008 and 2012, more than 100 staff members worked on Twitter outreach alone (@barackobama) (*The Economist* 2010; *New York Times* 2012). Current studies also show that the number of Japanese politicians using Twitter grew from three to 485 in under a year, while in Germany, 577 politicians opened Twitter accounts (Hong and Nadler 2011). Increasingly, politicians and elected officials are realizing the power of social media for communicating political information and interacting with citizens.

In considering the impact of social media in the political sphere, many researchers have explored how using SNSs such as Facebook and Twitter influences elections and public opinion poll results (Robertson et al. 2009; Hong and Nadler 2011; Tumasjan et al. 2010; O'Conner et al. 2010). These studies examine cases from the United States and European countries including Germany and the Netherlands. However, few studies from Asian countries were conducted. A case study on South Korea reviewed the evolution of hyperlinked networks, but did not explore use of Twitter during elections (Hsu and Park 2011). Findings and insights from empirical studies for different countries are needed to understand how citizens and politicians worldwide share political information and opinion via social media. This study investigates in particular political information-sharing in South Korea using Twitter.

The purposes of conducting this study are twofold: to explore retweeting (RT) information behavior for political messages by citizens in South Korea, and to compare the number and types of retweeted messages and the sentiments captured from these messages with the results of public opinion polling about leading political figures. This research allows us to better understand the role of Twitter in citizens' political information-sharing in South Korea, and offers insights into relationships between the message types and citizens' sentiments as expressed on Twitter and in public opinion polls.

Significance of Study

The year 2012 was a significant one in South Korea. With a general election in April 2012 and the presidential election in December 2012, *change of regime* issues engaged citizens in South Korea. The National Election Commission in South Korea lifted a strict ban on using SNSs such as Facebook and Twitter during election campaigns. The government expected that using social media would make it easier for citizens to obtain and share information on candidates and elections at low cost. With increased enthusiasm regarding this change in South Korea, the April 2012 election was considered an important test for the role of SNSs in political communication.

This chapter examines how citizens in South Korea used Twitter in sharing political information and opinions on three candidates running in the April 2012 general election, and investigates relationships between citizens' use of Twitter and the results of public opinion polls. This study compares South Korean citizens' retweeting of political messages about candidates in the April 2012 election with public opinion polling. The empirical findings add to the growing body of research on social media use in political communication.

Literature Review

Themes and research questions in this study concern the major concepts of Twitter as a social media tool, diffusion of innovation (DOI) theory and retweeting in Twitter, and use of Twitter and its impact on elections. Each will be examined for the further discussion.

Twitter as a Social Media Tool

Twitter was created in March 2006 and officially launched in July 2006. It is a fast-growing, real-time social media tool allowing people to find and share information on what is happening worldwide (Chang 2010). Twitter defines its service as "a real-time information network that connects you to the latest stories, ideas, opinions and news" (Twitter 2012). By January 2011, Twitter had more than 200 million users, and by October 2011 was handling more than 350 million tweets per day (Roosevelt 2012; *Los Angeles Times* 2011). Twitter's microblogging and messaging functionality has become a powerful tool for interpersonal, professional, and academic communication (Java et al. 2007; Thomas 2010; Dann 2010).

Twitter messages allow a maximum length of 140 characters, an average of 11 words per message (O'Connor et al. 2010). Messages, known as "tweets," can be made public or hidden, directed at another user by including the "@" symbol followed by another user's account name (e.g., @Friend_Username). Users can also share others' messages by RT, which copies and disseminates the original message to the user's followers (Zhao and Rosson 2009). Any message can be annotated with a topic or subject using hashtags (e.g., #Topic); clicking on or searching on a hashtag displays a choice of top tweets or all current tweets on Twitter that share the same hashtag. However, Twitter hashtags still suffer from their fragmentary and redundant nature (Chang 2010). Therefore, this study excluded hashtag keywords (#Keywords) in the data collection process.

Diffusion of Innovation Theory and Retweeting in Twitter

Rogers (1995, p. 5) defines diffusion of innovation as "the process by which an innovation is communicated through certain channels over time among the members of a social system." For this study, DOI provides a strong theoretical background to explain the phenomenon of adoption of innovation of political information-seeking and sharing via retweeting in Twitter.

According to Rogers (1995, p. 11), an innovation can be any "idea, practice, or object that is perceived as new by an individual or other unit of adoption." The diffusion process includes four key elements: innovation, the social system that the innovation affects, the communication channels of that social system, and time (Rogers 1962, 1995). The notion of innovation in DOI has also been expanded to include new products, ideas, services, methods, and inventions (Chang 2010). In this study, the innovation diffused among users particularly refers to the idea of seeking and sharing political information and opinions in Twitter through retweeting.

Communication is defined as "the process in which participants create and share information with one another in order to reach a mutual understanding" (Rogers 1995, p. 17). Mass media and interpersonal communications are two major communication channels in the dissemination process of innovation (Rogers 1962, 1995). Growing use of Twitter through creating and retweeting messages on computers and mobile devices can be seen as a major new pattern of mass-communication (Zhao and Rosson 2009). Dann (2010, p. 1) emphasizes that Twitter has rapidly "evolved through user innovations with the retweet (RT), reply (@) and hashtag (#) marks being introduced by consensus and community behavior." Roosevelt (2012) also mentions that retweeted messages should be analyzed using weighted measures since retweeting a message can be interpreted as agreement with that particular message, and can also spread the message faster and influence more users. Therefore, it is important to investigate the users' retweeting as community behavior of agreement and consensus in this study.

Rogers (1995, p. 23) defines a social system as "a set of interrelated units engaged in joint problem solving to accomplish a common goal," and further denoted characteristics of social systems as social norms, opinion leaders, change agents, and types of innovation decisions that can promote or hinder the diffusion of innovations. The time aspect is essential for explaining the innovation-decision process, the impact of innovators on adopters, and the growth rates of adoptions (Chang 2010; Rogers 1962, 1995). In this study, the time aspect offers findings on offline public opinion polling results in comparison with online users' concurrent retweeting of political messages for a comparative view of reflected political opinion over time.

Use of Twitter and Impact on Elections

Many researchers have studied how use of particular social networking sites (SNSs) by politicians and citizens relates to results of public opinion polls and elections (Hong and Nadler 2011; Tumasjan et al. 2010; O'Connor et al. 2010; Vergeer et al. 2011).

Tumasjan et al. (2010) argue that Twitter message content reflects the offline political landscape, thus potentially predicting actual election results. In a German case study, numbers of tweeted messages were observed to closely match ranking by share of the vote in election results, and nearly approximated results of traditional election polling. O'Connor et al. (2010) observed that sentiments in Twitter messages replicated 2008–9 US consumer confidence and presidential job approval polls. Hong and Nadler (2011) studied US politicians' use of Twitter and its impact on public opinion, and found that the impact of the number of tweets was not significant for any of the tested opinion polls. Vergeer et al. (2011) explored the relationship between using Twitter and gaining votes in the Netherlands. Although the study showed a positive relationship between the number of Twitter messages and the number of votes, the size of the Twitter network was noted to be a limited indicator for voting outcomes.

Although there is some research on Twitter in political communication and elections in the US, Germany, and the Netherlands, as yet little research has explored political use of Twitter within Asian countries. Furthermore, while existing studies have examined Twitter messages created by politicians and citizens that include particular keywords, there has not been research examining retweeted messages in particular. Therefore, this research studying retweeted messages in political communication in South Korea provides new insights into citizens' use of Twitter in the context of the national elections in South Korea.

Research Questions

The goal of this study is to investigate relationships between citizens' use of Twitter and public opinion polls, and to answer questions on how retweeting behavior in Twitter political communication may relate to public opinion polls.

RQ1: Does the number of citizens' retweeted messages correlate with results of concurrent public polls?

RQ2: Do the types of citizens' retweeted messages correlate with the results of public opinion polls?

RQ3: Do the sentiments of citizens' retweeted messages correlate with the results of public opinion polls?

Methodology

Data Capture and Storage

Python Twitter API was used to collect retweeted messages that included three specific keywords related to the general election of April 11, 2012, in South Korea, namely, the names of three leading political figures: Bak Geun-hye, Moon Jae-in, and Ahn Chul-soo (hereafter, Bak, Moon, and Ahn). The chosen keywords were appropriate in that these three leading political figures were expected to be the major candidates for the presidential election in December 2012. Initially, retweeted messages including the hashtags #BakGeunHye, #MoonJaeIn, and #AhnChulSoo were collected. However, those hashtags showed very low usage among Korean citizens, and the fragmentary and redundant nature of hashtags, as mentioned in Chang (2010), was also observed. Therefore, this study excluded hashtag keywords in data collection.

Python Twitter API collected tweets that included any one of the three presidential candidate names, automatically calculated the frequency of messages being retweeted every 100 seconds, sorted the top 200 messages based on the retweeting frequency, and stored them in the designated database. As Python Twitter API included Twitter messages for the most recent six days only, collected data needed to be stored in a different database.

Twitter messages were collected every five weekdays for six consecutive weeks, the same period as the collection of public opinion poll results. To study the relationships between Twitter messages and public opinion polling, correlation analysis was conducted.

Retweeted messages including the three keywords were harvested from April 2 to May 11, 2012, and resulted in a total of 556,675 messages. The most frequently retweeted 200 messages from each keyword class for each week were listed as a dataset of 600 messages, totaling 3,600 messages for the three classes for six weeks. From among these, sets of 120 messages, including the weekly top 40 retweeted messages for the three classes, were accumulated for six weeks. A total of 720 retweeted messages were analyzed for this study.

Messages were analyzed using two types of content analysis: (1) classifying message types and (2) identifying the general sentiment expressed in the messages. The results of content analysis for retweeted messages were compared with the results of public opinion polls through correlation analysis using SPSS 18.

Classification of Types of Message

Twitter messages are created and retweeted with multiple purposes and motivations. The objective in classifying types of messages was to understand the various purposes of citizens in their message-creating and retweeting behavior. Therefore, coding was conducted with a focus of studying the purposes as to why citizens created and retweeted particular messages.

Coding Scheme

The coding scheme was based on Robertson et al. (2009). Those authors examined linkage patterns of politically oriented community networking on Facebook, classifying five types of linkage motivation patterns observed on three presidential candidates' Facebook walls: evidence, rebuttal, action, joking and ridicule, and direct address. The study presented here showed the purposes for which posters created postings to share political information and opinions through Twitter.

In addition to adapting these five types of messaging from Robertson et al. (2009), three more types were created reflecting characteristics of the collected data set: media report, human report, and event report. Detailed explanations on codes and definitions are shown in Table 6.1 (hereafter, E, R, A, JR, DA, MR, HR, ER, respectively).

Reliability Testing

Content analysis requires that researchers make "replicable and valid inferences from texts to the contexts of their use" (Krippendorff 2004, 18). Methodological requirements of reliability and validity are critical demands in content analysis. This research undertook codebook development for content analysis through multiple intracoder reliability tests and an interactive sequence of codebook revisions.

Intracoder reliability

The initial coding scheme was based on Robertson et al.'s study (2009); additional codes were added as they emerged from the data to create a preliminary codebook. With the initial codebook, three rounds (six iterations) of intracoder reliability testing were conducted over a three-week period. A sample set of 60 messages was coded to classify message types, with a second coding of 60 messages carried out one week later. Differences between the two coding trials were discovered in 19 out of 60 messages (31.6 percent). After revising the definitions of codes based on the analysis, a third coding with a different set of 60 messages was conducted. A week later, a fourth coding was conducted, and differences between the third and fourth trial were discovered in 8 out of 60 messages (13.3 percent).

TABLE 6.1 Codebook of eight message types

Code	Sign	Definition
Evidence	E	Tweets written in order to *provide evidence for a particular opinion or simple fact.* It may include actual links to evidence such as newspaper, blog post, images, and video along with the texts.
Rebuttal	R	Tweets written in order to provide negative responses or comments to rebut others' ideas. It may sound like evidence, but it has additional components of *reaction or providing negative comments to specific persons or organizations.*
Action	A	Tweets written in order *to encourage others to take actions either on the Internet,* such as participating in a poll or joining a group, *or in the real world,* such as donating money or attending a rally.
Joking and ridicule	JR	Tweets written in order to *ridicule something or someone,* reveal something fully about them or their behavior, or simply point people to *satirical content.*
Direct address	DA	Tweets written in order to directly address *his/her own opinion or simply provide facts without any evidence.* It may include simple statements of his/her idea, facts, and opinions such as simple *messages of support or lack of support* as an expression.
Media report	MR	Tweets written in order to *cite and report the contents from a media report.* It is usually followed by *the actual links of the materials it* refers to, or can be written *in the form of a direct quotation (" ").* Even if the message itself includes neither links to the material it refers to nor direct quotations, indirect citations and reports of the contents from media can be coded as MR. The main purpose of MR is to distribute and circulate media content.
Human report	HR	Tweets written in order to *cite and report the contents from a human's remarks.* It is usually followed by an actual link to the material it refers to or can be written in the form of a direct quotation (" "). Even if the message itself includes neither links to the material it refers to nor direct quotations, indirect citations and reports of the contents from a human's remarks can be coded as HR. The main purpose of HR is to distribute and circulate the content of human remarks.
Event report	ER	Tweets written in order *to report and distribute real-time news events* or his/her own experience of an event. The main purpose of ER is to distribute the facts or news that happen as real-time events but are not likely to be broadcast by mainstream media.

The codebook was revised further, and a fifth coding with a different set of 60 messages was conducted. In the following week, a sixth coding was completed, with 100 percent agreement and no differences found between the coding results.

The main reason noted as a cause of inconsistencies was that multiple purposes could be employed in creating a single message. For example, a tweet could encourage people to vote by citing a politically important figure's remarks. In this case, this message could be coded as action (A) or human report (HR). It is important to consider that ideas or opinions can be expressed using multiple methods, such as giving examples, rebutting, or making a joke. This ambiguity is intrinsic in interpreting human language itself. If one message includes characteristics of two types, it is possible that one main purpose could be understood better and stressed more over the other purpose within the specific context so that each message can be coded as one specific type.

General Sentiment Identification

Tweeted messages include special features and conventions such as words, emoticons, and hashtags that represent the author's emotions and feelings within 140 characters (Agarwal et al. 2011; Tumasjan et al. 2010). These Twitter-specific features allow researchers to identify sentiments and opinions in tweeted messages. Sentiment analysis studies in Twitter are mainly conducted at the word level (Agarwal et al. 2011; Tumasjan et al. 2010; O'Connor et al. 2010). To measure the emotional meaning or degree in words and texts, researchers used predefined dictionaries, such as the Dictionary of Affect in Language (DAL), or other systems with embedded dictionaries, such as Linguistic Inquiry and Word Count (LIWC) or OpinionFinder, to classify words according to three categories: positive, negative, and neutral. This approach enables researchers to measure sentiments at the word level, and research has indicated that the sentiment word frequency in tweeted messages correlates with the public opinion polling results (O'Connor et al. 2010).

However, it is still difficult to analyze sentiments or opinions from tweeted messages at the message level. Branthwaite and Patterson (2011, p. 432) argue that "opinions are divided on the ability to code the underlying sentiments as positive or negative," and it is certainly difficult for machines to understand irony or sarcasm. Twitter features such as emoticons and hashtags add variation, so sentiment analysis requires human intervention and qualitative analysis to increase validity and accuracy at the message level (Branthwaite and Patterson 2011).

This study attempts to identify general sentiments understood and interpreted within political contexts. General sentiments within retweeted messages were sorted into three classes: positive, negative, and neutral. Sentiments expressed toward the three leading political figures can be interpreted as an indicator of how Twitter users perceived those leaders. Overall sentiments were identified considering the context in the messages, not by particular words or terms. Intracoder reliability was tested through the two trials of coding, and agreement without error was reached relatively easily.

Correlation with Public Opinion Polls

One of the most frequently referenced public opinion polls in South Korea is Korean Gallup (www.gallup.co.kr). Korean Gallup polls are administered through telephone and cell phone interviews to 1,550 citizens every day on weekdays. Impressions of the three leading political figures were collected from Korean Gallup polls for six weeks from April 2 to May 11, 2012. Correlation analysis was conducted to study the relationship between citizens' expressed opinions online on Twitter and offline through public opinion polls.

Findings

In answering the three research questions, general descriptive analyses including the magnitude of retweeted messages, classification of types of messages, and identification of sentiments were provided, with correlation analysis between results of content analyses of Twitter messages and the results of public opinion polls.

RQ1: Magnitude of Retweeted Messages and Public Opinion Polls

A total of 556,675 retweeted messages including the three keywords were collected for six weeks (April 2 to May 11, 2012). The total number of retweeted messages including Bak was 354,284 (63.64 percent), with 102,000 (18.32 percent) for Moon and 100,391 (18.03 percent) for Ahn (Figure 6.1). The number of top 40 most frequently retweeted messages including Bak for six weeks was 56,281 (53.69 percent); 24,880 (23.73 percent) for Moon; and 23,674 (22.58 percent) for Ahn (Figure 6.2).

The magnitude of the retweeted messages including the three keywords varied, and might depend on public awareness of the three leaders. Bak is a leader of the ruling party of Saenuri, and a daughter of the former president during the military dictatorship from the 1960s through the 1970s, JungHee Bak. Moon is the leader of the biggest opposition party of United MinJoo, and is well known as the successor of the former president, MooHyun Roh. Ahn is a non-partisan university professor without any official experience as a politician. The magnitudes of both total retweeted messages and top 40 retweeted messages showed one pattern: Bak was most frequently talked about by Twitter users, followed by Moon and Ahn.

Political Information-Sharing 99

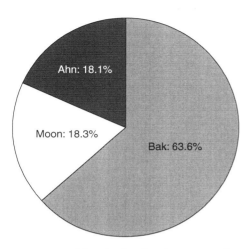

FIGURE 6.1 Magnitude of entire retweeted messages.

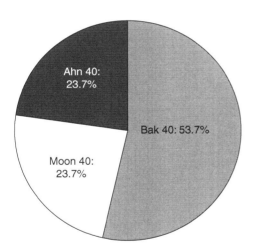

FIGURE 6.2 Magnitude of top 40 retweeted messages.

The extent to which the three leaders appeared in the Twitter timeline over the six weeks was not consistent with the percentages shown in public opinion polling results over the same period. Results from public opinion polls overall, as seen in Table 6.2, indicated that Bak obtained the most favorable impressions (averaging 36.83 percent), followed by Ahn (averaging 23 percent), and Moon (averaging 12.33 percent).

For correlation analysis, SPSS 18 was used. Total numbers of retweeted messages and of the top 40 most retweeted messages showed significant correlations with the percentages of public opinion polls (Table 6.3).

100 Lee, Ryu, Mon, and Park

TABLE 6.2 Results of public opinion polls for six weeks

	Week 1	*Week 2*	*Week 3*	*Week 4*	*Week 5*	*Week 6*	*Average*
BAK	34	36	39	36	38	38	36.83 (%)
MOON	15	13	11	13	11	11	12.33 (%)
AHN	23	23	25	23	23	21	23.00 (%)

Note: Public opinion poll results from nationwide data collection.

TABLE 6.3 Pearson correlation between retweeted message and public opinion poll

RT_all	RT_40	Poll
RT_all	0.985★★	0.676★★
RT_40		0.616★★
Poll		

Note: RT_all = number of all retweeted messages; RT_40 = number of top 40 retweeted messages; Poll = public opinion polls percentage.
**$p < .01$.

RQ2: Classification of Message Types and Public Opinion Polls

A total of 720 messages were classified into eight types according to the codebook. Direct address (326, 45.3 percent), human report (142, 19.7 percent), joking/ridicule (113, 15.7 percent), and evidence (54, 7.5 percent) were the most frequently assigned types (635/720, 88.2 percent) across all the retweeted messages. The results from classification of each type are shown in Figures 6.3 and 6.4.

- The main purposes of creating and retweeting were to directly address opinions and information without evidence (DA), distribute the cited contents from human remarks (HR), make jokes about or ridicule others' ideas (JR), and provide evidence (E).
- Three categories, media report, human report, and event report (198/720, 27.5 percent), approximately a quarter of messages, were created and retweeted to distribute and report cited contents from media, humans, and events. Media report, human report, and event report represented the tendency of citizens to rely on other sources such as trustworthy media or leading figures' remarks. Evidence (54/720, 7.5 percent) indicated messages created based on evidence. In sum, political messages identified with types of evidence, media report, human report, and event report (252/720, 35 percent) taken together demonstrated the tendency of citizens to circulate Twitter messages including supporting evidence.

Political Information-Sharing 101

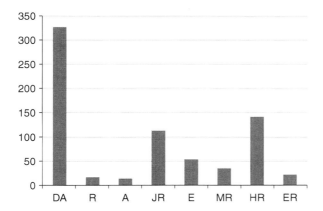

FIGURE 6.3 Results from classification of types of messages.

Note: D = direct address; R = rebuttal; A = action; JR = joking and ridicule; E = evidence; MR = media report; HR = human report; ER = event report. W1 means week 1 of five weekdays for which data collection is conducted.

- Rebuttal and joking/ridicule messages provided negative responses, comments, or jokes about others' ideas. Action messages sought to encourage people to take actions, and were usually created without including references or evidence. Direct address messages directly address opinions and information without evidence. These four types of messages, rebuttal, action, joking/ridicule, and direct address (468/720, 65 percent), provided ideas or opinion without supporting evidence or references.
- Overall classification of message types found two major clusters with four types each: supported (E, MR, HR, and ER; 35 percent) and unsupported (R, A, JR, and DA; 65 percent). Supported message types included references to an information source such as a link, image, or remarks from particular media or figures, while unsupported message types did not.

Results from message type classification are shown in Table 6.4 and Figure 6.5. A total of 240 tweeted messages for each political figure were analyzed.

- For Bak, direct address (114/240, 47.5 percent), joking/ridicule (50/240, 20.8 percent), and evidence (27/240, 11.3 percent) were the most frequently classified message types. Supported message types (E, MR, HR, ER) represented 65 (65/240, 27.1 percent) cases, while unsupported message types (DA, R, A, JR) represented 175 (175/240, 72.9 percent) cases.
- For Moon, direct address (118/240, 49.2 percent), joking/ridicule (36/240, 15 percent), and human report (36/240, 15 percent) were the most frequently assigned types. As the senior advisor of the biggest opposition party against the Saenuri Party, Moon is regarded as a progressive politician running against

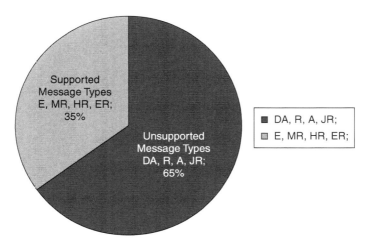

FIGURE 6.4 Clustering of supported and unsupported message types.

Note: D = direct address; R = rebuttal; A = action; JR = joking and ridicule; E = evidence; MR = media report; HR = human report; ER = event report. W1 means week 1 of five weekdays for which data collection is conducted.

> Bak. Supported message types (E, MR, HR, ER) represented 81 (81/240, 33.7 percent) cases, while unsupported message types (DA, R, A, JR) represented 159 (159/240, 66.3 percent) cases.

- For Ahn, direct address (94/240, 39.2 percent), joking/ridicule (27/240, 11.3 percent), and human report (86/240, 35.8 percent) were the most frequently assigned types. Unlike Bak and Moon, HR (86/240, 35.8 percent) was a dominant type for Ahn, and all of the HRs cite Ahn's own remarks. This suggests that Ahn's remarks were regarded as meaningful and influential among citizens, deserving repeated retweeting (RT). Even though unsupported types of DA, R, A, and JR (134/240, 55.8 percent) were observed more than supported types of E, MR, HR, and ER (106/240, 44.2 percent) cases, the contrast between two categories was more balanced than observed in the retweeted messages regarding Bak and Moon.

The eight types of Twitter messages did not show any correlation with results from public opinion polls (Table 6.5). Thus, retweeted (RT) messages as classified according to the purpose of the message did not relate to the public opinion poll results.

RQ3: General Sentiment Identification and Public Opinion Polls

Sentiments in retweeted messages were sorted into three classes: positive, negative, and neutral. Sentiments were identified from the overall sentiment observed

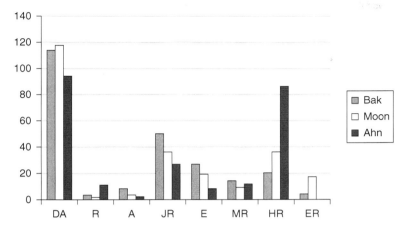

FIGURE 6.5 Classification of messages for three classes.

Note: D = direct address; R = rebuttal; A = action; JR = joking and ridicule; E = evidence; MR = media report; HR = human report; ER = event report. W1 means week 1 of five weekdays for which data collection is conducted.

in messages, not by coding for particular terms, and are shown in Table 6.6 and Figure 6.6.

- Among the total of 720 messages, 44.9 percent (323/720) conveyed negative sentiment, 46.1 percent (332/720) positive sentiment, and 9 percent (65/720) neutral sentiment.
- For Bak, 98.3 percent (236/240) of messages conveyed negative sentiment, and 1.67 percent (4/240) conveyed positive sentiment. It is clear that tweets about Bak, an icon of conservatism, primarily showed negative sentiments.
- For Moon, 18.8 percent (45/240) of messages conveyed negative sentiment, 75 percent (180/240) conveyed positive sentiment, and 6.5 percent (15/240) conveyed neutral sentiment. As a counterpoint to Bak, tweeted messages about Moon showed mostly positive sentiments.
- For Ahn, 17.5 percent (42/240) of messages conveyed negative sentiment, 61.7 percent (148/240) conveyed positive sentiment, and 20.8 percent (50/240) conveyed neutral sentiment. Although overall sentiment toward Ahn was positive, a high portion of neutral sentiment was captured in retweeted messages.

Positive and negative sentiment observed in retweeted messages showed significant correlation with percentages in public opinion polling; however, neutral sentiment did not show any correlation (Table 6.7).

TABLE 6.4 Results from classification of message types for three keywords

		DA	R	A	JR	E	MR	HR	ER	Sum
Bak	W1	20	0	4	5	8	1	2	0	40
	W2	21	1	4	6	6	0	2	0	40
	W3	20	2	0	7	7	2	1	1	40
	W4	18	0	0	7	4	5	4	2	40
	W5	15	0	0	11	2	5	6	1	40
	W6	20	0	0	14	0	1	5	0	40
Moon	W1	18	2	1	3	4	2	4	6	40
	W2	27	0	2	2	6	0	0	3	40
	W3	19	0	0	5	2	5	8	1	40
	W4	30	0	0	3	0	2	5	0	40
	W5	11	0	0	6	2	0	14	7	40
	W6	13	0	0	17	5	0	5	0	40
Ahn	W1	9	0	0	1	2	3	25	0	40
	W2	13	0	1	1	3	1	21	0	40
	W3	16	4	0	5	1	4	10	0	40
	W4	15	2	1	10	2	4	6	0	40
	W5	15	5	0	9	0	0	11	0	40
	W6	26	0	0	1	0	0	13	0	40
	Sum	326	16	13	113	54	35	142	21	720
	%	45.3	2.2	1.8	15.7	7.5	4.9	19.7	2.9	100.0

Note: D = direct address; R = rebuttal; A = action; JR = joking and ridicule; E = evidence; MR = media report; HR = human report; ER = event report. W1 means week 1 of five weekdays for which data collection is conducted.

TABLE 6.5 Pearson correlations among types of message and public opinion

DA	R	A	JR	E	MR	HR	ER	Poll
DA	−0.165	0.230	−0.274	0.050	−0.187	−0.569*	−0.122	−0.023
R		−0.104	0.090	−0.181	0.018	−0.041	−0.085	0.074
A			−0.193	0.666**	−0.331	−0.365	−0.067	0.232
JR				−0.015	0.029	−0.373	−0.177	0.237
E					−0.168	−0.487*	0.131	0.233
MR						0.004	−0.098	0.214
HR							−0.084	−0.233
ER								−0.370
Poll								

Note: D = direct address; R = rebuttal; A = action; JR = joking and ridicule; E = evidence; MR = media report; HR = human report; ER = event report. * $p < .05$; ** $p < .01$.

Political Information-Sharing **105**

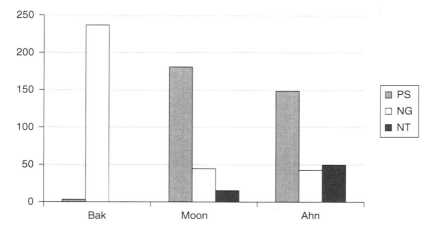

FIGURE 6.6 Results from sentiment identification.

TABLE 6.6 Results from sentiments identification

		NG	PS	NT	Sum
Bak	W1	39	1	0	40
	W2	40	0	0	40
	W3	40	0	0	40
	W4	40	0	0	40
	W5	38	2	0	40
	W6	39	1	0	40
Moon	W1	8	31	1	40
	W2	2	38	0	40
	W3	8	30	2	40
	W4	19	18	3	40
	W5	7	31	2	40
	W6	1	32	7	40
Ahn	W1	0	37	3	40
	W2	4	32	4	40
	W3	1	25	14	40
	W4	15	18	7	40
	W5	16	17	7	40
	W6	6	19	15	40
	Sum	332	332	65	720
	%	44.9	46.1	9.0	100.0

Note: NG = negative sentiment; PS = positive sentiment; NT = neutral sentiment.

TABLE 6.7 Pearson correlations among sentiments and public opinion

NG	PS	NT	Poll
NG	−0.962★★	−0.555★	0.842★★
PS		0.306	−0.869★★
NT			−0.288
Poll			

Note: NG = negative sentiment; PS = positive sentiment; NT = neutral sentiment.
★$p < .05$; ★★$p < .01$.

Conclusions

This study investigated political information-sharing on the social networking site Twitter during the 2012 South Korean general election. Retweeting as community behavior of agreement and consensus in Twitter was examined using both quantitative and qualitative approaches: counting the number (magnitude) of retweeted messages, using content analyses to classify types of messages and sentiments, and conducting correlation analysis between expressed opinions on Twitter and results of public opinion polls.

Although the magnitude of retweeted messages showed significant correlations with public opinion polling results over time, rankings of message magnitude differed from the rankings of public opinion polls. The magnitudes also appeared vulnerable to changes in political issues and events during the election campaign. The eight most frequently retweeted message types did not correlate with public opinion polling results. Contents in retweeted messages were highly subjective, complicated, and contextual as a representation of political communication. However, sentiments in retweeted messages, while also subjective and contextual, did show a correlation with public opinion polling results. This implies that capturing sentiments from retweeted messages dealing with broader political issues can be useful in gauging public opinion.

These findings require researchers to closely look at the content of Twitter messages to understand the purposes and underlying sentiments in context. From this perspective, the qualitative approach to classifying the purposes and sentiments of retweeted messages was appropriate for studying political communication via SNSs. The significant correlations between the use of Twitter and public opinion polls indicate possible potential for utilizing current SNSs to explore public opinion.

This study had several limitations. The sample used for this study may not be representative of the South Korean electorate as a whole, since not everyone uses Twitter. Tweets collected for this study were also limited only to those including names of three top political leaders. Other specifically topic-based keywords such as titles of specific policy or political issues could be employed to collect targeted

Note

1 This original research was first presented at the iConference in 2013, and is available online at http://hdl.handle.net/2142/38389; doi: 19.9776/13210.

References

Agarwal, A., B. Xie, I. Vovsha, O. Rambow, and R. Passonneau. 2011. Sentiment Analysis of Twitter Data. *Proceedings of the Workshop on Language in Social Media (LSM 2011)*: 30–8.

Branthwaite, A. and S. Patterson. 2011. The Power of Qualitative Research in the Era of Social Media. *Qualitative Market Research: An International Journal* 14(4): 430–40.

Chang, H.C. 2010. *A New Perspective on Twitter Hashtag Use: Diffusion of Innovation Theory*. Paper presented at the American Society for Information Science & Technology, Pittsburgh, PA.

Dann, S. 2010. Twitter Content Classification. *First Monday* 15(12), http://firstmonday.org/htbin/cgiwrap/bin/ojs/index.php/fm/article/view/2745/2681.

The Economist. 2010. Sweet to Tweet. *The Economist*, May 6, www.economist.com/node/16056612.

Grant, W.J., B. Moon, and J. Busby Grant. 2010. Digital Dialogue? Australian Politicians' Use of the Social Network Tool Twitter. *Australian Journal of Political Science* 45(4): 579–604.

Hong, S. and D. Nadler. 2011. *Does the Early Bird Move the Polls? The Use of the Social Media Tool "Twitter" by US Politicians and Its Impact on Public Opinion*. Paper presented at the 12th Annual International Digital Government Research conference: Digital Government Innovation in Challenging Times, College Park, MD.

Hsu, C. and H.W. Park. 2011. Sociology of Hyperlink Networks of Web 1.0, Web 2.0 and Twitter: A Case Study of South Korea. *Social Science Computer Review* 29(3), 354–68.

Java, A., X. Song, T. Finin, and B. Tseng. 2007. *Why We Twitter: Understanding Microblogging Usage and Communities*. Paper presented at the 9th WebKDD and 1st SNA-KDD workshop on web mining and social network analysis, San Jose, CA.

Krippendorff, K. 2004. Conceptual foundation. In *Content Analysis: An Introduction to its Methodology*, 2nd edn. Thousand Oaks, CA: Sage, pp. 18–43.

Los Angeles Times. 2011. Twitter, Launched Five Years Ago, Delivers 350 Billion Tweets a Day. *Los Angeles Times*, July 15, http://latimesblogs.latimes.com/technology/2011/07/twitter-delivers-350-billion-tweets-a- day.html.

New York Times. 2012. Campaigns Use Social Media to Lure Younger Voters. *New York Times*, October 8, www.nytimes.com/2012/10/08/technology/campaigns-use-social-media-to-lure- younger-voters.html.

O'Connor, B., R. Balasubramanyan, B.R. Routledge, and N.A. Smith. 2010. From Tweets to Polls: Linking Text Sentiment to Public Opinion Time Series. *Proceedings of the Fourth International AAAI Conference on Weblogs and Social Media*: 122–9.

Robertson, S., R.K. Vatrapu, and R. Medina. 2009. The Social Life of Social Networks: Facebook Linkage Patterns in the 2008 US Presidential Election. *Proceedings* of the 10th Annual International Conference on Digital Government Research, Puebla, Mexico: 6–15.

Roosevelt, C.M. 2012. Social Media Analytics: Data Mining Applied to Insurance Twitter Posts. *Casualty Actuarial Society E-Forum* 2: 1–36.

Rogers, E.M. 1962. *Diffusion of Innovations*, 1st edn. New York: Free Press.

Rogers, E.M. 1995. *Diffusion of Innovations*, 4th edn. New York: Free Press.

Thomas, L. 2010. Twitter at the Office: Social Eyes. *Journal of Web Librarianship* 4(1): 79–82.

Tumasjan, A., T.O. Sprenger, P.G. Sandner, and I.M. Welpe. 2010. Predicting Elections with Twitter: What 140 Characters Reveal about Political Sentiment. *Proceedings of the Fourth International AAAI Conference on Weblogs and Social Media*, www.aaai.org/ocs/index.php/ICWSM/ICWSM10/paper/view/1441.

Twitter. 2012. *About Twitter*, http://twitter.com/about.

Vergeer, M., L. Hermans, and S. Sams. 2011. Is the Voter only a Tweet Away? Microblogging During the 2009 European Parliament Election Campaign in the Netherlands. *First Monday* 16(8), http://firstmonday.org/htbin/cgiwrap/bin/ojs/index.php/fm/article/view/3540/3026.

Zhao, D. and M. B. Rosson. 2009. How and Why People Twitter: The Role That Microblogging Plays in Informal Communication at Work. *Proceedings of the ACM 2009 International Conference on Supporting Group Work*: 243–52.

PART III
Parties, Candidates, and Campaigns

7

MESSAGE REPETITION IN SOCIAL MEDIA

Presidential Candidate Twitter Feeds in the 2012 US General Election

Kate Kenski and Bethany A. Conway

When Rosser Reeves, a Republican Madison Avenue advertising consultant, was asked to advise General Dwight D. Eisenhower's presidential campaign in 1960, he attended a rally in Philadelphia and observed that the general was a "singularly inept speaker" who made 27 different points in a campaign speech. The end result was that no one knew what the general stood for. Reeves, who had created the repetitive but effective Anacin "fast, fast, fast relief" ad, turned the Eisenhower campaign around by having the general pick and focus on no more than three issues. Reeves' focused, "hard sell" strategy worked (*The 30-Second President* 1984). He maintained that regardless of how the public claimed to feel about an advertisement, repetition and focus were necessary for campaign effectiveness. More than 50 years later, the clutter of information with which members of the public are bombarded has increased exponentially, potentially making Reeves' repetition strategy more vital to a campaign's success than ever before. Part of this message bombardment occurs through social media, which have transformed the political campaign landscape (Gueorguieva 2008; Towner and Dulio 2012).

With these observations in mind, this chapter examines the 2012 general election tweets from the presidential candidates, Democrat Barack Obama and Republican Mitt Romney, their campaigns and advisors, and the Democratic and Republican parties for their message consistency via phrase repetition. Although campaigns overall need a theme or small set of themes to convey to the public, it remains an open question whether social media need to be a part of that campaign package in a coordinated fashion or whether social media messages are used most effectively by mobilizing supporters differently than messages found in other modes of campaign communication. It is reasonable to assume that some consistency in a campaign's message stream is useful, perhaps even necessary, for mobilization. We begin with a discussion of research on message repetition. We then turn our attention to the challenges and benefits of social media with a focus on Twitter. As will be shown later in this chapter, a notable percentage of the phrases in candidate tweets were duplicated in campaign feeds. The Democratic National Committee (DNC) also exhibited greater duplication rates with Obama and his campaign than did the Republican National Committee (RNC) with candidate Romney and his campaign. Further, candidate Obama and his campaign engaged in notable duplication of phrases from month to month on Twitter.

Message Repetition and Consistency

Repetition is an integral part of consistency. Without consistency, messages may appear unstructured and thus not be influential. In a "cluttered" environment, attention, recall, and positive cognitive response are difficult to obtain (Webb and Ray 1979). Repetition provides a sense of organization by structuring and priming what is most important in a message. Extensive research has demonstrated that overall repeated exposure to advertising increases a product's appeal. A consumer must receive multiple exposures to an advertisement in order for the advertisement to be effective (Stankey 1988; Yoo et al. 2009). At a rudimentary level, research has found that visuals that are easy to process, through visual priming or subtle increases in presentation duration, are found to be rated more highly than their counterparts (Reber et al. 1998; Winkielman and Cacioppo 2001). Exposure contributes to that ease of processing and thus preference.

Not only does repeated exposure affect preference, but it affects the perceived credibility of a statement (Koch and Zerback 2013). "Repeated presentation increases participants' subjective judgments of a statement's truth" (Dechêne et al. 2010, p. 255; see also Unkelbach 2007).

Although exposure repetition usually results in a positive effect for the source, there are numerous studies that suggest that there can be too much of a good thing. The magnitude of the positive reactions to a message are diminished if a person is exposed to the message or stimuli too many times. A curvilinear result appears if the repetition is too intense (Appel 1971; Cacioppo and Petty 1979; Calder and Sternthal 1980; Gorn and Goldberg 1980; Winter 1973). Grass and Wallace (1969) refer to this as a satiation effect. Too much repetition results in a weakening of the perceived credibility of the message as the targets of the message perceive that an overt persuasion attempt is being made (Koch and Zerback 2013). In a study on children, Gorn and Goldberg (1980) found that children's favorability toward a product was highest after moderate repetition to an advertisement (three exposures) but was lower when the children were exposed only once or after seeing the advertisement five times. A balance, therefore, must be sought in providing repeated exposure but not overdoing it to the point of satiation.

Message Repetition in Social Media **113**

One can potentially avoid audience "wear out" from exposure to a repeated message, resulting in a so-called "tedium effect," by offering some variation in the message. In one study by McCullough and Ostrom (1974), consumers were exposed to slightly varied print advertisements. The slight variation manipulation revealed that when repetition was increased, preference for the product also increased (see also Gorn and Goldberg 1980). The results suggest that the exact same message may result in feelings of tedium, but minor variations in the advertisements can mitigate such disengaging reactions. The types of variation resulting in greater influence from repetition can be cosmetic or substantive in nature (Schumann et al. 1990). Cosmetic variation is said to take place when an advertisement is changed in non-substantive ways, such as color, graphics, print fonts, or layout. Substantive variation takes place when the advertisement's message or argument is fundamentally changed. Schumann, Petty, and Clemons (1990) show that repeated ads are most effective for those whose motivation or involvement is low when the variations are cosmetic; when the product is highly relevant to the audience, that is, the individuals have high motivation to process the information, greater benefit from repetition is found when substantive variations in the message take place.

The social media environment is voluminous. The information stream produced on social media is fast and continuous, portending that candidates must strategize how to get their messages about themselves and their opponents to take hold in minds of members of the public when competing against many other ideas or "clutter." We therefore turn our attention to social media and their constraints and advantages to candidates.

The Challenges and Benefits of Social Networking Sites

Although some scholars observed that there was little evidence that social media "actually drove discussion, participation, or outcomes" in the 2008 election (Metzgar and Maruggi 2009, p. 141), increased and targeted web use by political campaigns after the 2008 election was anticipated (Towner and Dulio 2012). Between 2008 and 2012, social networking site (SNS) use increased by US adults. In April 2009, 46 percent of adult Internet users in the US reported using a SNS; by February 2012, this figure had increased to 66 percent—a 20 percent increase in under three years (Brenner and Smith 2013). Given their growth in adoption by American adults (Brenner and Smith 2013), SNSs were one such web tool that seemed a likely venue for candidates to place their messages and reach out to voters in subsequent campaigns. SNSs allow candidates to create profiles and display connections to voters. Displaying connections or relationships publicly is "a crucial component of SNSs" (boyd and Ellison 2008, p. 213). The connections convey information about the candidates.

Among SNSs, Twitter is unique because its platform constrains messages to 140 characters and allows the open viewing of messages, meaning that posted messages may be seen without account-owner permissions. Tweeters thus are assumed to establish connections for the "content rather than relationships" (Virk 2011, p. 19). Yet, Twitter has created possibilities for candidate–voter interaction with the "@username" function, which allows candidates to reply directly to other users and promote dialogue if they choose. Nevertheless, there is no social expectation that direct interaction between tweeters will happen necessarily (Marwick and boyd 2011). Those trying to build and maintain a networked audience, however, should recognize that such audiences need monitoring, feedback, and an understanding of followers' interests (Marwick and boyd 2011).

SNS platforms have potential limitations when it comes to delivering candidate messages. Social media have changed how messages are delivered, such that the source-message-channel-receiver (SMCR) model has become outdated and less relevant than before (Metzgar and Maruggi 2009). Loss of message control for candidates is a possible consequence (Gueorguieva 2008; Johnson and Perlmutter 2010; Stromer-Galley 2000). Scholars and pundits have also questioned whether the use of SNSs by politicians actually matters when it comes to influencing electoral outcomes (Baumgartner and Morris 2010; Ferenstein 2012; Kushin and Yamamoto 2010; Zhang et al. 2010). As Ferenstein (2012) put it, social media have "yet to make a real impact in politics." Although the number of Twitter users continues to increase, only a small portion of those users report using the social networking sites to read comments or posts by celebrities, politicians, or athletes (Smith 2011, p. 7). In October 2014, only 16 percent of registered voters followed candidates, political parties, or elected officials on SNSs such as Facebook or Twitter (Anderson 2015). Twitter and other SNSs are often supplemental to traditional sources (Towner and Dulio 2012) rather than the primary drivers of campaign information.

The benefits of SNSs as campaign tools include low-cost fundraising potential, enhanced recruitment of campaign volunteers, and increased possibilities for candidate exposure (Gueorguieva 2008). The most important benefit of using SNSs may be in organizing volunteers and activists, an aspect some maintain has been overlooked (Abroms and Lefebvre 2009; Sifry 2012). Social media also have the potential to allow politicians to bypass traditional media outlets (Lassen and Brown 2011; Conway et al. 2015). They offer opportunities to facilitate and develop connections with constituents and voters directly.

Twitter specifically is praised for its succinctness and frequency (Java et al. 2009). It is called a "microblog" because of its character constraint on user posts. Public relations professionals maintain that Twitter has "guerrilla marketing" potential, meaning that campaigns may be able to catch an audience's attention "by surprise, resulting in a high rate of impact and retention" (Virk 2011, p. 20) for a product or candidate. Successful Twitter strategies, however, have rarely been seen below the federal level with Obama's 2008 campaign paving the way (Abroms and Lefebvre 2009; Towner and Dulio 2012).

Scholars have investigated the incorporation of social media into the campaign package (Adams and McCorkindale 2013; Conway et al. 2013; Golbeck et al. 2010; Graham et al. 2013; Grant et al. 2010; Gueorguieva 2008; Johnson and Perlmutter 2010; Towner and Dulio 2012). Before Twitter was unveiled in 2006, candidates did not display a solid or consistent communication strategy in the political blogosphere. Although hyperlinks were common across blog posts, candidates and their staff members lacked an understanding of their utility, as demonstrated by contrasting campaign approaches (Lawson-Borders and Kirk 2005) and a lack of cohesion between blogs and candidate websites (Williams et al. 2006). The lack of understanding about the utility of online messaging appears to have followed into the social media arena. US primary candidates, for example, used links extensively in their tweets during the 2012 primary season (Conway et al. 2013). Nevertheless, candidates and campaigns have been struggling to harness SNSs, as suggested by dissimilar activity levels and a proclivity for unidirectional messaging (Aparaschivei 2011; Conway et al. 2013; Golbeck et al. 2010; Graham et al. 2013; Klinger 2013; Stromer-Galley 2014). Although some candidates tend to make use of social media's interactive features, many choose to use Twitter as a broadcast medium rather than a venue for discussion with voters (Stromer-Galley 2014). An investigation of Twitter use by members of Congress found that interaction through "retweets" or user mentions was rare. Instead, "Congress members are largely using Twitter to communicate the same information their offices would share in other media" (Golbeck et al. 2010, p. 1612).

The 2008 Obama campaign used digital technologies "to gain supporters and to mobilize them into action in ways that were unprecedented and untested in political campaigns" (Abroms and Lefebvre 2009, p. 415). The campaign created profiles on various new media sites early. On Twitter specifically, @BarackObama cultivated 112,474 followers in comparison to @JohnMcCain's 4,603 followers (Abroms and Lefebvre 2009). Given the success of the Obama campaign, it is not surprising that political candidates in 2012 realized the importance of web targeting and mobilization through social media. Yet, that recognition did not translate into a clear understanding of how to use them as effective communicative tools in the 2012 presidential primary (Conway et al. 2013). In their research on the blogosphere, Lawson-Borders and Kirk (2005, p. 557) observed that when new technologies are introduced, "many campaigns used them without knowing what specific communication they could serve. Some campaigns used them because it is considered hip, whereas others used them strategically or not at all."

Social Media Message Repetition by Candidates

With the lack of communicative norms for candidates on social media in mind, it is an open question as to how consistent candidates are in using Twitter—consistent with their campaigns, consistent with their parities, and/or consistent within their own presentations to the public. Given the importance of message consistency to the effectiveness of campaigns generally, the present study seeks to understand whether message consistency appeared on general election presidential candidate and campaign Twitter feeds.

Social media messages by candidates can be considered a form of advertising as well as a form of outreach to members of the public. Taken together, the social media literature and research on repetition suggest that effective social media campaign messages, such as messages through tweets, will involve some repetition, but not complete redundancy as too much redundancy may be perceived as tedious by message consumers. In political research, the findings suggest that repetition is beneficial when it is spaced, but it can backlash against an ad sponsor if the repetition is placed too closely (Fernandes 2013). Consequently, there should be some similarity between content posted by a candidate across different time periods. According to Ekström and Fitzgerald (2014, p. 82), "the distribution of single powerful phrases in texts, speeches and interviews is a proven signifying strategy in modern politics. Indeed the ability to 'staying on message' and produce 'sound bites' is a regular PR strategy adopted by politicians." Is it reasonable, however, to assume that a social medium that imposes a 140-character limit would be used by the 2012 presidential candidates in a way that keeps them "on message" in that medium?

As mentioned previously, Obama had a solid social media campaign in 2008 and set the bar for future political campaigns. His win was indicative of a successful media campaign overall. With his 2008 and 2012 wins in mind, we suspected that an examination of 2012 individual, campaign, and party tweets would reveal that Obama and the DNC had a greater presence on social media than did Romney and the RNC. But would the Obama/DNC presence also be more cohesive, especially given Obama's win? Some scholars have pointed out that the Republican Party has a "top-down, hierarchical organization" whereas the Democratic Party has been "more comfortable with ceding control to others outside the formal party hierarchy" (Metzgar and Maruggi 2009, p. 153). The more controlled hierarchical structure might be suggestive of one that has more coordinated repetition than does its counterparts.

Part of the effectiveness of tweets is to not only have those messages present in social media but to have followers acknowledge the messages through the act of retweeting them. Again based on the success of Obama's campaign in 2008 coupled with Obama's high tweeting frequencies in 2012 (Conway et al. 2013), we assumed that tweets from Obama, his campaign, and the DNC would be retweeted more than would Mitt Romney's, his campaign's, or the RNC's tweets. The act of retweeting a message is an act of intentional and acknowledged duplication or repetition of that message. When one retweets information, one is passing it along verbatim. One can, of course, also duplicate or repeat information in original tweets that happens to use or borrow phrases that have been previously uttered by one's self or others. Duplication is a form of repetition in which the same words are used exactly as they have appeared somewhere else. If a candidate has a strong message, it follows that he or she will use the same words in different contexts to convey the substance of the message.

Effective campaigns, even losing ones, should have some semblance of organization and message structure. We therefore anticipated that the candidates and their campaigns had coordinated their messages to some extent. We also assumed that the campaign advisers who were helping craft the messages and strategy should have some overlap in word selection to convey campaign themes. Although campaign finance rules imply parties are not supposed to have synonymous messages with their nominees' campaigns as that would suggest coordination beyond what is allowed, if candidates are reflective of party goals and values and if parties have a desire to see their candidates elected, some duplication in word choice should be anticipated. Some message duplication is expected to occur between candidates and their campaign feeds, parties of the candidates, and their lead campaign advisers.

Repetition in the Tweets of the 2012 General Election Presidential Candidates, Campaigns, and Parties

To investigate the repetition of the tweets in the 2012 presidential general election, tweets posted on individual candidate Twitter feeds, candidate campaign feeds, and the feeds operated by DNC and GOP were gathered over the same time period. The feeds at the start of the collection period were verified Twitter feeds as faux or imposter feeds did crop up from time to time. The feeds for candidates Barack Obama and Mitt Romney, their campaign feeds Obama2012 and TeamRomney, the feeds of advisors David Axelrod and Eric Fehrnstrom, and the party feeds were gathered from August 1, 2012 through November 6, 2012. Initially, tweets were gathered by downloading Twitter html data through the website's API on a regular basis. After Twitter made changes to the API in October 2012, tweets were aggregated and downloaded using Google Reader. These data were then entered into a spreadsheet, displaying the user's account name, the date a tweet occurred, and its complete content (n = 9,178). For August and September, retweet counts were also collected. Twitter content was also put into files that were then analyzed by a software called DupeFree Pro, which determined the percentage of explicit duplication between sources. Exact duplication matches were determined at three-word calibrations.

The data examined were not sample data. The data examined were the entirety of the time period. Given that a census was collected, statistical tests were not calculated. Differences that appear are the real differences between sources. While a notable amount of research uses statistical significance to determine substantive significance, such use is not an appropriate application for statistical tests, which

118 Kate Kenski and Bethany A. Conway

TABLE 7.1 Candidate, campaign, and party tweeting activity between August 1 and November 6, 2012

	Number of tweets					Average tweets per day
	Total	Aug	Sept	Oct	Nov	
Candidates						
Obama	2,219	512	530	811	366	22.6
Romney	322	83	81	123	35	3.3
Campaign teams						
Obama2012	1,753	477	799	340	137	17.9
TeamRomney	990	260	217	404	109	10.1
Campaign advisors						
Axelrod	184	61	54	48	21	1.9
Fehrnstrom	63	28	16	17	2	0.6
Parties						
DNC	1,603	343	458	691	111	16.4
RNC	2,044	464	628	782	170	20.9

can only connote whether or not a sample difference is likely to be different from a difference found in a population. Consequently, it is up to the reader to determine whether he or she thinks the numerical figures in this exploratory research are meaningful.

We first examined whether or not Obama, his campaign, and the DNC had greater social media presence than did Romney, his campaign, and the RNC. As shown in Table 7.1, Obama posted 6.9 times the number of tweets that his opponent did. Similarly, the Obama campaign was much more active on Twitter than was the Romney campaign, with 1.8 times the number of tweets. The RNC, however, was more active on Twitter than was the DNC; the Republican Party put forth 1.3 times the tweets that the Democratic Party did.

The candidate, campaign, and party messages that were retweeted provide repetition for the entities but through the slight variation of being presented by followers who passed along the messages. Table 7.2 shows that the sheer number of retweets for Obama and his team compared to those for Romney and his team was much greater in August and September. Obama's tweets were retweeted more than Romney's tweets (1,469,550 to 255,858) overall. Given how much less Romney tweeted, however, the average retweet rate was higher for Romney; Romney's tweets were spread by others more often on average when he did post. Obama2012 had more messages that were retweeted than did TeamRomney. Unlike for the candidates, however, it is important to note that TeamRomney's retweet average was lower than the average for Obama2012, suggesting that the campaign was not as successful at having followers spread its messages. A similar pattern was found for the DNC and the RNC in terms of sheer numbers and averages. The DNC messages were retweeted nearly twice as much as the RNC tweets.

Message Repetition in Social Media **119**

TABLE 7.2 Candidate, campaign, and party tweets between August 1 and September 30, 2012

	Number of times tweets retweeted	*Average a tweet was retweeted*
Candidates		
Obama	1,469,550	1410.3
Romney	255,858	1560.1
Campaign teams		
Obama2012	326,788	256.1
TeamRomney	19,618	41.1
Campaign advisors		
Axelrod	35,823	311.5
Fehrnstrom	1,583	36.0
Parties		
DNC	97,578	121.8
RNC	52,523	48.1

While Table 7.2 showed how often followers were passing along the candidates', campaigns', and parties' messages through the retweet feature, Table 7.3 looks at the frequency and nature of how the candidates, campaigns, and parties retweeted the original messages made by others. Retweeting posts made by others suggests that the person or entity is engaged in the medium beyond using it as a one-way delivery system for his or its messages. The data reveal that the candidates in particular did not retweet the messages of others very often. In other words, the candidates used Twitter in a top-down fashion. Obama and his campaign did not retweet at all in August or September; Obama retweeted 86 times in October and November. Romney only retweeted once during the time under investigation. TeamRomney retweeted significantly more than did candidate Romney with 24 percent of its tweets being retweets; @MittRomney was retweeted 24 times by TeamRomney. Nearly one in five of the DNC's tweets were retweets. The RNC retweeted 11.4 percent of the time. Interestingly, the RNC retweets were not from candidate Romney or TeamRomney often (@MittRomney was retweeted eight times from August to November; @TeamRomney was not retweeted); nearly two-thirds of the time the retweets were from @RNCResearch. The DNC, however, frequently retweeted messages from @BarackObama (86 times from August to November).

The collection of tweets from the sources in this study were put into comprehensive files. These files were then crossed against each other using plagiarism software (DupeFree Pro) in order to determine how often repetition occurred. We hypothesized that duplication of phrases would be seen between candidates and their campaign feeds, between candidates and parties of the candidates, and between candidates and their lead campaign advisers, which received support, as shown in Table 7.4. The level of duplication was just over a quarter for Obama and Obama2012

TABLE 7.3 Candidate, campaign, and party retweeting activity between August 1 and November 6, 2012

	Number of retweets	Retweets percentage	Who did entity retweet most often?
Candidates			
Obama	86	3.9%	@Obama2012
Romney	1	0.3%	@PaulRyanVP
Campaign teams			
Obama2012	0	0.0%	—
TeamRomney	238	24.0%	@MittRomney
Campaign advisors			
Axelrod	1	0.5%	@NKingofDC
Fehrnstrom	0	0.0%	—
Parties			
DNC	317	19.8%	@BarackObama
RNC	232	11.4%	@RNCResearch

(27 percent) and was just under a quarter for Romney and TeamRomney (24 percent). When it came to message repetition between the candidates and their parties, the percentages were somewhat smaller, with Obama and the DNC duplicating content at a rate of 18 percent and Romney and the RNC at a rate of 12 percent. There was a duplication rate of 14 percent between Obama2012 and the DNC and 9 percent between TeamRomney and the GOP. Duplication rates of the campaign advisers with their candidates and campaigns were small; David Axelrod's feed had a duplication rate of 7 percent with the Obama and Obama2012 feeds. While Eric Fehrnstrom's feed had a duplication rate of 5 percent with Romney's feeds, it had a 14 percent duplication rate with TeamRomney.

We wondered about the extent that phrases were duplicated from month to month inside a source's own set of tweets. In other words, did candidates, campaigns, parties, and advisors provide consistency from month to month in their ideas on Twitter? As shown in Table 7.5, the duplication rates were modest overall. This suggests that Twitter was not primarily used to drive campaign slogans. The feed with the highest duplication rate was Obama2012 in September and October (22 percent) and the second highest was Obama in October and November (17 percent). Romney and TeamRomney had duplication rates lower than those of Obama and Obama2012. The campaign advisers' feeds had extremely low to no duplications from month to month (no consistency).

Discussion

On Twitter, the messages and phrases offered in candidate, campaign, campaign adviser, and party feeds show some consistency, but not as much message repetition

Message Repetition in Social Media **121**

TABLE 7.4 Duplication percentages of August 1 through November 6, 2012 tweets between sources (three-word matches)

	Obama	Obama 2012	Romney	TeamRomney	DNC	RNC	Axelrod	Fehrnstrom
Obama	—							
Obama2012	27%	—						
Romney	11%	10%	—					
TeamRomney	7%	5%	24%	—				
DNC	18%	14%	8%	5%	—			
RNC	4%	3%	12%	9%	3%	—		
Axelrod	7%	7%	2%	3%	9%	3%	—	
Fehrnstrom	6%	5%	5%	14%	6%	8%	1%	—

TABLE 7.5 Duplication percentage between August tweets and September tweets within sources (three words)

	Aug/Sept	Aug/Oct	Aug/Nov	Sept/Oct	Sept/Nov	Oct/Nov
Candidates						
Obama	11%	12%	8%	15%	10%	17%
Romney	5%	5%	5%	10%	7%	13%
Campaign teams						
Obama2012	13%	11%	10%	22%	13%	8%
TeamRomney	6%	4%	3%	7%	4%	11%
Campaign advisors						
Axelrod	1%	1%	0%	1%	1%	0%
Fehrnstrom	1%	1%	0%	1%	0%	0%
Parties						
DNC	7%	8%	4%	9%	9%	13%
RNC	5%	4%	3%	4%	3%	9%

as perhaps found in other forms of campaign discourse (e.g., advertisements and speeches) that often reiterate campaign themes and slogans. While there was repetition between the candidates and their campaigns, driven in part by the retweet function on Twitter, coordination between the parties and their presidential nominees appeared somewhat limited, perhaps due to the needs of candidates at other levels of government whom the parties also serve. We suspected that the repetition rates would be higher than they were, but we also were not expecting complete redundancy. Had complete or very high redundancy been found, there would have been concerns regarding the authenticity of each feed as an independent voice and the campaign's ability to harness the novel features such a platform has to offer.

The candidates, campaigns, and parties were not as internally consistent with themselves across months as one might have expected. Obama and his campaign had higher rates of internal consistency (duplication) month to month in comparison to Romney and his campaign. Compared to the Romney team, when the Obama team posted messages online, it did so with greater consistency and, perhaps, the DNC helped them spread that message across the Twittersphere.

As with all studies, there were some limitations to the present study. First, we only analyzed three months' worth of data, and we only focused on Twitter. It is possible that other forms of social media (e.g., Facebook pages) might have exemplified greater rates of consistency than a mode that has a 140-character limitation. That said, given the limitation, we were somewhat surprised that consistent, pithy slogans did not appear more often than they did. Second, we did not collect data from the independent expenditure groups, which would be a rich area for future research. In this study, consistency was operationalized as retweets or repetition in three-word phrases. The rationale for the short length of the phrases was driven by the structural space limitations of Twitter. One could, however, define consistency in a way that does not require verbatim repetition.

The candidate with the most internal consistency within individual and campaign messages on Twitter happens to be the candidate who won the election in 2012. While there are undoubtedly more compelling non-Twitter explanations for the Obama win, this research observes that the candidate, campaign, and party with the most online message consistency may have benefited from it. By contrast, the candidate with some consistency between his candidate feed and his campaign feed but little verbal commonality with his party's Twitter feed lost the election, suggesting that there was a failure by the individual, campaign, and party to identify and articulate consistent online messages for the public to understand. In a complex mediated environment where thousands upon thousands of messages surround citizens, candidates have to have coordination among counterparts and well-articulated messages that are consistently presented to the public so that the citizens are able to identify what the candidate stands for. In 2012, Obama did just that.

References

The 30-Second President: A Walk through the 20th Century with Bill Moyers. 1984. Video. New York: Films Media Group.

Abroms, L.C. and R.C. Lefebvre. 2009. Obama's Wired Campaign: Lessons for Public Health Communication. *Journal of Health Communication* 14: 415–23.

Adams, A. and T. McCorkindale. 2013. Dialogue and Transparency: A Content Analysis of How the 2012 Presidential Candidates Used Twitter. *Public Relations Review* 39: 357–59.

Anderson, M. 2015. *More Americans Are Using Social Media to Connect with Politicians*. Pew Research Center, www.pewresearch.org/fact-tank/2015/05/19/more-americans-are-using-social-media-to-connect-with-politicians.

Aparaschivei, P. 2011. The Use of New Media in Electoral Campaigns: Analysis on the Use of Blogs, Facebook, Twitter, and YouTube in the 2009 Romanian Presidential Campaign. *Journal of Media Research* 2: 39–60.

Appel, V. 1971. On Advertising Wear Out. *Journal of Advertising Research* 11: 11–13.

Baumgartner, J.C. and J.S. Morris. 2010. MyFaceTube Politics: Social Networking Web Sites and Political Engagement of Young Adults. *Social Science Computer Review* 28: 24–44.

boyd, d.m. and N.B. Ellison. 2008. Social Network Sites: Definition, History, and Scholarship. *Journal of Computer-Mediated Communication* 13: 210–30.

Brenner, J. and A. Smith. 2013. *72% of Online Adults are Social Networking Site Users.* Pew Research Center, www.pewinternet.org/files/old-media/Files/Reports/2013/PIP_Social_networking_sites_update_PDF.pdf.

Cacioppo, J.T. and R.E. Petty. 1979. Effects of Message Repetition and Position on Cognitive Response, Recall, and Persuasion. *Journal of Personality and Social Psychology* 37: 97–109.

Calder, B.J. and B. Sternthal. 1980. Television Commercial Wearout: An Information Processing View. *Journal of Marketing Research* 17: 173–86.

Conway, B.A., K. Kenski, and D. Wang. 2013. Twitter Use by Presidential Primary Candidates during the 2012 Campaign. *American Behavioral Scientist* 57: 1596–610.

Conway, B.A., K. Kenski, and D. Wang. 2015. The Rise of Twitter in the Political Campaign: Searching for Intermedia Agenda Setting Effects in the Presidential Primary. *Journal of Computer-Mediated Communication* 20: 363–80.

Dechêne, A., C. Stahl, J. Hansen, and M. Wänke. 2010. The Truth about the Truth: A Meta-Analytic Review of the Truth Effect. *Personality and Social Psychology Review* 14: 238–57.

Ekström, M. and R. Fitzgerald. 2014. Groundhog Day: Extended Repetitions in Political News Interviews. *Journalism Studies* 15: 82–97.

Ferenstein, G. 2012. Waiting for the "Twitter Election"? Keep Waiting. *Advertising Age*, http://adage.com/article/digital/waiting-twitter-election-waiting/232965.

Fernandes, J. 2013. Effects of Negative Political Advertising and Message Repetition on Candidate Evaluation. *Mass Communication and Society* 16: 268–91.

Golbeck, J., J.M. Grimes, and A. Rogers. 2010. Twitter Use by the US Congress. *Journal of the American Society for Information Science and Technology* 61: 1612–21.

Gorn, G.J. and M.E. Goldberg. 1980. Children's Responses to Repetitive Television Commercials. *Journal of Consumer Research* 6: 421–4.

Graham, T., M. Broersma, K. Hazelhoff, and G. van 't Haar. 2013. Between Broadcasting Political Messages and Interacting with Voters. *Information, Communication & Society* 16: 692–716.

Grant, W.J., B. Moon, and J.B. Grant. 2010. Digital Dialogue? Australian Politicians' Use of the Social Network Tool Twitter. *Australian Journal of Political Science* 45: 579–604.

Grass, R.C. and W.H. Wallace. 1969. Satiation Effects of TV Commercials. *Journal of Advertising Research* 9: 3–8.

Gueorguieva, V. 2008. Voters, Myspace, and YouTube: The Impact of Alternative Communication Channels on the 2006 Election Cycle and Beyond. *Social Science Computer Review* 26: 288–300.

Java, A., X. Song, T. Finin, and B. Tseng. 2009. Why We Twitter: An Analysis of a Microblogging Community. *Advances in Web Mining and Web Usage Analysis: Lecture Notes in Computer Science* 5439: 118–38.

Johnson, T.J. and D.D. Perlmutter. 2010. Introduction: The Facebook Election. *Mass Communication and Society* 13: 554–9.

Klinger, U. 2013. Mastering the Art of Social Media: Swiss Parties, the 2011 National Election and Digital Challenges. *Information, Communication & Society* 16: 717–36.

Koch, T. and T. Zerback. 2013. Helpful or Harmful? How Frequent Repetition Affects Perceived Statement Credibility. *Journal of Communication* 63: 993–1010.

Kushin, M.J. and M.Yamamoto. 2010. Did Social Media Really Matter? College Students' Use of Online Media and Political Decision Making in the 2008 Election. *Mass Communication and Society* 13: 608–30.

Lassen, D.S. and A.R. Brown. 2011. Twitter: The Electoral Connection? *Social Science Computer Review* 29: 419–36.

Lawson-Borders, G. and R. Kirk. 2005. Blogs in Campaign Communication. *American Behavioral Scientist* 49: 548–559.

Marwick, A.E. and d. boyd. 2011. I Tweet Honestly, I Tweet Passionately: Twitter Users, Context Collapse, and the Imagined Audience. *New Media & Society* 13: 114–33.

McCullough, J.L. and T.M. Ostrom. 1974. Repetition of Highly Similar Messages and Attitude Change. *Journal of Applied Psychology* 59: 395–7.

Metzgar, E. and A. Maruggi. 2009. Social Media and the 2008 US Presidential Election. *Journal of New Communications Research* 4: 141–65.

Reber, R., P.Winkielman, and N. Schwarz. 1998. Effects of Perceptual Fluency on Affective Judgments. *Psychological Science* 9: 45–48.

Schumann, D.W., R.E. Petty, and D.S. Clemons. 1990. Predicting the Effectiveness of Different Strategies of Advertising Variation: A Test of Repetition-Variation Hypotheses. *Journal of Consumer Research* 17: 192–202.

Sifry. M.L. 2012. How Social Media Is Keeping the GOP Primary Going. *TechPresident*, http://techpresident.com/news/21841/how-social-media-keeping-gop-primary-going.

Smith, A. 2011. *Why Americans Use Social Media*. Pew Research Center, www.pewinternet.org/Reports/2011/Why-Americans-Use-Social-Media/Main-report.aspx.

Stankey, M.J. 1988. Using Advertising Media More Effectively. *Business* 38: 20–7.

Stromer-Galley, J. 2000. On-Line Interaction and Why Candidates Avoid It. *Journal of Communication* 50: 111–32.

Stromer-Galley, J. 2014. *Presidential Campaigning in the Internet Age*. New York: Oxford.

Towner, T.L. and D.A. Dulio. 2012. New Media and Political Marketing in the United States: 2012 and Beyond. *Journal of Political Marketing* 11: 95–119.

Unkelbach, C. 2007. Reversing the Truth Effect: Learning the Interpretation of Processing Fluency in Judgments of Truth. *Journal of Experimental Psychology: Learning, Memory, and Cognition* 33: 219–30.

Virk, A. 2011. Twitter: The Strength of Weak Ties. *University of Auckland Business Review* 13(1): 19–21.

Webb, P.H. and M.L. Ray. 1979. Effects of TV Clutter. *Journal of Advertising Research* (June): 7–14.

Williams, A.P., K.D. Trammell, M. Postelnicu, K.D. Landreville, and J.D. Martin. 2006. Blogging and Hyperlinking: Use of the Web to Enhance Viability during the 2004 US Campaign. *Journalism Studies* 6: 177–86.

Winkielman, P. and J.T. Cacioppo. 2001. Mind at Ease Puts a Smile on the Face: Psychophysiological Evidence That Processing Facilitation Elicits Positive Affect. *Journal of Personality and Social Psychology* 81: 989–1000.

Winter, F.W. 1973. A Laboratory Experiment of Individual Attitude Response to Advertising Exposure. *Journal of Marketing Research* 10: 130–40.

Yoo, C., H.-K. Bang, and Y. Kim. 2009. The Effects of a Consistent Ad Series on Consumer Evaluations: A Test of the Repetition-Variation Hypothesis in a South Korean Context. *International Journal of Advertising* 28: 105–23.

Zhang, W., T.J. Johnson, T. Seltzer, and S.L. Bichard. 2010. The Revolution Will Be Networked: The Influence of Social Networking Sites on Political Attitude and Behavior. *Social Science Computer Review* 28: 75–92.

8

CAMPAIGNING ON TWITTER

The Use of Social Media in the 2014 European Elections in Italy

Sara Bentivegna and Rita Marchetti

The Case of the 2014 European Elections in Italy

As is well known by scholars and political actors, the European elections do not normally arouse great interest among citizens and voters. Distance from the decision-making centers and complexity in the application of the decisions do not contribute to attracting citizens to this European institution. However, in more recent years, the economic crisis and the EU-driven austerity measures have made a strident entry into the national political debate in various member states, including Italy, where the restrictions imposed by the European Council often appear in the political debate. For various reasons, therefore, the 2014 elections concluded a campaign that saw the contending parties discuss the role of Europe and alternative proposals for changing its policy.[1]

At the same time, the electoral result was presented and expected to have significant consequences in relation to domestic politics. Various political actors interpreted it in this way. First among them was Matteo Renzi, current prime minister and secretary of the Democratic Party (DP), who sought legitimization through a popular vote after having assumed government without being first elected. Furthermore Renzi, in his role as secretary of the DP, had to avoid at all costs being overtaken by the populist Five Stars Movement (M5S), which would thus have become the first party in Italy. Conversely, the M5S, after the extraordinary consensus received in 2013, had precisely the opposite aim: that of overtaking the party led by Renzi. Less ambitious but nonetheless difficult objectives were pursued by Forza Italia (FI), a party in serious difficulties following the sentencing of Berlusconi and his decline as a senator, as well as the birth of new center-right parties. Another aspect interweaving the national dimension was concern about overcoming the 4 percent barrier[2] by new small parties (NCD, FDI, L'Altra Europa con Tsipras).

Besides matters of a political nature, there was the question of the centrality of the web imposed by the electoral success of the M5S in 2013. This centrality is not merely instrumental, it is also ideological: for Beppe Grillo, the spokesperson of the M5S, the web makes it possible to sidestep the news media. It enables monitoring of those in power and the self-organization of citizens so they can challenge the state (Bordignon and Ceccarini 2013). Aside from the ideologization of the web by M5S, it is clear that the new relationship between citizens and political actors that can be created on digital platforms has been seen as a sort of obligatory and challenging route.

Another element useful in reconstructing the campaign context relates to the current electoral system for European elections in Italy: a party-centered system with open lists and two votes to cast. It is therefore a system that rewards candidates and encourages them to seek greater public attention and build a good reputation so as to obtain more preferential votes. From the point of view of a candidate, the availability of a platform like Twitter is useful: It is a communication tool that is entirely controlled and managed by the user. Indeed, it cannot be ruled out that having a Twitter account is simply an expression of communicative conformism: just a status symbol shown to keep up with the times.

The final background features concern the size of the Twitter user audience and the centrality of the platform in the Italian media ecosystem. The user base is decidedly limited (10 percent of Italian Internet users[3]). Moreover, to be noted is that users mostly belong to the traditional elites (politics and the media), the techno-elite (Castells 2001), active minorities, and non-elites. They are young (19.1 percent are aged between 14 and 29, 12.7 percent between 30 and 44; Censis and Ucsi 2015) with high educational levels. These user characteristics show that Twitter is still a "niche" platform. But it is a niche platform that has achieved a central role in the Italian media ecosystem, especially in regard to the political dimension, creating an evident and widespread form of media hybridization (Chadwick 2013). Almost every day, television programs and newspaper articles cite tweets by political parties, which they use to reconstruct and recount political events (Bentivegna 2014b; Mancini and Mazzoni 2014). A presence on Twitter, therefore, can be a formidable opportunity for candidates to gain visibility. The features briefly outlined thus far make it sufficiently clear that the context in which the electoral campaign took place was particularly favorable to the adoption of Twitter by all candidates.

In order to verify the propensity to use Twitter during the election campaign, the first step was to map the accounts of candidates on the platform. This was followed by an analysis of the communication strategies adopted by selecting a statistically representative sample of the tweets posted. The accounts were identified by consulting the party websites, where the candidates are listed and often accompanied by links to social networks. At the same time, checks were carried out on the lists of candidates provided by the Ministry of the Interior. The availability of candidates' accounts was ascertained in two phases—as soon as the candidacies were formalized (mid-April) and halfway through the electoral campaign (mid-May) to intercept any new accounts. The timelines of all the candidates with a Twitter account were downloaded for five weeks using Twitter API, going in reverse time order up to the threshold of 3,200 tweets. Out of a total of 825 candidates 517 accounts were identified. The total number of tweets produced from 22 April to 25 May was 111,509. A statistically representative sample of 3,816 tweets was selected from the universe of tweets produced by the candidates. A content analysis of the tweets was carried out using a specially designed coding scheme. Guiding the data collection and analysis was the hypothesis that adoption of the platform is now so widespread that the traditional variables of political affiliation are no longer relevant. This was a consequence of both the Italian context and the political rise of social media as an instrument for enhancing egalitarianism, which was possible due to low cost and ease of use (Gibson and McAllister 2014). We then hypothesized that the generalized adoption of the platform had given rise to an unprecedented blend of tradition and innovation in the communication styles adopted. Thus, after identifying "who" was on Twitter, we considered "how" the platform was used and "what" was published during the campaign. The data collected and their processing enabled us to construct a typology comprising three different Twitter styles: *Personal Marketing*, *Re-intermediation*, and *Impression Management*.

All Aboard the Twitter Bandwagon

The entry of Twitter into the politician's toolkit in Italy took place between 2011 and 2012, when the platform emerged from the shadow of Facebook. To give an idea of this change, it is sufficient to note the increase in members of parliament with a Twitter account from 9.7 percent (92 MPs) during the previous legislature to 72 percent (684 MPs) in the current one (Corbo 2015). Unfortunately, there are few studies regarding its use in electoral campaigns, and they focus mostly on the use of the platform by political leaders (Bentivegna 2014a) and the characteristics of their followers (Vaccari and Valeriani 2015). This study will take a broader view of the use of Twitter by candidates for the 2014 European elections, rather than its use by leaders alone.

Of the 825 candidates[4] identified, 517 were found to have a Twitter account. This percentage (62.6 percent) places Italy in line with (if not slightly ahead of) the figures for other countries, such as the United States (Gainous and Wagner 2014). After a first analysis of actual use, however, the number of candidate users was found to be 442 (53.6 percent). With regard to the candidates' parties on Twitter, Table 8.1 shows very clearly how the traditional variables associated with presence on the web are of little consequence: both established parties (FI) and new and fringe parties (FDI, Altra Europa con Tsipras) are on Twitter, as well as opposition parties (5SM, Lega) and governing parties (DP, NCD). If we consider

TABLE 8.1 Active users, Twitter users and tweet productivity by political party

Political party (abbr*)	Number of active users	Number of candidates	Tweet productivity%
Partito Democratico (PD)	65	73	17.3
Movimento Cinque Stelle (M5S)	64	73	8.4
Forza Italia (FI)	50	73	17.8
Scelta Europea (SE)	46	73	5.2
Nuovo Centro Destra—Udc (NCD)	45	73	6.3
L'Altra Europa con Tsipras (Tsipras)	45	71	7.8
Fratelli d'Italia (FDI)	33	68	15.3
Verdi Europei—Green Italia (Verdi)	31	66	9.7
Italia dei Valori (IDV)	26	68	1.8
Lega Nord –Die Freiheitliche (Lega)	22	65	7.8
Other parties	15	122	2.6
Total	442	825	111,509

* Some abbreviations are official; some are unofficial for presentation purposes.

that in the past the parties most recalcitrant in adopting Internet were FI and those of the center-right in general (Bentivegna 2006; Vaccari 2012), these findings are indicative of the profound transformations that have characterized the Italian political context. It is likely that the spread of technological literacy in the country has played a significant role in heightening awareness of the centrality of the web in the electoral context, just as the professionalization of electoral campaigns has led to the inclusion of Twitter in a candidate's toolkit. It is equally probable, however, that impetus for the adoption of Twitter has also been imparted by the victorious example of the M5S, a party born on the web and that has become one of the country's principal parties in the space of just a few months. In any case, the empirical data support the hypothesis that generalization of the adoption of Twitter during this electoral campaign was accompanied by the disappearance of traditional political and party variables.

Obviously, the widespread adoption of the platform by candidates does not entail uniformity of use. In this regard, significant differences emerge if one considers the level of Twitter use by the candidates (Table 8.1): fully 50.4 percent of all tweets were produced by the members of three parties (DP, FI, and FDI). This figure is unexpected and suggests very different styles of use. Contrary to expectations, in fact, M5S is not particularly active on the platform, despite being one of the parties with the highest number of candidates possessing a Twitter account. Also to be noted is the insignificant contribution by IDV candidates,

130 Sara Bentivegna and Rita Marchetti

TABLE 8.2 Types of tweet by party*

Type of tweet	PD	M5S	FI	Lega	Tsipras	FDI	Greens	NCD	Other parties	Total
Original	53.1	69.4	42	35.7	59.5	40.2	35.6	52.8	62.9	48.9
Retweet	34.5	18.3	44.4	32.5	36.1	39.2	55.2	43.7	30.8	37.7
@reply	12.4	12.2	13.6	31.8	4.4	20.5	9.2	3.5	6.3	13.4
Total	(699)	(278)	(691)	(305)	(296)	(584)	(413)	(229)	(381)	(3816)

* Because of the low number of cases, IDV and SC have been aggregated with other parties.

which reflects the party's electoral decline mirrored by the divestment in the web after being a vanguard in its adoption in the past (Bentivegna 2006).

One aspect of the analysis of the candidates' Twitter accounts, was identifying their creation date. This makes it possible to determine whether ongoing use is made of the platform or whether it is for purely electoral purposes. With the exclusion of the 23 percent of candidates who opened a Twitter account only a few months before the elections—which is evidence of an account's electoral purposes—the majority are distributed over time, with a peak of 24.7 percent in 2012, confirming that year as the turning point in the adoption of the platform in Italy.[5] Multi-year, as well as more recent, experience of the platform is apparent for candidates of all parties, even if the early adopters belong to a greater extent to political parties that have shown interest in the web for some time (DP and Greens), while the newcomers belong to newly founded parties (FDI, NCD, Altra Europa con Tsipras) and ones traditionally averse to technology such as Lega Nord.

The data tell us little about the type of communication the candidates engaged in, or "how" the 140 characters were used. Elementary information in this regard is provided by tweet formats,[6] which divide among an original tweet, a retweet (RT), and an @reply (Table 8.2). Among these three formats, @reply may be considered an indicator of a discursive interaction in which the candidate has participated on his or her own initiative, or accepting the invitation of others, while the original tweet pertains to a one-way mode of communication.

These data indicate a marked propensity for the transmission/sharing of information rather than interaction with the user, with the partial exception of Lega Nord (31.8 percent) and FDI (20.5 percent), i.e., parties engaged in strident protest against the national government and that of Europe. The opportunity for direct exchanges with citizens afforded by the platform, which "activates the 'small world' phenomena through which distant people are in remarkably close reach" (Bennett 2012, p. 28), is seldom taken by candidates, confirming a resistance to direct interaction that is common to political parties in many countries (Enli and Skogerbø 2013; Goldbeck et al. 2010; Larsson and Moe, 2012; 2013; Parmelee and Bichard 2013; Strandberg 2013).

We can safely say that the platform is now a tool generally employed in electoral campaigns, and its adoption is no longer a distinctive feature of particular parties. Nonetheless, some parties are more active in its use than others. The variants of Twitter presence identified are indicative of different styles of the platform's use, from both the formal (frequency and volume of use) and relational (interaction) points of view. In what follows, we shall consider the extent to which interpretations of the platform by candidates result from a simple "translation" of old communicative strategies or from effective "innovation" of the forms, contents, and opportunities of electoral campaigning in the age of social media.

Basic Patterns of Electoral Tweets

To analyze the communication flows produced and distributed during the election campaign, and the role of the platform in the candidate's communication strategies, we considered the content of the tweets published by the candidates. From the universe of tweets (111,509 items) we extracted a statistically representative sample[7] of 3,816 tweets. We analyzed the sample using a coding scheme designed to register the following characteristics:[8] the presence and type of hashtags (thematic, personal electoral, party electoral, European campaign electoral, referring to the leader, topical, pointless babble, media-related, geolocation), images (photographs, cartoons, videos), links (legacy media, online media, candidate or party platform, other platforms); tone (formal, informal); communicative style (referential; humorous, ironic; conversational, participatory; sarcastic, provocative); function (campaign promotion, information diffusion, political and non-political news reporting, position-taking, personal, mobilization); and topic (political issues, policy issues, campaign issues, personal issues, issues related to current events). The variables used in the analysis referred to both competence in the platform's grammar (Murthy 2013)—for example in the use of images, links, and hashtags—and to elements pertaining to the political dimension of the election—for example, the publicizing information, position-taking, interaction, and attempts to mobilize voters.

Analysis of the structural elements of the tweets revealed some unexpected features: in fact, in the "age of the selfie," it was reasonable to expect the constant and widespread use of images to recount the campaign or other events. The data, however, confounded this expectation and recorded the presence of images in only one case in four (24.3 percent). Equally sporadic was the use of links (36.3 percent), which are normally used to overcome the constraint of 140 characters and to expand the information content. Also to be noted is that when links were present, 62 percent of them referred to other platforms created by the candidate or the party. In short, the majority of the tweets posted by the candidates did not use visual imagery, nor did they expand the richness of their content through the link device. Such an "elementary" supply suggests a certain lack of experience in use of the platform—confirmed in many cases by the recent opening of a Twitter account.

Even more significant confirmation of scant familiarity with the grammar of Twitter was provided by the sporadic or haphazard use of hashtags, which were present in only 49.7 percent of cases. Considering that it is through the adoption and use of a hashtag that people join a community of users (Burgess and Bruns 2012) with which they interact and through which they expand their communicative networks, the inevitable marginality on the platform, as well as the degree of amateurism, are evident. This limitation is all the more significant if one considers that 47.3 percent of the candidates had no more than 250 followers: that is, a number equal to that of an ordinary user—who, however, unlike a politician engaged in an election campaign, is uninterested in building consensus and acquiring greater visibility. When present, hashtags related to the party (#M5S, #DP), to specific themes (#netneutrality, #job), to the candidate (#Salvini, #Meloni) or, more generally, to the European elections (#europee2014) or geolocations (#Roma, #Milano). This last type of hashtag indicating the candidate's presence in the various localities of the constituency relates to conduct of the campaign, and it suggests interpretation of the platform as serving the purpose of self-promotion through publicizing of the candidate's agenda. Besides this direct form of campaigning, to be noted are the high values attributed to the hashtags referring to the party and the candidate, which testify to double-track electioneering (impersonal in the former case, personal in the latter).

Significant differences in the use of hashtags emerge in relation to the candidates' membership of the various parties (Table 8.3). For example, M5S candidates almost exclusively used the party hashtag, thus confirming the party's prevalence over the candidate, traditionally presented as an ordinary citizen engaged in politics with no specific individual features. Conversely, the Lega candidates use personal hashtags and ones referring to the party leader, namely Salvini (the party secretary). With regard to the Lega, also of interest is the frequent use of hashtags related to the media and used to signal Salvini's presence on television programs. This is also the practice of FDI candidates, who make abundant references to the party—which must be made known to voters—and the leader, the only well-known figure in the party. In short, these data indicate a diversified presence on the platform that suggests the existence of numerous types of communication strategy related, at least in part, to the party of membership. We shall see later the extent to which the parties are associated with specific communication styles and the extent to which other variables are of greater significance.

To continue the analysis of the tweets, there is an informal tone (72.9 percent of cases) that translates into a communicative style that is participatory (43.9 percent), referential (41.7 percent), provocative (11.7 percent), or humorous/ironic (2.7 percent). The variety of styles suggests that there is a wide range of communicative registers adopted, either to share information or simply to transmit it, chat informally, or engage in quarrelsome and aggressive discussion. This

Campaigning on Twitter 133

TABLE 8.3 Hashtag use by party

Hashtag	PD	M5S	FI	Lega	Tsipras	FDI	Greens	NCD	Total*
Thematic	20.6	17.2	23.2	18.5	33.6	25.8	27.5	21.8	23.9
Personal	23.2	5.4	29	42.4	6.6	19.6	3.6	27.9	19.5
Party	32.8	75.3	21.3	37	45.3	69	71	29.9	44.9
Leader	3.1	4.3	9.8	10.9	2.2	24	2.5	1.4	7.6
Current issues	6.3	7.5	6.8	2.2	8.8	5.2	9.8	7.5	6.9
Pointless babble	7.3	11.8	8.5	7.6	5.8	9.6	11.2	12.9	9.1
Media	3.4	2.2	8.5	15.2	5.8	17.7	5.4	5.4	7.7
European elections	26	10.8	23.5	18.5	16.8	12.2	10.5	20.4	19.4
Europe	7	2.2	9.3	5.4	2.2	5.9	2.9	12.2	6.5
Geolocation	21.6	11.8	17.5	20.7	13.9	15.1	6.2	24.5	15.8
Total	(384)	(93)	(366)	(92)	(92)	(271)	(276)	(147)	(3046)

* Percentages and totals are based on tweet cases.

diversification relates to the many nuances that differentiate a broadcast communication model from a conversational one. In this ambience, which alternates between the transmission of information and communicative exchange, the candidates engage in different functions:[9] campaign updating—as communication intended to inform voters about the candidate's activities; self-promotion—i.e., the relaying of interviews, statements or communications relative to the candidate him/herself; information dissemination—publicizing general information on political and current affairs; position-taking—i.e., intervention on political and campaign issues and problems; emotionalization—in the classic sense of incursion into the candidate's private life (Van Santen and Van Zoonen 2010), sharing gossip and emotions with voters; and finally mobilization—i.e., urging commitment by supporters (Table 8.4).

Among the functions identified, not surprisingly the most common one is position-taking (46.1 percent), i.e. a variant of what Castells (2009) has termed "mass autocommunication," whose purpose in this case is to circulate opinions and proposals, as well as to join the mainstream media in a form that closely resembles the traditional "sound bite." At least in theory, therefore, position-taking is characterized by two dimensions: one on the platform, the other in the mainstream media. Another particularly common function is promotion of the candidate's agenda (25.7 percent). Decidedly unusual, however, is the high number of cases (18.4 percent) relatable to the emotionalization function. In the choice and combination of the functions assigned to tweets, candidates behaved differently according to whether they belonged to the government or opposition parties, established parties, or new parties. The candidates of the DP, NCD—i.e., the parties supporting the government—favored campaign-updating and position-taking, while those of the opposition parties—M5S, Lega, FDI—also

TABLE 8.4 Functions of tweets by party

Functions	PD	M5S	FI	Lega	Tsipras	FDI	Greens	NCD	Total*
Campaign updating	41	29.9	24.5	24.6	31.1	18.5	11.6	30.6	25.7
Self-promotion	9.7	21.2	13.5	8.5	14.9	16.3	9.4	13.5	13.7
Information disseminating	5.2	6.8	5.9	7.5	7.1	4.1	13.3	7.9	7.3
Position-taking	42.6	32.7	50.8	42.6	40.9	47.4	60	48.5	46.1
Emotionalization	16.6	22.3	16.9	25.9	13.9	25.9	15	14	18.4
Mobilization	7	8.6	11	9.8	9.8	9.2	6.1	7	8.5
Other	0.1	1.4	0.4	0.7	0.3	0.2	0.2	0	0.6
Total	(669)	(278)	(691)	(305)	(296)	(584)	(413)	(229)	(3816)

* Percentages and totals are based on tweet cases

engaged in emotionalization and mobilization. The greater variety of functions associated with the tweets of candidates belonging to the opposition parties indicates greater investment in communication on the platform, in both traditional and innovative forms.

Finally, the great majority of the topics discussed regard campaigning issues (60.5), updates on, or descriptions of, the campaign's management and progress; followed by policy issues (18.5 percent), specific issues to address and resolve; personal issues and pointless babble (12.8 percent), thoughts and jokes prompted by the tweeters' personal views; political issues (3.5 percent), matters concerning the relationship between parties and political institutions; and current affairs (5 percent). The large preponderance of campaigning issues is closely bound up with the campaign-updating function (see Chapter 9, this volume). This was the principal function of the tweets, and it distinctively characterized use of the Twitter platform by candidates for personal marketing. Hence it was in direct continuity with the communicative tradition of electoral campaigns. The innovation offered by Twitter—especially in terms of a different, more conversational and casual, relationship with voters—seems to have been grasped by only a minority of candidates.

Campaigning in 140 Characters

The number of variables thus far illustrated separately were used to conduct, first, a factor analysis, and then a cluster analysis that led to identification of three types of tweets posted by candidates. The first cluster—the largest, with 48.7 percent of the tweets analyzed—was given the label "Personal Marketing"; the second, with a percentage weight of 32.9 percent, that of "Re-intermediation" (in reference to the intermediary role assumed by the candidate); the third, of decidedly smaller size (18.4 percent), that of "Impression Management".

The first cluster is a clear example of communication for the purpose of personalization and self-promotion: 86.1 percent of the topics pertained to campaigning issues, and in 62.9 percent of cases the function of the tweet was campaign updating and self-promotion (publication of election pledges, participation in television or radio programs; transmission of interviews given by the candidate; accounts of campaign events; and publication of activities on other social media). Not coincidentally, this cluster recorded the highest value for candidates' personal hashtags, together with those referring to geolocation (signaling of election events), the European elections, and the party in general.

The second cluster, Re-intermediation, was characterized more by the position-taking function (average value 74.7 percent versus 37 percent overall), defined as intervention on political and non-political issues, the signaling of problems to be addressed, identification of issues to be resolved in Europe, attacks on other candidates and parties, or emphasis of the party leader's role. Predominant among the topics were policy issues (41 percent), which recorded a value more than twice that of general issues (18.2 percent). The topics most debated were the governance of Europe and whether Italy should remain in the Eurozone, environmental issues, work and the economic crisis, and immigration. Analysis of the hashtags contained in the tweets confirmed the importance of policy issues (15.2 percent) and showed a closer focus on the party of reference rather than the individual candidate (19.4 percent).

Finally, the third cluster, Impression Management, was characterized by a participatory, emotional, and colloquial communicative style (79.9 percent), an informal tone in almost all cases (96.7 percent), and a propensity to interaction (50.4 percent of the tweets had an @reply format). The main aim of these tweets was emotionalization (84.2 percent versus 16.2 percent of the total): i.e., accounts of campaign events from a personal point of view; incursion into private life in relation to work, family and friends; the sharing of emotions, moods, desires, and especially the exchange of greetings, pleasantries, and jokes. In keeping with the tweet's function, the topics discussed were mainly personal issues and pointless babble (62.1 percent).

The different tweet construction styles were associated with political variables (party affiliation of the account holder) and experience in using the platform. As regards the party, tweets published by the candidates of the government parties (DP, NCD) and those belonging to political parties such as Altra Europa con Tsipras and M5S (largely unknown to the electorate) were characterized by a style centered on personal marketing. The reintroduction of the preferences system is likely to have influenced choice of a Twitter use mode aimed at the circulation of the candidate's name amid fierce competition among parties and within the party itself. However, tweets related to the Re-intermediation style were published by all candidates, with a significant peak in the case of those belonging to the Green Party (52.3 percent), who presumably used the platform to try and impose discussion frames related to the issue that characterizes their party (protection of

136 Sara Bentivegna and Rita Marchetti

TABLE 8.5 Tweeting style by party

Tweeting style	PD	M5S	FI	Lega	Tsipras	FDI	Greens	NCD	Other Parties	Total
Personal marketing	55.5	55.4	48.6	39.7	59.5	40.4	33.9	54.6	57	48.7
Re-intermediation	28.1	24.5	34.7	30.5	27	32.5	52.3	31.9	30.5	32.9
Impression management	16.4	20.1	16.6	29.8	13.5	27.1	13.8	13.5	12.5	18.4
Total	(699)	(278)	(691)	(305)	(296)	(584)	(413)	(229)	(381)	(3816)

the environment). Finally, it is notable that tweets from opposition parties like the Lega (29.8 percent), FDI (27.1 percent), and M5S (20.1 percent) were concentrated in the Impression Management cluster. These are the parties that have shown the greatest capacity to use the opportunities offered by the platform to interact with users and expand their follower bases.

Besides the specificities of the parties that tended to adopt one style rather than another, the three clusters were also differentiated by the candidates' experience in the use of Twitter. Data on the year of account creation confirm the specificity of the Impression Management style with respect to the other two (Table 8.6). Tweets belonging in this cluster had been published by candidates with an account created in 33.6 percent of cases in 2011, 30.6 percent in 2012, and 23.9 percent before 2011. Instead, the opening of accounts just prior to the elections was associated with tweets using the Personal Marketing style and, second, that of Re-intermediation.

Description of the characteristics of the three types of Twitter presence cannot conclude without considering their efficacy, at least in communicative terms. In this regard, the simplest and clearest indicator is undoubtedly the increase in the number of followers, which is now one of the metrics used to describe the progress of an election campaign in the age of the social media (Owen 2013). On Twitter, in fact, the size of the network of followers is a clear indicator of the potential circulation—and, therefore, the visibility—of the tweets posted and their author.

Comparison between the number of followers at the beginning and the end of the campaign shows that, in a significant proportion of cases (47.5 percent), there was substantial stability, i.e., an increase of fewer than 50 followers. This modest performance is associated with tweets for the purpose of Personal Marketing (57.3 percent), which confirms that tweeting solely for self-promotion does not pay off in terms of expanding the relational network or, more generally, the candidate's visibility. More successful, albeit again to only a modest extent, is the posting of tweets for Re-intermediation purposes, with increases of about 200 followers (35.7 percent). A significant increase, however, is associated with tweets pertaining to the Impression Management strategy: from 201 to 600 followers

Campaigning on Twitter   137

TABLE 8.6 Tweeting styles and year of account creation

Year of creation:	Personal Marketing	Re-intermediation	Impression Management	Total
Before 2010	27.4	28.9	23.9	27.2
2011	20	22.8	33.6	23.4
2012	23.3	25.3	30.6	25.3
2013	14.4	9.3	5.6	11.1
2014	14.9	13.7	6.3	12.9
Total	(1859)	(1255)	(702)	(3816)

TABLE 8.7 Tweeting styles by number of followers acquired during the campaign

Increase in followers	Personal Marketing	Re-intermediation	Impression Management	Total
Up to 50	57.3	41.8	31.6	47.5
From 51 to 200	26.2	35.7	33.3	30.6
From 201 to 600	9	14.8	23.9	13.7
601 and more	7.5	7.7	11.1	8.2
Total	(1859)	(1255)	(702)	(3816)

in 23.9 percent of cases and more than 600 in 11.1 percent. Hence, from the communicative point of view, there is no doubt that the impression management strategy was the one most appreciated by users, and that it increased the size of the network. But the extent to which it was efficacious in electoral terms is difficult to determine: in fact, the three communicative styles were used both by candidates who were elected and those who were not.

Italian Candidates between Tradition and Innovation

Given that 53.6 percent of candidates had an active Twitter account during the campaign, the European elections of 2014 can undoubtedly be considered the first Twitter elections in Italy. The data have confirmed the initial hypothesis of a generalized and participatory adoption of Twitter across the various political parties. This can be interpreted as a consequence of the platform's place in the country's media ecosystem, and of the importance given to social media in the political arena, especially since the surprising success of M5S. It is likely that it was the combination of these elements that induced candidates to adopt the platform to conduct a campaign aimed at winning preference votes. Context variables, therefore, and considerations concerning the platform's cheapness and ease of use, created the conditions for the generalized adoption of Twitter, annulling the importance of the party-based traditions of Web 1.0 use. Hence, in a very short time, candidates from parties usually alien to the web (the Lega, for example) reversed course and established a presence on the platform, certainly not for display but for everyday use.

The use of Twitter by candidates from all parties certainly marked the platform's definitive entry into the electoral "toolkit," and it will be difficult to do without Twitter in the future. This recognition, however, does not imply uniformity of use, and it should not divert attention from a legitimate question concerning the nature of communication performed with 140 characters. As described by the data, such communication is largely one-directional (with a 48.9 percent presence of original tweets) with sporadic shifts to the conversational style (with a 13.4 percent presence of @replies). This obviously gainsays the rhetoric that the social media have restored a direct relationship between politicians and citizens. In short, the broadcast model of the old media has often been replicated on Twitter, turning the platform into a yet another opportunity for politicians to take center-stage.

The three clusters that we proposed on analyzing the data have made it possible to highlight different styles of Twitter use, ranging from a more "traditional" type of communication to one that is decidedly more innovative. Candidates prefer the broadcast communication model. This is also designed to publicize events in the candidate's campaign, turning the Twitter account into a kind of bulletin board announcing future events and reporting past ones. This type of communication (the most common, with a value of 48.7 percent), which we termed Personal Marketing, combines the typical features of one-to-many communication with those of the mere publication of electoral information. The anchoring to "tradition" is manifest in both the communicative model and the content, evidencing that the adoption of Twitter has involved the simple transfer of old patterns to a new platform. A less traditional use of the platform is the one that we have called Re-intermediation (32.9 percent) in order to emphasize the intermediation that political actors seek to resume with citizens. In this case, candidates use Twitter to communicate opinions and points of view directly to citizens. They thus act as intermediaries on political issues between the world of politics and that of voters. Moreover, for the best-known candidates, Twitter is another opportunity to gain space and visibility in the legacy media. Decidedly innovative, finally, is the Twitter use that we have called Impression Management (18.4 percent), characterized by a conversational model and an interpretation of the relationship between politicians and citizens inspired by a less formal and institutional sharing of politics.

We have distinguished tweets among three types of communication identified with reference to highly diversified investments in the platform: mere transfer of consolidated campaign practices, opportunities for speech-making and visibility in others, activation of an informal and conversational relationship in others. In this regard, it should be borne in mind that candidates differed in their behaviors according to their membership of the government or opposition parties, established parties, or new parties. The candidates of the

DP and NCD—i.e., parties supporting the government—preferred functions like campaign updating and position-taking, while those of the opposition parties—M5S, Lega, FDI—gave ample space to emotionalization and mobilization. In short, the picture that emerges from the data is not homogeneous, and it constantly oscillates between tradition and innovation. In many respects, such oscillation resembles that of political parties on the one hand committed to confirming an institutional image, sometimes of government, and on the other, seeking to convey an image of opposition across the board, also by attempting to distance themselves from traditional politics to approach the everyday lives of voters. Given these contradictory movements, the experience of the 2014 election campaign is difficult to define: it was a sort of campaign in progress, with uncertain and blurred features.

Notes

1   Research for this chapter was conducted as part of a project, "Guardare la tv, parlare di politica. I networked publics tra media broadcast e media sociali," funded by the University of Rome "Sapienza" (2013).
2   For entry into the European Parliament there is a 4 percent threshold in Italy.
3   Data released by http://wearesocial.sg/blog/2015/01/digital-social-mobile-2015 and Censis and Ucsi (2015).
4   In reality, the total number of candidates was 930, reduced to 825 on account of multiple candidatures.
5   Specifically, 20.6 percent of candidates were already on Twitter from 2007 to 2010. They were joined in 2011 by another 15.8 percent and in 2013 by a further 15.6 percent.
6   For the purposes of this analysis, it was decided not to consider the MT format, i.e., an RT with a comment by the user.
7   The sampling parameters were the following: confidence level 99 percent, margin of error 2 percent.
8   The coding was carried out by a team of two coders. The intercoder reliability test was based on a set of tweets taken from a random sample of 10 percent of the total. Cohen's kappa was used to estimate intercoder reliability. The reliability scores for the average pairwise Cohen's kappa were as follows: conversation's tone 0.66, style 0.76, function 0.77.
9   Within each tweet it was possible to identify and record up to a maximum of four functions. In the majority of cases, however, the functions were fewer than two.

References

Bennett, W.L. 2012. The Personalization of Politics: Political Identity, Social Media, and Changing Patterns of Participation. *The ANNALS of the American Academy of Political and Social Science* 644(1): 20–39.

Bentivegna, S. 2006. *Campagne elettorali in rete*. Rome: Laterza.

Bentivegna, S. 2014a. Far finta di essere social: La campagna elettorale dei leader nel 2013. In S. Bentivegna (ed.), *La politica in 140 caratteri: Twitter e spazio pubblico*. Milan: FrancoAngeli, pp. 105–24.

Bentivegna, S. (ed.). 2014b. *La politica in 140 caratteri: Twitter e spazio pubblico*. Milan: FrancoAngeli.

Bordignon, F. and L. Ceccarini. 2013. Five Stars and a Cricket: Beppe Grillo Shakes Italian Politics. *South European Society and Politics* 18(4): 427–49.

Burgess, J. and A. Bruns. 2012. (Not) the Twitter Election: The Dynamics of the #ausvote Conversation in relation to the Australian Media Ecology. *Journalism Practice* 6(3): 284–402.

Castells, M. 2001. *The Internet Galaxy: Reflections on the Internet, Business, and Society.* New York: Oxford University Press.

Castells, M. 2009. *Communication Power.* New York: Oxford University Press.

Censis and Ucsi. 2015. *L'economia della disintermediazione digitale.* Rome: FrancoAngeli.

Chadwick, A. 2013. *The Hybrid Media System: Politics and Power.* New York: Oxford University Press.

Corbo, A. 2015. *Onorevole Twitter.* Unpublished dissertation, University of Rome.

Enli, G.S. and E. Skogerbø. 2013. Personalized Campaigns in Party-Centered Politics. *Information, Communication & Society* 16(5): 757–74.

Gainous, J. and K.M. Wagner (eds.). 2014. *Tweeting to Power: The Social Media Revolution in American Politics.* New York: Oxford University Press.

Gibson, R.K. and I. McAllister. 2014. Normalising or Equalising Party Competition? Assessing the Impact of the Web on Electronic Campaign. *Political Studies* 63(4): 529–47..

Goldbeck, J., J.M. Grimes, and A. Rogers. 2010. Twitter Use by the US Congress. *Journal of the American Society for Information Science and Technology* 61(8): 1612–21.

Larsson, A.O. and H. Moe. 2012. Studying Political Microblogging: Twitter Users in the 2010 Swedish Election Campaign. *New Media & Society* 14(5): 729–47.

Larsson, A.O., and H. Moe, 2013. Representation or Participation? Twitter Use during the 2011 Danish Election Campaign. *Javnost: The Public* 20(1): 71–88.

Mancini, P. and M. Mazzoni, 2014. Politici e social network: Un trampolino per i media mainstream; Un sistema ibrido (tutto) italiano. In S. Bentivegna (ed.), *La politica in 140 caratteri: Twitter e spazio pubblico.* Milan: FrancoAngeli, pp. 41–56.

Murthy, D. 2013. *Twitter: Social Communication in the Twitter Age.* Cambridge: Polity Press.

Owen, D. 2013. The Campaign and the Media. In J.M. Box-Steffensmeier and S.S. Schier (eds.), *The American Elections of 2012.* New York: Marlowe, pp. 21–47.

Parmelee, J.H. and S.L. Bichard. 2013. *Politics and the Twitter Revolution: How Tweets Influence the Relationship between Political Leaders and the Public.* Lanham, MD: Lexington Books.

Strandberg, K. 2013. A Social Media Revolution or Just a Case of History Repeating Itself? The Use of Social Media in the 2011 Finnish Parliamentary Elections. *New Media & Society* 15(8): 1329–47.

Vaccari, C. 2012. From Echo Chamber to Persuasive Device? Rethinking the Role of the Internet in Campaigns. *New Media & Society* 15(1): 109–27.

Vaccari, C. and A. Valeriani, 2015. Follow the Leader! Direct and Indirect Flows of Political Communication during the 2013 General Election Campaign. *New Media & Society* 17(7): 1025–42.

Van Santen, R. and L. Van Zoonen, 2010. The Personal in Political Television Biographies. *Biography* 33(1): 46–7.

9

CANDIDATE USE OF TWITTER AND THE INTERSECTION OF GENDER, PARTY, AND POSITION IN THE RACE

A Comparison of Competitive Male/Female Senate Races in 2012 and 2014

Marion R. Just, Ann N. Crigler, and Rose A. Owen

Introduction

Election campaigns form the foundation of representative democracy as they take diverse candidates and interests and transform them into patterns of governing. In his 1996 book, *Senators on the Campaign Trail*, Richard Fenno argues that candidates build representational connections that "create the underlying infrastructure of a representative democracy" (Fenno 1996, p. 332). Specifically, he examines how diverse politicians communicate with potential voters to nurture connections. He finds that successful politicians are able to negotiate with constituents effectively through sharing more or less policy-oriented or personal messages. For example, during two open-seat elections in 1980, Fenno observed Pennsylvania Republican Arlen Specter, who referenced his three-inch thick sheaf of issue positions during any and all appearances. In contrast, Alabama Democratic candidate Jim Folsom ran a more personal whistle-stop campaign using only a single page of "issue positions" (Fenno 1996, pp. 6–7). Fenno elaborates further on representatives' communication imperatives on the campaign trail in his 2000 book, *Congress at the Grassroots: Representational Change in the South, 1970–1998*. He states that: "All representatives are context interpreters" (Fenno 2000, p. 6). By the nature of their jobs, they must be able to grasp quickly the circumstances in which they are operating and adjust their actions or strategies accordingly. How applicable are Fenno's observations to the social media campaigns of the current era? Does the context of the campaign still shape candidates' interpretations and subsequent messages? For example, how does leading or trailing affect messaging? What are the priorities of the electorate and political parties? Are there particular issues that dominate the political debate? With whom are they communicating in a given medium? These factors constitute some of the dynamic contexts of elections over time.

Fenno's (1996, 2000) case studies were selected to capture differences in partisan affiliation and incumbency (among other factors). He did not focus on gender differences or on new media—understandably so, since there were few women candidates and no new media. Fenno (1996, 2000) observed representatives in face-to-face communications with constituents where interpretation may be facilitated by direct contact. While the campaign trail is still filled with face-to-face communications, candidate diversity and campaign contexts have broadened to include more women and an important electronic domain in which candidates communicate directly with their followers.

Today, there are 20 women senators and even more women who run as candidates. We take advantage of the increased media and gender diversity in our study of the 2012 and 2014 US Senate campaigns to examine how men and women candidates use social media to communicate with constituencies. Both years were marked by a large number of male and female contests. We examine two years so that there is variation in gender by party and position in the race. To include different gender campaign contexts, we also include single gender candidate pairs during each election. In 2012, we include six male/female pairs, three male pairs, and one female pair. In 2014, the study includes eight races with male/female candidates, one male pair, and one female pair. Both years were marked by an increasing role for social media in campaign communication. Candidates have increasingly relied on social media since 2008, when Barack Obama's presidential campaign used "My Barack Obama" to mobilize supporters. That same year, YouTube emerged as a campaign tool. In the 2010 midterm elections many candidates began to use Facebook and Twitter to keep in touch with their supporters. By 2012, Twitter became a visual medium and its use only grew more significant by 2014.

We focus on the elements of representational connections to analyze how men and women candidates portray themselves and reach out to potential constituents. To assess Fenno's (1996, p. 335) "constituency connections," we look for gender differences in the amount of Twitter activity (tweets, retweets, and favorites) and in what Fenno (1996, 2000) called "policy connections" or "issues agendas." We explore the personal connection by looking at who is pictured with candidates on Twitter. The paper also considers candidates' partisan affiliation and position in the race (leading/trailing) as these factors shape the context in which candidates communicate.

In the televised advertising campaign, candidates are somewhat removed from constituents, particularly their followers. Television spots are aimed at people who are on the fence or those who can be discouraged from turning out for opponents. Not surprisingly, TV ads are predominantly negative, particularly those sponsored by political action committees (PACs). Twitter, however, is more like

Intersection of Gender, Party, and Position **143**

the face- to-face communication that Fenno (1996, 2000) describes as the bed-rock of representation. Since the conversation on Twitter is directed at follow-ers, it is more likely to be about connections rather than attacks. To support this expectation, we explore the frequency of attacks and the relationship to gender, party, and position in the race.

Theoretical Approach and Previous Research

This study takes a social constructionist theoretical perspective to argue that can-didates use social media to construct messages that will help them win elections (Just et al. 1992). We argue that candidates' gender, party identity, and perceptions of vulnerability in the polls shape the ways in which they communicate with potential constituents. Past research suggests that the amount, content, and con-nections that candidates choose to use in constructing their campaign commu-nications differ across gender, party, and position in the race as well as over time.

Historically Twitter users were more male than female, especially in discus-sion of new technology, which was an early trend in Twitter topics (Duggan and Brenner 2013). In recent years, women have drawn even with men in overall use. Now there are more women than men Twitter users (75 percent versus 69 per-cent) who report regularly seeing posts about national government and politics, according to a 2015 Pew Research Center study (Barthel et al. 2015, p. 10). Jeff Gulati and Christine Williams (2011) find that by the election of 2010, most House candidates had a presence on all three major social network sites—Twitter, Facebook, and YouTube. Their study showed that both party and gender were not associated with adoption of social media. Research by Heather Evans, Victoria Cordova, and Savannah Sipole (2014) on the use of Twitter in 2012 House elec-tions found that women candidates were 15 percent more likely to have Twitter accounts and to tweet more often (mean = 107) than men (mean = 82). In con-trast, our earlier work on the 2012 Senate elections did not find significant gender differences in the use of social media by men and women candidates (Just and Crigler 2014). Given these findings, we do not expect a gender difference in the use of Twitter by Senate candidates. These expectations are expressed in H1 below.

H1: Men and women candidates will use Twitter equally.

Incumbents and candidates in competitive elections are significantly more likely to use Twitter during the campaign. Sky Amman's (2014) study of the 2010 Senate elections found that those in competitive races were more likely to use Twitter than those in non-competitive elections. Previous research on social media use by Congressional candidates indicates that weaker candidates use social media more than strong candidates (Gulati and Williams 2011). Relatedly, scholars have found that candidates who are trailing in the polls, tend to take risks and "go negative" (attack opponents) (Druckman et al. 2009, p. 344) and to use electronic media more than those who are leading (Lassen and Brown 2011; Bystrom 2014). These findings lead to our second hypothesis:

> *H2: On Twitter, trailing candidates will post more messages than candidates leading in the race and will also attack more than leading candidates.*

Previous research shows that women's campaign styles are, by and large, similar to men's, but some differences have emerged particularly in terms of candidates' message focus and the discussion of issues on the campaign trail (Dabelko and Herrnson 1997; Herrnson et al. 2003). Evans, Cordova, and Sipole's (2014) study of the 2012 House elections on Twitter finds that women candidates emphasized campaigning, issues, mobilization, and attacking the opponent more often than men (although gender differences in attacks disappear when controlling for incumbency and competitiveness of the election). In fact, recent research finds that candidates predominantly use Twitter to mobilize voters online and provide their followers with opportunities to volunteer and to get involved with the campaign (Abroms and Lefebvre 2009). John Parmelee and Shannon Bichard (2012) showed that most of the candidates included in their sample were using their accounts to refer to their campaigns, commenting on political opponents and making calls for action. Further, they tended to use Twitter to inform their followers about media appearances, quotes and to post links to campaign related information (Parmelee and Bichard 2012).

Although studies of other media found gender differences on issues, researchers have not come to consensus about social media, perhaps because of changes over time and across platforms. Kathleen Dolan's analyses of Congressional candidates' websites, for example, have found that men and women do not differ in their issue emphasis (Dolan 2009, 2014). In Dolan's research, party considerations were more important than gender in deciding which issues to emphasize (2014, pp. 160, 171). Kim Fridkin and Patrick Kenney (2014) largely agree that there are few gender differences in issue emphasis in their study of House, Senate, and gubernatorial candidates. In the Senate, however, they do find that women candidates are more likely to discuss emerging issues, such as women's health (Fridkin and Kenney 2014). Reviews of the literature lead to our next hypotheses:

> *H3a: All candidates, regardless of gender, party or position in the race will use Twitter primarily to communicate about the campaign.*
> *H3b: Gender will have only a modest effect on candidate policy connections.*

Research based on experimental data shows that candidates—regardless of gender—are seen as better able to handle "compassion issues" if they express traits of warmth and expressiveness. In general, these are embraced more by female than male candidates (Huddy and Terkildsen 1993). In addition to communicating warmth, previous research found that women are more likely to treat the audience as peers using "we" and "our"—a "feminine strategy" of online communication (Bystrom et al. 2004, p. 151). In social media, reaching out to the audience as peers may take several forms including interacting more with diverse constituents, having followers who interact with the campaign by retweeting, and marking messages as favorites. These findings suggest the following hypotheses.

> *H4a: Women candidates will connect more with constituents on social media than men candidates particularly in terms of the images they project on Twitter.*
> *H4b: Gender, party and position combine to influence retweeting and other interactions with the public.*

Data and Methods

In order to test our hypotheses about the gendered uses of social media, we analyzed the tweets for ten US Senate races in each year (six male–female races in 2012 and eight in 2014). In 2012 we coded one week during the height of the campaign season (October 9–16, 2012) and the last week of the campaign (October 31–November 6, 2012). The sampled two weeks of the 2012 campaign contained 2,392 Twitter messages. For 2014, we coded a 10 percent sample of tweets from Labor Day until the day before Election Day. The sample of 2014 campaign tweets contained 897 Twitter messages from the 20 candidates in the ten state races. The candidates and states included in the study are shown in Table 9.1.

The 2012 and 2014 content analyses were conducted by two teams of three student coders. Each message was coded for: the main focus of the message, issues, and images. To assess personal connections, we analyzed who was pictured with the candidates in their Twitter messages (by race, gender and age). In addition, we counted the numbers of retweets and favorites to assess which tweets were particularly effective in resonating with constituents by creating a "wide and divergent network of distribution" and fostering public engagement (Gainous and Wagner 2014, p. 77). To investigate the effect of candidates leading or trailing in their races, we created a variable to reflect the candidates' positions in the race midway through the campaign. Based on Nate Silver's FiveThirtyEight Senate projections of October 13, 2012 (Silver 2012b), and again in 2014, we divided candidates into categories of modestly leading, in a dead-heat, or modestly losing in these highly competitive races. The complete codebook is available from the authors.

Intercoder reliability was excellent for both years. In 2012, percent agreement among coders was 97 percent, or coding 228 out of 233 questions exactly the same. The only differences occurred one time for any particular question and

146 Just, Crigler, and Owen

TABLE 9.1 US Senate candidates for 2012 and 2014 elections

Election Year	State	Republican candidate	Democratic candidate
2012	Nevada	Dean Heller	Shelley Berkley
	Missouri	Todd Akin	Claire McCaskill
	Wisconsin	Tommy Thompson	Tammy Baldwin
	North Dakota	Rick Berg	Heidi Heitkamp
	Massachusetts	Scott Brown	Elizabeth Warren
	Connecticut	Linda McMahon	Chris Murphy
	Arizona	Jeff Flake	Richard Carmona
	Hawaii	Linda Lingle	Maizie Hirono
	Indiana	Richard Mourdock	Joe Donnelly
	Virginia	George Allen	Timothy Kaine
2014	Georgia	David Perdue	Michelle Nunn
	Iowa	Joni Ernst	Bruce Braley
	Kansas	Pat Roberts	Greg Orman
	Kentucky	Mitch McConnell	Alison Grimes
	Louisiana	Bill Cassidy	Mary Landrieu
	Michigan	Terri Lynn Land	Gary Peters
	North Carolina	Thom Tillis	Kay Hagan
	New Hampshire	Scott Brown	Jeanne Shaheen
	Oregon	Monica Wehby	Jeff Merkley
	West Virginia	Shelley Moore Capito	Natalie Tennant

were typically off by only one point on a scale. In 2014, inter-coder reliability was measured with Kronbach's Alpha > 0.89 for each variable.

Results

H1: Gender and Tweets

In general our findings confirm previous research on technology diffusion. In 2012, there was a small difference by gender and party in the candidates' use of Twitter but by 2014 there were no significant differences in the mean number of tweets sent by women and men candidates ($T = 1.44$) or by Democratic and Republican candidates ($T = 1.43$). In 2012, the most frequent Twitter users in our sample were: Republicans Richard Mourdock (445), Linda Lingle (390), and Dean Heller (316). The least frequent of those who used Twitter were: Democrats Shelley Berkley (5) and Claire McCaskill (9), and Republican George Allen (17). During the 2014 general election campaign, the most frequent Twitter posters were Democrats Bruce Braley (1172) and Mary Landrieu (1036), and Republican Pat Roberts (1042). The least frequent Twitter users were Democrat Jeff Merkley (101), and Republicans Monica Wehby (112), Bill Cassidy (134), and

Intersection of Gender, Party, and Position **147**

TABLE 9.2A US Senate candidates' use of Twitter during the 2012 General Election (October 9–16, 2012 and October 31 to November 6, 2012)

State	Candidates	Sample tweets	Sample retweets	Sample favorites
Arizona	Richard Carmona	41	491	49
	Jeff Flake ☙	0	0	0
Connecticut	Chris Murphy ☙	45	547	169
	Linda McMahon	225	1410	1159
Hawaii	Mazie Hirono ☙	42	166	35
	Linda Lingle	390	458	45
Indiana	Joe Donnelly ☙	0	0	0
	Richard Mourdock	445	2236	206
Massachusetts	Elizabeth Warren ☙	107	11400	2483
	Scott Brown	58	2097	529
Missouri	Claire McCaskill ☙	9	595	171
	Todd Akin	62	1463	854
Nevada	Shelley Berkley	5	4	3
	Dean Heller ☙	316	794	503
North Dakota	Heidi Heitkamp ☙	128	368	905
	Rick Berg	42	139	18
Virginia	Timothy Kaine ☙	43	385	70
	George Allen	17	152	30
Wisconsin	Tammy Baldwin ☙	203	1209	228
	Tommy Thompson	216	1175	191

☙ – Winner

Mitch McConnell (192). The numbers of retweets and favorites do not correlate with the frequency of tweeting from the campaign. In 2012, Democrat Elizabeth Warren was retweeted and favorited more than any other candidate. In 2014, Democrat Alison Grimes outdistanced all other candidates in numbers of retweets and favorites, followed by Thom Tillis, Michelle Nunn, and Scott Brown. (See Tables 9.2a, 9.2b, and Table 9.3).

H2: Trailing Candidates and Tweets

We found (see Tables 9.2a and 2b and Table 9.3) that some of the biggest tweeters lost their races. Table 9.3 indicates that trailing women candidates tend to send more tweets in both years that we studied. In 2012, Republican women were more than twice as likely as the other gender party groups to use Twitter, averaging 308 tweets. In 2014, when the Democrats were the beleaguered party in the polls and media coverage repeatedly threatened loss of the Senate from the Democratic majority, Democratic women sent more tweets—an average of 55 tweets, but this difference is not statistically different from the men. We note that

148 Marion R. Just, Ann N. Crigler, and Rose A. Owen

TABLE 9.2B US Senate candidates' use of Twitter during the 2014 General Election (September 1 to November 3, 2014)

State	Candidates	Total tweets	Sample tweets	Sample retweets	Sample favorites
Georgia	Michelle Nunn	413	41	1403	711
	David Perdue ✍	463	46	717	331
Iowa	Bruce Braley	1172	117	1167	261
	Joni Ernst ✍	338	33	735	226
Kansas	Greg Orman	216	21	505	391
	Pat Roberts ✍	1042	104	667	268
Kentucky	Alison Grimes	455	45	4158	2266
	Mitch McConnell ✍	192	19	434	205
Louisiana	Mary Landrieu	1036	103	678	306
	Bill Cassidy ✍	134	13	169	75
Michigan	Gary Peters ✍	247	24	167	57
	Terri Lynn Land	322	32	280	125
North Carolina	Kay Hagan	422	42	1190	417
	Thom Tillis ✍	630	63	1819	553
New Hampshire	Jeanne Shaheen ✍	558	55	525	276
	Scott Brown	392	39	764	736
Oregon	Jeff Merkley ✍	101	10	118	17
	Monica Wehby	112	11	152	77
West Virginia	Natalie Tennant	434	43	216	120
	Shelley Moore Capito ✍	361	36	114	158

✍ – Winner

TABLE 9.3 Sample mean tweets, retweets, and favorites by gender and party of candidates in 2012 and 2014 (rounded to the nearest tweet)

Partisanship and gender	Mean tweets		Mean retweets		Mean favorites	
	2012	2014	2012	2014	2012	2014
Dem. male	32	43	356	489	72	182
Dem. female	82	55	2,290	1,362	638	683
Rep. male	145	47	1,007	762	291	542
Rep. female	308	28	934	320	602	147

being a trailing candidate is comparable to the political climate in which each party's candidates find themselves in the election. In the case of social media, it appears candidates (or their staffs) increase their online activity and presence when they are behind (see Gulati and Williams 2011).

Previous research shows that candidates go negative when they are afraid that they are losing. An analysis of attack tweets shows that in 2012, gender was not

FIGURE 9.1 Sample tweet.

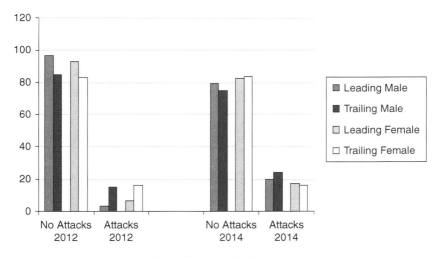

FIGURE 9.2 Attacks by gender and position in the race.

significantly related to political attacks regardless of position in the race, but in 2014, gender did influence Twitter attack strategies. Men were significantly more likely to attack when in the toss-up or trailing position than women. Figure 9.1 shows a sample tweet from Thom Tillis, the Republican winning challenger in North Carolina. He used humor to soften the attack on Obama and, by association, his opponent, the Democrat incumbent Senator Kay Hagan. We note that there was an increase in attacks in 2014, but only for male candidates—and this may represent the more significant trend.

H3: All Candidate Tweets Focus on the Campaign

Previous research suggests that women and men focus on somewhat different topics while campaigning. Women tend to emphasize social issues while men focus more on their own accomplishments. The results for Twitter were rather different. The main focus of Twitter messages was almost identical for men and women candidates during both years. For all candidates, the most prominent category of messages was the campaign process. Twitter messages about the campaign process dwarfed mentions of any other specific topic. In both years, there were three times as many tweets about the campaign as there were about issues of any kind. In 2012, male candidates are slightly more likely than women to focus on issues, and female candidates are slightly more likely than men to focus on the campaign. There were no statistically significant gender differences in main focus of tweets in 2014. See Table 9.4.

In 2012, men sent far more messages about the economy than women (37 percent to 23 percent), while women mentioned jobs more often than men (37 percent to 30 percent). While both are economic issues, jobs is a more personalized view of the economy. See Figure 9.3.

Women rarely mentioned abortion. We know that in the case of the Missouri and Wisconsin races, the issue of women's reproductive health was raised in the summer, before the campaigns were in full swing, and reproductive issues may have been thoroughly aired prior to our period of study. Women candidates had little incentive to focus on those issues during the fall campaign as their opponents had already experienced a strong backlash on their comments about "legitimate rape" and "no exceptions" for abortion (Black 2012, Silver 2012a). For 2014, only 13 percent of the Twitter messages were about issues and therefore the tables had very few observations for particular issues. There were two exceptions: women tended to tweet more about energy (including fracking and alternative energy) than the male candidates.

Tables 9.4 and 9.5 demonstrate that the use of Twitter by candidates is less about issues and slightly more about the campaign and getting out the vote. Twitter's 140 characters do not accommodate candidate Arlen Specter's three-inch stack of issue statements. These are replaced by campaign process tweets aimed at mobilizing followers to support and spread the word about their candidate through social networks.

H4: Gender and Tweeted Images

While candidates do not appear to use social media to emphasize policy positions, social media do provide relatively easy access for establishing connections between candidates and their supporters. Unlike advertising campaigns or news coverage, SNS empower users to participate and engage with candidates and their staffs. Direct exchanges are rare on campaign SNS. Candidates generally do not reply

TABLE 9.4 Gender by focus of tweets, 2012 and 2014

	Self		*Self and opponent*		*Issues*		*Campaign process*		*Other*		*Attack opponent*		*Endorsement*		*Total*	
	2012	*2014*	*2012*	*2014*	*2012*	*2014*	*2012*	*2014*	*2012*	*2014*	*2012*	*2014*	*2012*	*2014*	*2012*	*2014*
Male count	67	23	31	23	156	49	551	205	99	3	183	105	183	44	1270	452
Row %	5.3	5.1	2.4	5.1	12.3	10.8	43.4	45.4	7.8	0.7	14.4	23.2	14.4	9.7	100	100
Female count	82	23	20	19	64	65	511	197	73	3	143	73	189	58	1082	438
Row %	7.6	5.3	1.8	4.3	5.9	14.8	47.2	45.0	6.7	0.7	13.2	16.7	17.5	13.2	100	100
Total count	149	46	51	42	220	114	1062	402	172	6	326	178	372	102	2352	890
Row %	6.3	5.2	2.2	4.7	9.4	12.8	45.2	45.2	7.3	0.7	13.9	20.0	15.8	11.5	100	100

2012: Pearson Chi-square 38.12, p < .0002014: N.S.

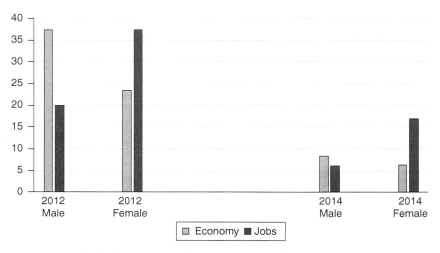

FIGURE 9.3 Gender by mention of economy versus jobs in candidate tweets.

to messages tweeted by followers. However, they do tweet images of themselves on the campaign trail with groups of people to show connections are being made with potential constituents. In addition, Twitter followers are able to connect with candidates by posting messages, retweeting, and marking tweets as "favorites." On Twitter, the ability to retweet and "favorite" a candidate has been used to indicate how candidates' messages are resonating with their potential constituency. We use these to measure the positive personal connections between candidates and their prospective constituents.

Candidates tweeted pictures of themselves with many people—most of whom were white (in 2012, 72 percent of people pictured with candidates were white; in 2014 the percentage dropped to 66.7 percent). There were, however, significant gender and party differences in the race of people shown with the candidates in their tweets (See Table 9.6). In both 2012 and 2014, Republican candidates were significantly more likely to be pictured with white supporters than Democratic candidates, who tended to include a broader racial/ethnic diversity. In 2012, gender and party interacted: Republican men candidates were more likely to show images of themselves with whites only (87.3 percent compared to 51.2 percent for Republican women). In 2014, party differences were still there, but Republican men and women did not differ significantly.

H5: Gender, Party, and Position

Examining how candidates' tweets resonated with potential constituents, the analysis looks at favorites and retweets by party, gender, and position in the race. We

TABLE 9.5 Mean retweets by candidate gender, party, and position, 2012 and 2014

	Economy		Jobs		Immigration		Healthcare		Energy		Abortion		State issues		Other issues		Total	
	2012	2014	2012	2014	2012	2014	2012	2014	2012	2014	2012	2014	2012	2014	2012	2014	2012	2014
Male count	41	4	20	3	2	4	25	6	19	1	5	1	0	0	44	30	156	49
Row %	26.3	8.2	12.8	6.1	1.3	8.2	16.0	12.2	12.2	2.0	3.2	2.0	0	0	28.1	61.2	100	100
Female count	7	4	13	11	0	3	6	5	2	6	0	0	8	3	26	33	63	65
Row %	11.1	6.2	20.6	16.9	0	4.6	9.5	7.7	3.2	9.2	0	0	12.7	4.6	41.3	50.7	100	100
Total count	48	8	33	14	2	7	31	11	21	7	5	1	8	3	70	63	219	114
Row %	21.9	7.0	15.1	12.3	.9	6.1	14.2	9.6	9.6	6.1	2.3	.9	3.7	2.6	32.5	55.2	100	100

2012: Pearson Chi-square 38.12, p < .0002014: N.S.

TABLE 9.6 Party by race of people in candidates' Twitter images, 2012 and 2014

	Caucasian only		Mixed races		People of color only		Total	
	2012	2014	2012	2014	2012	2014	2012	2014
Republican count	300	89	72	16	25	2	397	107
Row %	75.6	83.2	18.1	15.0	6.3	1.9	100	100
Democrat count	114	89	57	64	7	7	178	160
Row %	64.0	55.6	32.0	40.0	3.9	9.4	100	100
Total count	414	178	129	80	32	9	575	267
Row %	72.0	66.7	22.4	30.0	5.6	3.4	100	100

2012: Pearson Chi-Square = 14.064, p < .001; 2014 Pearson Chi-Square = 21.921, p < .000.

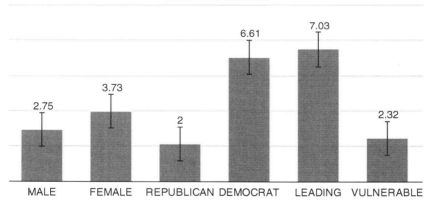

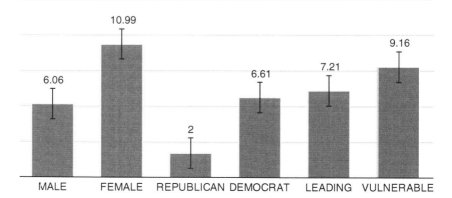

FIGURE 9.4 Mean favorites by candidate gender, party, and position in the race.

found that these factors differed depending on which aspect of public participation was involved. For example indicating that candidates' tweets were "favorites" in 2012, party and position in the race but not gender were significant factors, and in 2014, gender, and party but not position were significant factors in favoring a candidate.

We found a similar discrepancy between 2012 and 2014 regarding retweeting. All three factors—party, gender, and position in the race—were significant factors in retweeting a candidate's tweets in 2012, and party and gender were significant factors in public connections via retweeting in 2014.

It is important to recognize that although we looked at Senate elections in both 2012 and 2014, there was a significant difference in the context of these two elections. The elections of 2012 took place in a presidential election year, in which the Democratic incumbent Barack Obama defeated the Republican challenger, Mitt Romney. As Fenno (2000) argued, candidates must interpret the electoral context for their campaigns. The result may lead as it did in the case of 2012, to different Twitter strategies. By looking at both years, we were able to tease out the importance of different factors that overlapped so considerably in 2012. In that year most of the women were Democrats and won their races, while we had a variety of women and men who won their races in 2014.

Conclusion

We conclude that time is a factor in and of itself in candidate Twitter behavior, and for Twitter, as Bob Dylan sang, "the times, they are a-changing." With more women in the mix and different party prospects, candidate behavior reflects the electoral context in which a candidate competes. Candidates' emphasis on connecting with their constituents through Twitter is governed in part by their gender, party, and position in the race. Women and men candidates use Twitter with about the same frequency and Tweets focus on the same topics. Women, however, stimulate public connections more consistently across various measures and years. They are seen with more racially diverse people. Women's tweets are generally favorited and retweeted at a greater rate than men's. It is possible that underlying this observation is the behavior of groups such as Emily's List in stimulating women candidates' constituents to participate actively on Twitter. We note for example that the candidates with the most retweets—in 2012, Elizabeth Warren, and in 2014, Alison Lundergan Grimes and Kay Hagan—were key Emily's list-supported candidates.

While there were no statistically significant gender differences in the use of attacks on Twitter in 2012, by 2014, men in the trailing position were significantly more likely than women to send attack tweets. Candidates, regardless of gender, attack more when they are in a toss-up or trailing position than candidates who are leading. Position in the race and the urge to pull out all the stops occurs on two levels—for the individual candidate and also the party's vulnerability in that

156 Just, Crigler, and Owen

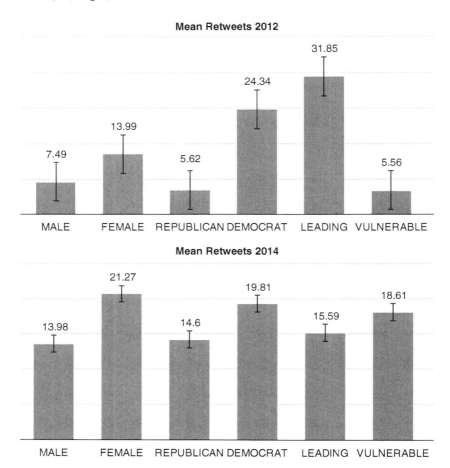

FIGURE 9.5 Mean favorites by candidate gender, party and position in the race.

election year. A study of the Twitter behavior of Tea Party and MoveOn supported candidates in 2014 also found that being a member of Tea Party contributed to underdog behavior only by Tea Party candidates who were running against the Republican Party establishment (Crigler and Hua 2015).

Which party is favored in the Senate elections and intra-party controversies influence candidate connections with potential voters. Another aspect of context that may have influenced our results is the type of Senate election that 2012 and 2014 represented. The elections of 2012 took place in the context of the presidential election and to some extent Senate candidates reflected the conversations at the top of the ticket. The Senate elections of 2014 reflected more state-wide issues, although many Republican candidates continued to criticize the Obama presidency. In both years, we confirm Fenno's (2000) argument that candidates clearly take into account the context of the campaign in strategizing their social media communications with constituents. We would expect that 2016 will combine the variety of gender and party candidates that we saw in 2014 and that the Twitter conversations may reflect some of the contextual factors of a presidential race that we saw in 2012.

The use of Twitter has evolved over time as well. It has become mainly a campaign tool for mobilizing supporters. Tweeting about issues appears to have decreased in the time period we studied and we expect that it will continue that pattern in the future. Since Twitter users must take a positive action to follow a candidate it is not surprising that candidates' tweets are mostly read by supporters. Candidates respond accordingly and tailor their Twitter communication to mobilization. Twitter may not communicate a great many attacks, compared to televised ads, but neither do candidate tweets have a great deal of substance. This channel of communication now involves what Fenno (1996, 2000) calls the personal rather than policy connections. Other channels will have to carry the burden of the policy connections necessary to effect representation.

References

Abroms, L.C. and R.C. Lefebvre. 2009. Obama's Wired Campaign: Lessons for Public Health Communication. *Journal of Health Communication* 14(5): 415–23.

Amman, S.L. 2014. Why Do They Tweet? http://ssrn.com/abstract=1725477.

Barthel, M., E. Shearer, J. Gottfried, and A. Mitchell. 2015. *The Evolving Role of News on Twitter and Facebook.* Pew Research Center, www.journalism.org/2015/07/14/the-evolving-role-of-news-on-twitter-and-facebook.

Black, J. 2012. Rape Remarks Sink Two Republican Senate Hopefuls. *NBC News*, http://nbcpolitics.nbcnews.com/_news/2012/11/07/14980822-rape-remarks-sink-two-republican-senate-hopefuls?lite.

Bystrom, D. 2014. Advertising, Websites, and Media Coverage: Gender and Communication along the Campaign Trail. In S.J. Carroll and R.L. Fox (eds.), *Gender and Elections: Shaping the Future of American Politics*, 3rd edn. New York: Cambridge University Press, pp. 241–64.

Bystrom, D.G., L.L. Kaid, T.A. Robertson, and M.C. Banwart. 2004. *Gender and Candidate Communication: Videostyle, WebStyle, NewsStyle.* New York: Routledge.

Crigler, A. and W. Hua. 2015. *Social Media Populism? A Comparison of Tea Party and MoveOn in Competitive 2014 US Senate Campaigns.* Paper presented at Conference on New Populism's Political Communication, CNRS, Paris, June 26–27.

Dabelko, K.C. and P.S. Herrnson 1997. Women's and Men's Campaigns for the US House of Representatives. *Political Research Quarterly* 50(1): 121–35.

Dolan, K. 2009. The Impact of Gender Stereotyped Evaluations on Support for Women Candidates. *Political Behavior* 32: 69–88.

Dolan, K. 2014. *When Does Gender Matter? Women Candidates and Gender Stereotypes in American Elections.* New York: Oxford University Press.

Druckman, J., M. Kifer, and M. Parkin. 2009. Campaign Communications in US Congressional Elections. *American Political Science Review* 103(3): 343–66.

Duggan, M. and J. Brenner. 2013. *The Demographics of Social Media Users—2012.* Pew Research Center,http://pewinternet.org/Reports/2013/Social-media-users/The-State-of-Social-Media-Users.aspx.

Evans, H., V. Cordova, and S. Sipole. 2014. Twitter Style: An Analysis of How House Candidates Used Twitter in Their 2012 Campaigns. *PS: Political Science and Politics* 47(2): 454–63.

Fenno, R. 1996. *Senators on the Campaign Trail: The Politics of Representation.* Norman: University of Oklahoma Press.

Fenno, R. 2000. *Congress at the Grassroots: Representational Change in the South, 1970–1998.* Chapel Hill: University of North Carolina Press.

Fridkin, K. and P. Kenney. 2014. *The Changing Face of Representation: The Gender of US Senators and Constituent Communications.* Ann Arbor: University of Michigan Press.

Gainous, J. and K. Wagner. 2014. *Tweeting to Power: The Social Media Revolution in American Politics.* New York: Oxford University Press.

Gulati, G. and C. Williams. 2011. *Diffusion of Innovations and Online Campaigns: Social Media Adoption in the 2010 US Congressional Elections.* Paper presented at the General Conference of the European Consortium for Political Research, Reykjavik, August 25–27.

Herrnson, P.S., C.J. Lay, and A.K. Stokes. 2003. Women Running "as Women": Candidate Gender, Campaign Issues, and Voter-Targeting Strategies. *Southern Political Science Association* 65(1): 244–55.

Huddy, L. and N. Terkildsen. 1993. Gender Stereotypes and the Perception of Male and Female Candidates. *American Journal of Political Science* 37(1): 119–47.

Just, M. and A. Crigler. 2014. *Gender and Self-Presentation in Social Media: An Analysis of the 10 Most Competitive 2012 US Senate Races.* Paper presented at the annual meeting of the American Political Science Association, Washington, DC, September.

Just, M., A. Crigler, D. Alger, T. Cook, M. Kern, and D. West. 1992. *Crosstalk: Citizens, Candidates and the Media in a Presidential Campaign.* Chicago: University of Chicago Press.

Lassen, D.S. and A.R. Brown. (2011). Twitter: The Electoral Connection. *Social Science Computer Review* 29(4): 419–36.

Parmelee, J. and S. Bichard. 2012. *Politics and the Twitter Revolution: How Tweets Influence the Relationship between Political Leaders and the Public.* Lanham, MD: Lexington Books.

Silver, N. 2012a. Akin Comments Could Swing Missouri Senate Race. *New York Times*, August 19.

Silver, N. 2012b. GOP Senate Hopes Fade, Even as Romney's Rise, Polls Show. *New York Times*, http://fivethirtyeight.blogs.nytimes.com/2012/10/13/g-o-p-senate-hopes-fade-even-as-romneys-rise-polls-show/?_r=0.

10

WHO GETS TO SAY #AREYOUBETTEROFF?

Promoted Trends and Bashtagging in the 2012 US Presidential Election

Joel Penney

In a media landscape characterized by the growing significance of participatory digital platforms like Twitter, the process of electioneering is undergoing dramatic transformations. Political marketing professionals, who operate on behalf of major parties and candidates, have been developing a range of tactics to exploit these platforms for promotional gain (Loader and Mercea 2011; Serazio 2015). However, they are quickly learning that the shift from a top-down to a peer-to-peer model of message dissemination is redefining the relationship between campaigns and the voting public. These shifting dynamics became readily apparent in the 2012 US presidential election cycle, when a series of public battles broke out over the uses and meanings of paid promotional hashtags on Twitter. Known as Promoted Trends, the marketing tool was adopted for the first time for electioneering purposes by the Republican Party and the Mitt Romney campaign, only to be swiftly co-opted and subverted by supporters of opposing candidate Barack Obama. These incidents—examples of a practice known as *bashtagging*—offer a productive opportunity to reflect on the changing shape of communication power and citizen-level electoral participation in the age of Twitter.

The following analysis of the bashtagging phenomenon considers how Twitter users have come to function not only as active participants in political marketing—or *brand advocates* in the parlance of the promotional industries (Fuggetta 2012)—but also as interpretive agents with the capacity to resist preferred meanings of promotional texts and actively oppose them through practices of creative appropriation. Furthermore, the chapter discusses how bashtagging emerges from the logics and practices of culture jamming, which I argue fosters a style of political participation that is increasingly focused on seizing the apparatus of promotional culture (Wernick 1991; Banet-Weiser 2013) for peer persuasion

160 Joel Penney

purposes. While the popularization of culture jamming in mainstream electoral contexts may ultimately support the efforts of political marketers to draft supporters as foot soldiers—or "meme warriors" (Lasn 1999, p. 129)—in media-centered persuasion battles, it also empowers citizens to wrest more control over the process, potentially undermining the force of campaign advertising expenditures as well as the elite interests that typically underwrite them.

Promoted Trends, Bashtagging, and the Variable Role of Grassroots Intermediaries

In contemporary digital marketing practice, both commercial and political, taking advantage of the voluntary media-spreading labor of brand advocates (or "evangelists") has become a central concern. Henry Jenkins, Sam Ford, and Joshua Green, who refer to these peer-to-peer agents of media circulation as *grassroots intermediaries*, note that such a strategy "demonstrate[s] how audiences become part of the logic of the marketplace" (Jenkins et al. 2013, p. 7) as their engagement with brands takes on an increasingly public and conspicuous character via social media. With regard to political marketing on social media platforms, Michael Serazio (2015, p. 1919) explains that "as part of wider ambitions by the advertising industry to colonize these spaces, [political] consultants are eagerly pursuing the recruitment of evangelists there, which represents ... 'the holy grail for campaigns.'" In other words, the promotional industries have come to understand platforms like Twitter as spaces for users to promote brands—and branded candidates—to one another, and they are more than eager to provide the tools and templates to help kick-start the process.

One key tactic to emerge in this context is Twitter's Promoted Trends program, which enables brands and organizations to pay to place their promotional hashtags alongside other featured trending hashtags on the platform. On its website, Twitter extols the value of Promoted Trends by emphasizing the high level of visibility given to the advertisers' branded hashtags:

> Because these Trends are placed prominently next to a user's timeline, they get mass exposure ... Your Promoted Trend is featured at the top of the list [of current Trends] for an entire day ... Because of their reach, Promoted Trends are extremely effective.
>
> ("Promoted Trends" 2015)

In addition to this wide-ranging visibility, however, Twitter also promises advertisers that Promoted Trends will foster positive word-of-mouth among consumers as they adopt and personalize the hashtags and share them with their followers: "Exposure to Promoted Trends turns Twitter users into brand advocates, making them more likely to speak positively about a brand and to retweet its messaging." To support this claim, Twitter cites a 2013 internal study of 35 Promoted

Trends that showed an average 22 percent increase in brand-related conversations on Twitter, a 30 percent increase in positive mentions, and a 32 percent increase in retweets (Molchanov 2013). The program is thus presented as a rather simple, straightforward solution to the contemporary marketer's dilemma of how to shape online word-of-mouth in an environment where peer recommendations are seen as far more trustworthy than traditional one-way advertising (Mangold and Faulds 2009).

Of course, such an effort assumes that users who voluntarily share branded marketing messages with their peers do so out of a sheer admiration for the brand in question and that their media-spreading activities will therefore support its promotional agenda. However, this is not always the case. Jenkins, Ford, and Green (2013, 7) are quick to point out that while grassroots intermediaries "often serve the needs of content creators" by extending the flow of branded messages and lending a sense of authentic personal endorsement, they "also may act counter to corporate goals". By beckoning consumers to spread the brand gospel through user-generated content and digital customization, marketers leave the door open for hostile, as well as supportive, forms of participation.

This point was demonstrated rather dramatically in one of the first high-profile cases of bashtagging in the commercial marketing field, which involved Twitter users targeting the perennially controversial fast food chain McDonald's. In January 2012, the company launched a participatory marketing campaign on Twitter that centered on the Promoted Trend #McDStories; the goal of the campaign, as *Forbes* put it, was to "inspire heart-warming stories about Happy Meals" for loyal customers to share with their peers (Hill 2012). Very quickly, however, Twitter users seized the #McDStories Promoted Trend as an opportunity to publicly mock and embarrass the company with gross-out tweets such as "Fingernail in my Big Mac once #McDStories," as well as more politically charged retorts from animal welfare groups like PETA (Roberts 2012). In response, the company removed the Promoted Trend from Twitter within two hours to halt the deluge of bad publicity (Hill 2012). As the #McDStories incident illustrates, providing opportunities for users to spread marketing messages on platforms like Twitter not only invites the participation of effusive brand advocates but also of a range of critics.

In the field of political marketing—a practice that by its very nature faces an uneven reception among a contentious public—the risk of this sort of critical intervention appears to be even more pronounced. The 2012 US presidential campaign cycle marked the first time that Promoted Trends on Twitter were used to advertise on behalf of a political candidate, and the bashtagging response was so swift and immense that the future viability of the tactic was left unclear. A few months prior to the election, The Republican National Committee (RNC) purchased the Promoted Trend #AreYouBetterOff, echoing the Romney campaign's message that voters were in fact *not* better off than they had been four years prior when rival candidate Barack Obama was elected president. According

162 Joel Penney

to *Ad Week*, the hashtag advertisement cost a pricey $120,000 a day to run on Twitter (Heine 2012). While the launch of the hashtag appeared to be a success on the surface—appearing in more than 31,000 tweets in a matter of days (Roston 2012)—efforts to frame its use in the service of Republican brand advocacy proved to be far less achievable. An analysis from *BuzzFeed* found that tweets that affixed the word "yes" to the #AreYouBetterOff hashtag outnumbered those with the word "no" by a ratio of nearly five to one, leading the reporter to conclude that "when you crunch the numbers, Romney's stacks up as one of the worst bashtags Twitter's seen" (Brandom 2012). In addition to simple "yes" responses, Twitter users who opposed the Romney campaign found many creative ways to subvert its intended meaning. For example, one Twitter user responded by tweeting "I have health insurance, a car, a college degree, and PELL [grant] getting to my BA and beyond. #AreYouBetterOff I know I am" (Fenn 2012). Another tweet adjoined the hashtag to the cheeky line "No. Signed, Osama Bin Laden," a reference to the Obama administration's capture of the terrorist leader (Roston 2012). Pivoting attention to the 2012 Republican presidential ticket's much-discussed private wealth, another Twitter user posted "I'd like to see #Romney and #Ryan's assets from 2008, compare them to today, and ask them #AreYouBetterOff??" (Roston 2012).

As if the sensational backfiring of #AreYouBetterOff was not enough, the Romney campaign endured another round of bashtagging a month later when the campaign paid for the hashtag #CantAfford4More to appear on Twitter during a national televised debate with Obama. Once again, the prominent positioning of the Promoted Trend provided an all-too-easy target for oppositional voices, and—as reported by *Ad Week* in a piece with the suggestive title, "Promoted Tweets a Waste of Money?"—the hashtag #CantAfford4More was quickly "hijacked" for a bevy of anti-Romney mockery (Coffee 2012). In yet another bashtagging incident from the 2012 election cycle suffered by the Republican side, the conservative "Super PAC" Americans for Prosperity (funded by billionaire David Koch) purchased the Promoted Trend #16TrillionFail during the Democratic National Convention to encourage criticism of the Obama administration's spending, only to be met with critical responses like "#16TrillionFail is how much delusional billionaires will spend to defeat #Obama and what the result will be for them" (Hiatt 2012).

This series of so-called Twitter "fails" stands a cautionary tale for the political marketing field, suggesting that the Promoted Trends tactic may simply be avoided in future election campaign cycles. However, beyond simply underlining the axiom that promotional hashtags will inevitably be targeted by critics as bashtags, the #AreYouBetterOff incident and its ilk signal how the power of political campaigns to "sell" their agendas through corporate-style marketing and branding is challenged by the shift from traditional one-way, mass-media advertising to the participatory tactics of social media-based promotion. As political marketers begin transitioning to a framework in which the audience is called upon, as Sarah Banet-Weiser (2013, p. 7) puts it, to "coproduce brands via digital forms of

Who Gets to Say #AreYouBetterOff? **163**

message sharing and customization," their ability to exert control over the political communication process appears to be increasingly destabilized.

Political Marketing and the Agency of Audiences/Users

Such a shift is particularly significant given the fact that for many years, scholars have framed the relationship between institutional political marketing and its audiences in rather stark and oppressive terms. Specifically, critics have expressed fears over the power of elites to sway the public mind through manipulative and deceptive tactics that exploit the allure of modern communication technologies. This line of critique can be traced back at least as far as the early twentieth century era of mass propaganda, when Frankfurt School figures like Theodor Adorno (1985) warned of the dangerously seductive spectacle of fascism and how it could spread to democratic countries like the United States via powerful culture industry platforms like television. Jürgen Habermas, another key Frankfurt School member, famously decried the use of twentieth-century mass media by political elites for what he termed "manipulative publicity" (1991, p. 178), arguing that the growth of mass-mediated political theater quells deliberative dialogue and fosters uncritical acceptance of dominant ideologies. Some decades later, the Frankfurt School-influenced critic Stuart Ewen lambasted the television-fueled "politics of image" of the Reagan era as leading to "the dominance of surface over substance" (1990, pp. 269–71) and a subsequent disengagement of the citizenry from the realities of public life. Taking specific aim at the tactics of modern electoral campaign marketing, Bob Franklin (1994) further echoed the Frankfurt School tradition by arguing that "packaging politics" via the style-heavy discourses of advertising fundamentally weakens the quality of the democratic process.

However, this well-established body of criticism has been challenged in recent years by scholars who invoke the framework of the active audience popularized in cultural studies research. For instance, Richard Huggins (2002, pp. 146–7) finds that contrary to a model of top-down manipulation and control, young voters are largely "savvy about the communications genres in which political discourse is now framed" and "quite skilled in negotiating the postmodern terrain which is the electronic campaign." In other words, Huggins appeals to the interpretative and meaning-making agency of what he refers to as the "political audience," mirroring the encoding/decoding framework of media reception advanced by Stuart Hall (1980). In a parallel vein, Barrie Axford (2002) calls into question the Frankfurt School's assumptions regarding mass-mediated political communication, noting its tendency to "treat audiences as mere consumers, victims of promotional culture." As he posits, "the considerable weight of evidence that now points to the interpretative capacity of diverse audiences and the savvy manner in which they attach meanings to, but also distance themselves from, promotional messages is often unremarked." At the same time, however, Axford wonders whether this acknowledgement of agency on the part of the political audience "can still leave

164 Joel Penney

them without the means and perhaps the desire to affect the process" of mediated political persuasion (2002, p. 7). Interpretative agency at the point of reception may enable citizens to resist the manipulative appeals of political marketing, so it would seem, yet this alone does not necessarily redirect its broader lines of force.

However, networked digital media, characterized by what Axel Bruns (2008) calls "produsage," or the eliding of distinctions between producers and users of content, have emerged as the key technological means by which citizens can send as well as receive persuasive messages and thus potentially seize a degree of control over the political communication process. Such a development takes the notion of an agentive political audience a considerable step further, moving from a model of active *interpretation* to one of active *participation* in political marketing. Following Nico Carpentier (2011, p. 130), the former can be understood as a form of media interaction, while the latter constitutes true media participation in the sense that citizens take on a *co-deciding* role in the production of content.

It is important to stress, however, that the nature of this participation may vary depending on the differing subject positions of different new media "produsers," and that participation itself does not always necessarily equate with a democratization of communication power. Applying Hall's encoding/decoding model to interactive new media technologies, Adrienne Shaw (2015) outlines three different "using positions" following Hall's reading positions for media reception: *dominant/hegemonic use*, where "intended uses and emergent uses match," *negotiated use*, where the text or technology is used "correctly but not necessarily as intended," and oppositional use, which refers to "unexpected uses" such as hacking. In the case of Promoted Trends on Twitter, this model would suggest that those who use a political campaign hashtag like #AreYouBetterOff as intended (i.e., supporting the brand advocacy goals of its creators) would constitute a dominant using position. On the other hand, those who engage in bashtagging practices like those described above would appear to fall somewhere between the negotiated and oppositional positions, since while the hashtag is being used "correctly" on the surface, it is done in a way that not only undercuts the intentions of the creators but also disturbs the Promoted Trends advertising model of Twitter itself. Bashtagging is only one of many potential examples of a negotiated or oppositional using position with regard to the participatory political marketing tactics of the digital age—circulating parodic remixes of a campaign's online viral video efforts also springs to mind—yet it quite handily illustrates the agency of new media users to meaningfully intervene in these promotional processes.

Bashtagging and the Culture Jamming Tradition

In order to place this kind of resistant use of Twitter-based marketing in its appropriate context, it is necessary to consider how bashtagging stems from the broader phenomenon of culture jamming, a set of practices and corresponding

Who Gets to Say #AreYouBetterOff? **165**

logics that has been building in popularity within activism circles in recent decades. While the term itself was first coined in the 1980s by the experimental musicians Negativland (Carducci 2006, 117), its origins have been traced to the French Situationist movement of the 1960s and its strategy of *detournement*. As Christine Harold (2004, p. 192) explains, *detournement* literally means "detour" or "diversion," but also has connotations of "hijacking" and "misappropriation." The Situationists, whose ranks included Marxist media critic Guy Debord, became known for pranks such as defacing public signs and storefronts in order to create images that were playfully critical of consumer culture. The practice of culture jamming reached wider exposure beginning in the 1990s through *Adbusters* magazine, whose advertising parodies have been celebrated for "destabiliz[ing] and challeng[ing] the dominant messages of multinational corporations and consumer capitalism" (Warner 2007, pp. 18–19).

As these examples indicate, culture jamming has historically focused on undermining the hegemonic power of advertising and consumer culture. In publications such as *Adbusters*, culture jamming practitioners take aim at the manipulative tactics of the promotional industries, such as the use of seductive images and emotional appeals to "achieve automatic, unreflective trust in the branded product" among consumers (Warner 2007, p. 18). Of course, such advertising tactics are not exclusive to the domain of commercial marketing. Rather, they have also been roundly embraced by generations of political campaigners to promote electoral candidates and parties (Franklin 1994; Wernick 1991). In her work on what she terms "political culture jamming," Jamie Warner suggests how this adoption of commercial advertising tactics by political campaigners has spurred artists and activists to co-opt these very practices as a means of critiquing them: "As politicians and political parties increasingly utilize the branding techniques of commercial marketers to 'sell' their political agendas, it follows that similar jamming techniques could be employed to call those branding techniques into question" (Warner 2007, p. 19).

Indeed, situating Twitter bashtagging practices in the tradition of "political culture jamming" helps to draw out the broader structural tensions that undergird them. In this context, the act of subverting the #AreYouBetterOff hashtag can be understood as a critical response to the Romney campaign's intensive efforts to market the candidate (as well as tarnish the brand of his opponent), which reached record-breaking heights in the 2012 election cycle. According to *The Washington Post*, a total of $492 million was spent on television ads supporting Romney's presidential candidacy in 2012, a figure that exceeds both that of his opponent, Barack Obama, as well as every other previous campaign in US political history (*The Washington Post* 2015). As commentators were quick to point out, much of this record spending on behalf of Romney's candidacy was a direct outgrowth of the highly controversial 2010 *Citizens United* Supreme Court decision, which strongly deregulated corporate campaign contributions and allowed new "Super PAC" groups to raise unlimited amounts of money from undisclosed sources,

166 Joel Penney

largely for media promotion purposes (Marcus 2012). Furthermore, an overwhelming 91 percent of TV ads in support of Romney were in the oft-bemoaned genre of negative attack ads, also setting a record for a US presidential campaign (Little 2012). For those dissatisfied with the direction of modern political marketing and branding in the US, the 2012 Romney campaign thus offered an outsized target for criticism like none other that came before.

Of course, even at $120,000 a day, Promoted Trends on Twitter like #AreYouBetterOff only constituted a tiny fraction of the overall money spent in support of Romney's candidacy. However, the high-profile and historic nature of this particular ad buy was one likely reason why it became an immediate flashpoint for Romney's detractors. Moreover, while voters were effectively powerless to stop the deluge of negative TV campaign advertising unleashed by record levels of corporate cash, they *were* able to intervene in efforts to spread big-ticket attack ads to the peer-to-peer arena of Twitter. In this case, obstructing the message was as simple as adopting the sponsored hashtag and turning it against itself.

According to Harold, this sort of media sabotage constitutes one of two major characteristics of culture jamming more broadly. As she explains, its practitioners typically aim to clog or glut dominant cultural systems with counter-messages as a means of negating their power and influence. Harold (2004, p. 190) likens this to "monkey-wrenching," a term that refers to how industrial workers would destroy or block the functioning of factory equipment as a means of protest and resistance. In the examples of bashtagging outlined above, the element of sabotage is rather clear: In each case, critics of the organization in question attempt to literally clog the stream of tweets featuring its promotional hashtag with messages that run counter to the dominant message. The uses of the #AreYouBetterOff Promoted Trend for anti-Romney messaging thus suggest a deliberate effort to neutralize or nullify the RNC's message as well as its pricey Twitter advertising expenditure, effectively wasting the party's time and money in order to undermine its chances at electoral victory.

However, in addition to this dynamic of sabotage and negation, Harold emphasizes that culture jamming may also involve more productive forms of appropriation that center on the building of new cultural meanings. As she argues, culture jamming "need not be seen only as a damming, or a stopping" of dominant cultural systems, but also as "an artful proliferation of messages, a rhetorical process of intervention and invention" (Harold 2004, p. 192). In other words, culture jammers often appropriate dominant messages as the raw materials for their own creative expressions, interjecting new perspectives and ideas in the process. This too is observable in the practice of bashtagging on Twitter, including the example of #AreYouBetterOff. As noted above, Twitter users who appropriated this Promoted Trend used the opportunity to inject a variety of issue-based narratives into the online discourse surrounding the election, from sharing positive experiences with President Obama's healthcare policy to launching critical discussions of wealth disparity and inequality in the US. Following Harold, we can thus understand bashtagging not only as an act of social media sabotage that attempts to subtract from an organization's peer-to-peer marketing efforts, but also as an act of creative addition that appropriates these efforts to introduce alternative voices and perspectives into the online discourse.

Such tactics, to be clear, are not limited to any one communication technology or platform. Prior to the advent of social media sites like Twitter, practitioners of culture jamming like the editors of *Adbusters* tended to rely on traditional mass media channels to circulate their subversive messages. For instance, in his 1999 manifesto, appropriately titled *Culture Jam*, *Adbusters* co-founder Kalle Lasn recounts a series of so-called "subvertisements" that his group placed in outlets such as network television and mass-circulation magazines to spread anti-consumerist ideas to the public (Lasn 1999, p. 128). However, this top-down tactic was quite expensive, limiting participation only to well-funded activist organizations; in his book, Lasn even provides aspiring activists with a sample rate card for purchasing ad time on national and local TV networks, and the prices are not cheap (1999, p. 184). On the other hand, looking towards the digital future, Lasn notes how the Internet revolution opens up significant new opportunities for the widespread propagation of culture jamming, emphasizing that "the internet is one of the most potent meme-replicating mediums ever invented" (1999, p. 132).

Indeed, these oppositional practices have been greatly facilitated by the changing technological infrastructure of message dissemination. In peer-to-peer digital media networks like Twitter, each node, or link in the chain of circulation, is a potential point of rupture and dissention. However, in addition to changes in media technology, we must also take account of the broader cultural factors that shape how these technologies are used. Specifically, high-profile Twitter bashtagging incidents like #AreYouBetterOff draw our attention to how culture jamming has become mainstreamed over time as a popular rhetorical tactic for counteracting the force of the promotional industries, as well as the powerful social, economic, and political interests that they represent. For those who wish to challenge the pervasive influence of branding and marketing techniques, commercial, political, or otherwise, the sabotage and appropriation of cultural jamming has come to serve as a readily available cultural script for engineering interventionist critical responses.

Conclusion: Electoral Participation and the "Meme Warrior" Model

This proliferation of culture jamming in mainstream online political discourse suggests how citizens are adapting to conditions of what Axford and Huggins (1997, p. 6) call the "mediatized politics in promotional cultures," which characterize many contemporary Western-style democracies. Rather than buckle under

168 Joel Penney

the weight of an ever-swelling flood of campaign branding and advertising messages funded by powerful interests, members of the voting public are opting to use participatory platforms like Twitter to co-opt the media marketing process and reshape it in their own interests. In *Culture Jam*, Lasn introduces the term "meme warriors" (1999, p. 129) to describe media activists who disseminate political counter-rhetoric by mimicking professional marketing techniques, and it has proved to be quite prescient. In a contemporary digital landscape characterized by the grassroots circulation of political viral videos, image macro memes, and trending hashtags, "meme warriors" serves as an apt description for an emergent generation of engaged citizens who adopt the peer-to-peer marketing model to gain entrance into the process of political persuasion.

While the "meme warriors" concept can be applied to a wide variety of citizen-level online political activity, from signing and sharing e-petitions to posting social movement advocacy symbols as profile pictures, it has particular resonance for culture jamming-oriented practices like Twitter bashtagging. In the case of #AreYouBetterOff, the use of the hashtag to spread either the anti-Obama message originally intended by its creators, or alternative messages that directly counter these intensions, form the lines of a semiotic battle over the meaning of this particular Twitter meme. Furthermore, the ranks of the "meme warriors" who participate in Twitter hashtag battles may be much larger and more diffuse than in prior iterations of culture jamming. Due to the open-access nature of the platform, any Twitter user can potentially contribute to the critical appropriation of a promotional hashtag at virtually no cost, and without the need for any formal organizing.

However, while thousands of Twitter users ostensibly acted as "meme warriors" to either support or subvert the #AreYouBetterOff message in the 2012 US election, the degree to which these peer-to-peer marketing practices are redefining the nature of citizen participation in elections remains an open question. Due to the fact that politically oriented interaction on social media platforms can serve a wide range of possible functions for users, from entertainment and social status-seeking to information-gathering and deliberative dialogue (Papacharrissi 2010), the role of deliberate peer-to-peer political persuasion in the vein of the "meme warrior" model is not always clear. For instance, a study of Twitter users who created fake parody accounts of Australian politicians found that these citizens largely had no interest in sending persuasive political messages to their followers, and framed their activities more in terms of playful entertainment to amuse fellow "political junkies" (Wilson 2011). Along these lines, we can question whether at least some who co-opted the #AreYouBetterOff hashtag did so as a form of parodic play rather an instrumental form of semiotic warfare.

Furthermore, the latter approach may not be as popular in the big picture of political Twitter use as the #AreYouBetterOff story might suggest. A study of Twitter use during the 2012 Dutch parliamentary election campaign concluded that "persuasive campaigning is observed to a lesser extent among citizens than among politicians," and that "citizens regard Twitter more as an outlet for expressing discontent than as a medium for negative campaigning" (Hosch-Dayican et al. 2014). On the other hand, an interview study with Twitter users who shared an anti-Romney video clip during the 2012 US presidential election cycle revealed a multifaceted web of individual motivations, of which peer persuasion was a considerable, if not all-encompassing, component. In particular, those who had prior experience with persuasive communication in other areas of life, such as formal election campaign volunteering as well as commercial advertising and public relations experience, were more likely to frame their political Twitter activities within a marketing-like model of peer persuasion (Penney 2014). Although the nascent body of empirical research provides a complicated and sometimes contradictory picture, it appears that deliberate participatory campaigning via platforms like Twitter is a distinct reality for some citizens—but certainly not all—who use these platforms to communicate about political topics like elections.

However, regardless of its exact level of uptake at the present moment, this style of engagement in the electoral process is likely to gain more and more traction due to the broader structural dynamics at work. Indeed, a "meme warrior" approach is *precisely* what the institutional architects of political marketing are seeking to cultivate via brand advocacy tactics like Promoted Trends, even as they struggle to control the results in a peer-to-peer digital landscape. Ironically, practices like Twitter bashtagging may be easily absorbed into the dominant model of political marketing, in which rival campaigns attempt to one-up each other in an ever-building media arms race. It is not unreasonable to imagine that in future election cycles, various techniques of social media sabotage and critical appropriation will be actively encouraged—even directed—by professional electioneers as a way of combating the brand advocacy tactics of the opposing side. Such a prediction would not be unexpected for critics of culture jamming more broadly, who have argued that efforts like *Adbusters'* advertising parodies do little to upset the fundamental dynamics and patterns of contemporary marketing, "a mode of power that is quite happy to oblige subversive rhetoric" (Harold 2004, p. 191). Indeed, one can assume that the official Obama campaign organization took no small degree of delight in the relentless bashtagging of #AreYouBetterOff and other pro-Romney Twitter hashtags, as it played into the textbook political marketing strategy of "selling" one candidate by bashing the other. Thus, like many culture jamming practices that have come before, the phenomenon of Twitter bashtagging is susceptible to the critique of perpetuating the very systems and logics that it purportedly attempts to challenge and disrupt.

At the same time, it is important to recognize how increasing citizen participation in political marketing via hashtags and other personalized, peer-to-peer tactics complicates the relationship between communication power and spending power in the context of elections. In countries like the US that have moved to vastly deregulate campaign fundraising and promotional media spending, there is a growing fear that "if we allow markets to control the political process, we lose democracy" (Greenwood 2010). While such concerns are undoubtedly valid, the

170 Joel Penney

case of #AreYouBetterOff suggests that a one-to-one formula equating campaign marketing expenditures with political influence may be undercut in the transition from top-down communication formats like television to a peer-to-peer model that increasingly relies on the voluntary participation of grassroots intermediaries. As stressed in the burgeoning literature on networked digital media and participatory culture (Jenkins et al. 2013), these intermediaries retain the agency to not only actively interpret and resist, but also meaningfully alter the flow of media messages to support their interests. On this shifting terrain, the notion of being able to simply buy viral influence with a well-positioned campaign hashtag appears to be increasingly untenable.

References

Adorno, T. 1985. Freudian Theory and the Pattern of Fascist Propaganda. In A. Arato and E. Gebhardt (eds.), *The Essential Frankfurt School Reader.* New York: Continuum, pp. 118–37.

Axford, B. 2002. The Transformation of Politics or Anti-Politics? In B. Axford and R. Huggins (eds.), *New Media and Politics.* London: Sage, pp. 1–29.

Axford, B. and R. Huggins. 1997. Anti-Politics or the Triumph of Postmodern Populism in Promotional Cultures? *Javnost: The Public* 4(3): 5–27.

Banet-Weiser, S. 2013. *Authentic TM: The Politics of Ambivalence in a Brand Culture.* New York: NYU Press.

Brandom, R. 2012. How Romney Learned the Hard Truth About Promoted Hashtags. *BuzzFeed*, www.buzzfeed.com/tommywilhelm/how-romney-learned-the-hard-truth-about-promoted-h#.vje2Nr5GV.

Bruns, A. 2008. *Blogs, Wikipedia, Second Life, and Beyond: From Production to Produsage.* New York: Peter Lang.

Carducci, V. 2006. Culture Jamming: A Sociological Perspective. *Journal of Consumer Culture* 6(1): 116–38.

Carpentier, N. 2011. *Media and Participation: A Site of Ideological-Democratic Struggle.* Bristol: Polity.

Coffee, P. 2012. Promoted Tweets a Waste of Money? *Ad Week PR Newser*, October 3, www.adweek.com/prnewser/cantafford4more-are-promoted-tweets-a-waste-of-money/47593.

Ewen, S. 1990. *All Consuming Image: The Politics of Style in Contemporary Culture*, revised edn. New York: Basic Books.

Fenn. M. 2012. Republican-Sponsored Hashtag "#AreYouBetterOff" Backfires When Twitter Users Answer "Yes." *The Daily Dot*, September 5, www.dailydot.com/politics/hashtag-areyoubetteroff-sponsored-backfire.

Franklin, B. 1994. *Packing Politics: Political Communication in Britain's Media Democracy.* London: Edward Arnold.

Fuggetta, R. 2012. *Brand Advocates: Turning Enthusiastic Consumers into a Powerful Marketing Force.* Hoboken: John Wiley & Sons.

Greenwood, D. 2010. Money Is Speech: Why the *Citizens United v. FEC* Ruling Is Bad for Politics and the Market. *Dissent*, March 3, www.dissentmagazine.org/online_articles/money-is-speech-why-the-citizens-united-v-fec-ruling-is-bad-for-politics-and-the-market.

Habermas, J. 1991. *The Structural Transformation of the Public Sphere*. Trans. T. Burger and F. Lawrence. Cambridge, MA: MIT Press.

Hall, S. 1980. Encoding/Decoding. In S. Hall, D. Hobson, A. Lowe, and P. Willis (eds.), *Culture, Media, Language: Working Papers in Cultural Studies, 1972–1979*. London: Hutchison, pp. 117–27.

Harold, C. 2004. Pranking Rhetoric: "Culture Jamming" as Media Activism. *Critical Studies in Media Communication* 21(3): 189–211.

Heine, C. 2012. Romney First Presidential Candidate to Run Pricey Twitter Ad. *Adweek*, August 29, www.adweek.com/news/technology/romney-first-presidential-candidate-run-pricey-twitter-ad-143202.

Hiatt, A. 2012. #16TrillionFail Heard "Cross the World." *Huffington Post*, September 7, www.huffingtonpost.com/anna-hiatt/16trillionfail-trending-topic_b_1860056.html.

Hill, K. 2012. #McDStories: When a Hashtag Becomes a Bashtag. *Forbes* January 2, www.forbes.com/sites/kashmirhill/2012/01/24/mcdstories-when-a-hashtag-becomes-a-bashtag/.

Hosch-Dayican, B., C. Amrit, K. Aarts, and A. Dassen. 2014. How Do Online Citizens Persuade Fellow Voters? Using Twitter during the 2012 Dutch Parliamentary Election Campaign. *Social Science Computer Review*, November 11.

Huggins, R. 2002. The Transformation of the Political Audience? In B. Axford and R. Huggins (eds.), *New Media and Politics*. London: Sage, pp. 127–50.

Jenkins, H., S. Ford, and J. Green. 2013. *Spreadable Media: Creating Value and Meaning in a Networked Culture*. New York: NYU Press.

Lasn, K. 1999. *Culture Jam: The Uncooling of America*. New York: Eagle Brook.

Little, M. 2012. Negative Ads Increase Dramatically During 2012 Presidential Election. *The Los Angeles Times*, May 3, http://articles.latimes.com/2012/may/03/news/la-pn-drastic-increase-in-negative-ads-during-2012-presidential-election-20120503.

Loader, B.D. and D. Mercea. 2011. Networking Democracy? Social Media Innovations and Participatory Politics. *Information, Communication, & Society* 14(6): 757–69.

Mangold, W.G. and D.J. Faulds. 2009. Social Media: The New Hybrid Element of the Promotion Mix. *Business Horizons* 52(4): 357–65.

Marcus, R. 2012. Romney Benefits from Post-*Citizens United* Spending. *The Center for Public Integrity*, October 10, www.publicintegrity.org/2012/10/10/11360/romney-benefits-post-citizens-united-spending.

Molchanov, D. 2013. Study: The Value of Promoted Trends. *Twitter Advertising Blog*, September 11, https://blog.twitter.com/2013/study-the-value-of-promoted-trends.

Papacharrissi, Z. 2010. *A Private Sphere: Democracy in a Digital Age*. Malden, MA: Polity Press.

Penney, J. 2014. Motivations for Participating in "Viral Politics": A Qualitative Case Study of Twitter and the 2012 US Presidential Election. *Convergence: The International Journal of Research into New Media Technologies*, May 7.

Twitter for Business. 2015. *Promoted Trends*. San Francisco: Twitter, https://biz.twitter.com/en-gb/products/promoted-trends.

Roberts, H. 2012. #McFail! McDonalds' Twitter Promotion Backfires as Users Hijack #McDStories Hashtag to Share Fast Food Horror Stories. *The Daily Mail*, January 24, www.dailymail.co.uk/news/article-2090862/McDstories-McDonalds-Twitter-promotion-backfires-users-share-fast-food-horror-stories.html.

Roston, M. 2012. Republicans Ask "Are You Better Off?" and Many Reply "Yes." *The New York Times*, September 4, http://thecaucus.blogs.nytimes.com/2012/09/04/republicans-ask-are-you-better-off-and-many-reply-yes/?_r=0.

Serazio, M. 2015. Managing the Digital News Cyclone: Power, Participation, and Political Production Strategies. *International Journal of Communication* 9: 1907–25.

Shaw, A. 2015. Dialectics of Affordances: Stuart Hall and the Future of New Media Studies. *Culture Digitally*, June 10, http://culturedigitally.org/2015/06/dialectics-of-affordances-stuart-hall-and-the-future-of-new-media-studies.

Warner, J. 2007. Political Culture Jamming: The Dissident Humor of *The Daily Show with Jon Stewart. Popular Communication* 5(1): 17–36.

The Washington Post. 2015. Mad Money: TV Ads in the 2012 Presidential Campaign. *The Washington Post*, www.washingtonpost.com/wp-srv/special/politics/track-presidential-campaign-ads-2012.

Wernick, A. 1991. *Promotional Culture: Advertising, Ideology, and Symbolic Expression.* London: Sage.

Wilson, J. 2011. Playing with Politics: Political Fans and Twitter Faking in Post-Broadcast Democracy. *Convergence: The International Journal of Research into New Media Technologies* 17(4): 445–61.

11

PARTIES, LEADERS, AND ONLINE PERSONALIZATION

Twitter in Canadian Electoral Politics

Tamara A. Small

Like their American counterparts, Canadian political parties began using digital technologies as a tool for political communication in the early 1990s, albeit with less intensity and success. While websites and social media are now standard for Canadian parties, we have not seen the same sort of innovation in online campaigning as Barack Obama in 2008 or even Howard Dean in 2004. The numbers of Canadians engaging with parties online are small. Data from the 2014 *Canadian Online Citizenship Survey* shows that only 13 percent of survey respondents had visited a political party or politician website in the year previous (Jansen et al. 2014). Social media use is even lower: 6 percent of respondents friended or followed a political actor on Facebook, while less than 4 percent followed one on Twitter. Given Canada's highly regulated campaign finance laws, online fundraising is minimal. Canadian parties are more likely to follow online practices developed in the previous American election.

Around 2008, Canadian political actors began using Twitter. With the rise of social media, Canadian party leaders began to maintain social media accounts distinct from those of the parties they lead. This is curious given that Canada, unlike the United States, is quite party-centered. This has also occurred in other party-centered Westminster systems including the United Kingdom and Australia and in several Canadian provinces. This development is likely in part because, unlike a website or an email listserv, social media are essentially free. However, the multiple social media accounts beg the question whether leaders and parties in Canada have different communication strategies when using digital technologies. The "personalization of politics" presents a theoretical lens to explore this digital reality. Personalization refers to the phenomena where individual politicians become the "main anchor of interpretation and evaluation" in politics (Adam and

174 Tamara A. Small

Maier 2010, p. 213). There is a debate in the literature suggesting that the focus on leaders is at the expense of political parties, organizations, and institutions (Van Aelst et al. 2012). With regards to political communication, the individual politician becomes the strategic focus of party communication, while individual politicians may present themselves in terms of more non-political or private traits.

Given the two types of accounts, we might expect more personalization in the leaders' tweets. As will be discussed, party leaders play an enormously important role in Canadian politics and there is evidence of personalization in political communication. Moreover, some believe that Twitter is by definition a personalized media (Kruikemeier 2014). As such, leaders can strategically share information from a personal or private perspective, allowing citizens a deeper insight into his or her life (Zamora Medina and Zurutuza Muñoz 2014). This chapter seeks to contrast the levels of personalization on the Twitter feeds of parties and leaders during the 2011 federal election. The 2011 campaign was described as Canada's first "Twitter Election." According to Canada's main news agency, Twitter was "the new 'amplifier' for political leaders aiming to mobilize supporters and keep the pressure on opponents" (Canadian Press 2011). The chapter asks to what extent is there a difference between leaders' and parties' tweets in terms of the emphasis on personalization? Do parties focus less on leader-oriented political communication than the leaders? Do party leaders use Twitter to present non-political traits? We answer these questions through a content analysis of Twitter feeds.

The chapter makes two contributions to the discussion of Twitter and elections. First, little is known about online personalization in Canada and internationally. This chapter increases our knowledge of that phenomenon. Second, the chapter moves beyond the dominant focus in the Canadian literature on Twitter interactivity.

The chapter develops in several sections. It begins with a brief literature review on the use of Twitter in Canadian elections. This is followed by an overview of electoral politics in Canada with attention paid to the importance of party leaders. Then the concept of personalization and its relationship to digital politics is explored. Next the methodology and data are outlined. Following this are the results of the analysis. The chapter finds little difference between party and leader Twitter accounts—both parties and leaders are topics of campaign tweets. There is evidence of personalization on Twitter in the sense that attention is given to the party leaders, but this has not been at the expense of the party organization.

Twitter in Canadian Elections

As Twitter has become more popular, the literature on politicians' use of Twitter has grown. In Canada, academic research has generally focused on the extent to which parties have embraced its interactive capacities. Because interactivity is built into the architecture of social media, it has been argued that social media

Parties, Leaders, Online Personalization **175**

like Twitter can create new opportunities for participation by allowing for more direct connection between the public and political actors (Effing et al. 2011). Interaction on Twitter is typically assessed by looking at the combination of @ replies and retweets (see Parmelee and Bichard 2011). A study of the 2011 federal election found that party leaders were only interactive on Twitter one-third of the time (Small 2014). Although it is noted that the leader of the Green Party, which only won one seat in that election, significantly skews interaction levels; when the Green leader's tweets are removed, only 18 percent of tweets of the other leaders are interactive. Similar results are found in the province of Québec in the 2012 election. Exploring the Twitter feeds of six political parties, Giasson et al. (2013) show that 40 percent of tweets are interactive. However, the analysis indicates that some parties are considerably more interactive than others. While many of the major parties retweeted or replied infrequently, the two smallest Québec parties were interactive more than 60 percent of the time. Both studies conclude despite interactive use by small parties, broadcasting information is the main goal of Twitter. Studies on the Ontario provincial election in 2011 have contradictory results on the issue of interactivity. One study that explored political party accounts during the election found that, like the federal study, around 30 percent of tweets were interactive with very minor Ontario Green Party was far more interactive than the others (Giasson and Small 2014). On the other hand, when Cross et al. (2015) examined the Twitter feeds of three Ontario party leaders, they found that the two main leaders were very interactive 40 percent of the time. Putting the two Ontario studies together, there are differences in the use of Twitter between the leaders and the parties they lead. As such, we might expect differences in personalization between the two types of accounts in this analysis.

Elections, Parties, and Leaders in Canadian Politics

The 2011 federal election was held on May 2. Although Canada has a non-constitutional fixed election date, convention allows elections to be called at the discretion of the prime minister, and may be held at any time if the government loses the confidence of the legislature (i.e., responsible government). In 2011, the prime minister requested the dissolution of parliament after the House of Commons passed a motion of non-confidence finding the minority government in contempt of parliament. The official campaign period was 38 days. At the time of the election, the House of Commons was comprised of 308 members. As in the US, members are elected using the single-member plurality electoral system, where the candidate that receives more votes than any other candidate is the winner. Unlike the US, Canada has a multiparty system. There were four parties with members in the House of Commons in 2011: the governing Conservative Party (CPC), the Liberal Party (LPC), the New Democratic Party (NDP) and the Bloc Québécois (BQ).

176 Tamara A. Small

Political parties are the dominant players in both legislative and electoral politics in Canada. As a parliamentary democracy, typically the party that wins the largest number of seats becomes the government. According to law, a political party must have at least 12 sitting members to be a "recognized party" in the House of Commons. This entitles them to funding, committee membership and allocation of questions in Question Period (Bédard and Robertson 2008). Due to the convention of responsible government, Canada has high levels of party discipline. That is, individual legislators almost always vote according to the wishes of their party. Electoral competition is also structured around parties. "Registered" parties receive significant benefits under the Canada Elections Act, including free broadcast time, the ability to issue tax receipts, expense reimbursement, and access to the voters list. Parties have a near monopoly over recruitment and candidate selection (Cross 2004); it is almost impossible to be elected without the backing of a political party.

Despite the importance of parties, party leaders are considered "the superstars of Canadian politics" (Clarke et al. 1991, p. 89). It is important to remember here that all party leaders including the prime minister and the leader of the opposition are merely members of parliament (MPs), who ran as a candidate in a local constituency election as all MPs do. However, party leaders preside over party, parliamentary, and governmental affairs (Gidengil et al. 2012). Canadian campaigns are also leader-centered. The "leaders' tour" is the focal point of the national campaign (Bélanger et al. 2003). The main leaders crisscross the country attending rallies, giving speeches, and making policy announcements in a highly orchestrated media spectacle. Since the media pay for a seat on a leader's campaign bus or plane, the activities and pronouncements of leaders dominate media coverage each day of the campaign. Leaders debates are another high point of the campaign. Here the leaders of the legislative parties participate in at least two debates, one in each official language. The debates are the sole opportunity for voters to see the leaders together and attract significant viewership. Canadian voters recognize the importance of party leaders. Data from several Canadian election surveys show that leader evaluations are a significant determinant of voting preference; while the effect of leader evaluations on overall vote share is modest, the more one likes a particular leader, the more likely they are to vote for the leader's party (Gidengil et al. 2012). Clearly party leaders are important in Canada, and therefore there is potential for the personalization of online politics to be applicable to the Canadian case. The next section looks to clarify the concept of personalization and its relationship to digital politics in more detail.

The Personalization of Politics: Media and Digital Technology

The concept of personalization refers to changes in political practice where the individual politician, rather than parties, organizations, or institutions, are increasingly at the center of politics (Adam and Maier 2010). There is some debate around the newness of this change, although some suggest that personalization is a contemporary feature of politics that is increasing (McAllister 2007). Personalization is generally seen as the result of two interrelated factors: (1) the decline in parties and party membership and (2) the rise of the electronic media, especially television (Van Aelst et al. 2012). Rahat and Sheafer (2007) suggest there are three distinct types of personalization. Institutional personalization refers to changes in political rules and mechanisms that put less attention on parties/institutions and more on the individual. In media personalization, there are changes in the presentation of politics in the media that place the attention on individual politicians at the expense of parties/institutions. Behavioral personalization focuses on changes in behavior; politicians may act more as an individual in their political activities and voters may make voting decisions based on individuals rather than parties.

This analysis fits squarely in the category of media personalization, though the choice by a Canadian leader to have a Twitter feed separate from the party can be considered behavioral personalization. In highly media-centered political environments such as Canada, it is argued that individual politicians have become the focus of both journalistic accounts of politics and the communication strategies of political actors. Scholars have made further distinctions within the conceptualization of media personalization (see Rahat and Sheafer 2007; Van Aelst et al. 2012). First, there is a focus in political communication on the politician as a private person including his or her personal characteristics, non-political traits and personal interests. This is known in the literature as "privatization." Next, there is heightened attention on individual politicians in terms of political characteristics and activities where the attention remains political. This is referred to as "individualization." In both cases, however, parties and institutions are diminished as the focus on political communication. There is considerable scholarly attention of personalization in media reporting; while it has not been found in every case, it does appear to be present in the coverage of Canadian political leaders especially with regards to female political leaders (Trimble et al. 2013; Lalancette et al. 2014).

With the growing importance of digital technologies, scholars have begun exploring whether (media) personalization has moved online. Van Santen and Van Zoonen (2010) suggest digital media have the ability to facilitate a direct link between individual politicians and citizens, which make it ideal for personalization. Moreover, digital technologies are relatively inexpensive and face fewer campaign regulations than other communication technology (Davis et al. 2008), which might also incentivize use by individual politicians. There is some evidence to suggest that personalized online content is beneficial. For instance, Kruikemeier et al. (2013) conducted experiments exploring the relationship between candidate personalization on websites and political engagement in the Dutch political context. The research concludes that personalized online communication does

178 Tamara A. Small

increase the political involvement of citizens. And in a similar experimental study of personalization on Twitter, Lee and Oh (2012) find that personalized tweets significantly enhance message recall and create a sense of intimacy with the candidate among individuals with the same partisan affiliation as the candidate.

The literature on online personalization in election campaigns is small.[1] Some of the earliest work comes from several studies in the book *Making a Difference: A Comparative View of the Role of the Internet in Election Politics* (Davis et al., 2008). Overall, the results were inconclusive. In election campaigns in Italy (1996–2006) and the Netherlands (2002–3), party leaders operated their own separate websites (Bentivegna 2008; Voerman and Boogers 2008), which provided more private types of leader information and overshadowed the party sites as a source of information and voter contact. However, personalization was not evident in the online campaigns in Germany (2002, 2005) and Belgium (2002, 2006) (Schweitzer 2008; Hooghe and Vissers 2008). Hermans and Vergeer (2012) studied the web personalization on campaign websites of candidates from 17 countries in the European elections in June 2009. The research shows that candidates mostly share professional information and some information about their family life. Contrary to expectations, the provision of private information (e.g., recreation, sports, and religion) was far less common. There were some cross-national differences, with post-communist countries being more open to personalization. Sanne Kruikemeier (2014) looked at personalization on Twitter by candidates around the 2010 election in the Netherlands. Consistent with expectations, personalization of all types was commonplace. Indeed, the tweets by Dutch candidates were more often about their emotions (34.4 percent), private life (17.1 percent), and professional activities (24.7 percent) than about the campaign. The study concludes by suggesting that Twitter is mainly a vehicle to present a candidates' private persona. A study of the use of Twitter by the two leading party leaders in the 2011 Spanish election found limited personalization, with both leaders using Twitter to spread their party's main political agenda and proposals (Zamora Medina and Zurutuza Muñoz 2014). They conclude that Twitter was used for politics rather than for making personal connections with voters. Given the limited amount of research on the topic of online personalization during election campaigns, it is difficult to come to any conclusions about the state of this literature beyond noting that personalization, to some degree, has gone digital.

Methods and Data

In order to assess online personalization in Canada, we contrast the Twitter accounts of three main political parties and leaders during the 2011 federal election.[2] This is accomplished using content analysis. Content analysis is a method of "measuring or quantifying dimensions of the content of messages," which is useful for describing and making inferences "about the sources who produced those messages, or [to] draw inferences about the reception of those messages by their audiences"

TABLE 11.1 Tweeting in the 2011 federal election by account

	Account	Tweets
Leader		
Harper (CPC)	@pmharper	111
Ignatieff (LPC)	@M_Ignatieff	97
Layton (NDP)	@jacklayton	85
Total		293
Party		
LPC	@liberal_party	506
NDP	@NDP_ElectionHQ	49
Total		555

(Benoit 2011, pp. 268–9). Five accounts are analyzed (Table 11.1). The Liberal Party and the NDP operated an account for both the party and their respective leaders (Michael Ignatieff and Jack Layton); the governing Conservatives operated a single account for their leader, prime minister Stephen Harper. By including both sets of feeds, the analysis will provide for an assessment of the levels and types of personalization by party leaders and whether this differs from party accounts.

The main unit of analysis is the individual tweet, which has a 140-character limit. A lot can be conveyed in this limited space including policy proposals, personal information, reaction to other tweets, links, and hashtags (Parmelee and Bichard 2011). Every tweet from the five accounts between the day the writ dropped[3] (March 23, 2011) and Election Day (May 3, 2011) was collected.[4] Given the small number of tweets produced by the five accounts (Table 11.1), all tweets are analyzed. Additionally, the number of tweets and followers was recorded every week of the campaign.

This analysis draws on Van Aelst, Sheafer, and Stayner's (2012) work on personalization in mediated environments to assess personalization on the campaign tweets. As discussed, they make a distinction between two dimensions of personalization: privatization and individualization. With the former focusing on non-political traits of an individual politician and the latter focusing on political activities of a politician. Similar categories are employed in this analysis to assess the tweets produced by the parties and leaders (Table 11.2). The category of partization was developed to capture tweets that were not personalized in any way and still focus on the party organization. Each tweet, from party and leader feeds, was analyzed using the mutually exclusive categories listed in Table 11.2. To be sure, there is no way to determine who is actually doing the tweeting—the leader or a staff person. Nevertheless, the data do provide insight into how politicians and their campaigns conceive of Twitter as a communication tool. The purpose of this content analysis is to empirically assess the level of personalization in the Canadian Twitterverse.

180 Tamara A. Small

TABLE 11.2 Tweet personalization coding scheme

Tweet type	Description
Privatization	Tweets that focus on the politician as a private individual and are unrelated to politics or the election campaign.
	For example, pmharper: Departing for Toronto shortly. Laureen & I were thrilled to meet Maria Aragon and her family. Maria, you have a bright future ahead of you!
Individualization	Tweets that are related to politics or the election campaign that focus on the party leader.
	For example, jacklayton: Unlike @pmharper, I'll give small businesses a break – & create Cdn jobs. Watch the ad: http://ndp.ca/hhuni #Cdn-poli #NDP #elxn41
Partization	Tweets that are on politics or the election campaign, where the leader is not mentioned.
	For example, M_Ignatieff: Liberals stand with police and victims of crime. We're the only party that will defend the gun registry. #elxn41 #lpc
Other	Tweets that do not fit in any other category including replies and non-party retweets.

TABLE 11.3 Twitter followers in the 2011 federal election

	Week 1	Election Day	New followers	% of change
@pmharper	107,125	132,866	25,741	24.0
@M_Ignatieff	64,704	98,180	33,476	51.7
@jacklayton	60,796	98,469	37,673	62.0
Total	232,625	329,515	96,890	41.7
Average	77,542	109,838	32,297	
@liberal_party	7,217	11,334	4,117	57.0
@NDP_Elec-tionHQ	475	1,613	1,138	239.6
Total	7,692	12,947	5,255	68.3
Average	3,846	6,474	2,628	

Results

Follow the Leader

Before moving to our research questions, it is worth exploring those people who receive and read partisan tweets during an election campaign. While it is difficult to determine the audience of Twitter, we look to the number of followers as a

Parties, Leaders, Online Personalization **181**

good measure of a candidate's impact within the electorate (Parmelee and Bichard 2011). Some might criticize this number, as it does not indicate how many people actually read a tweet. However, the number of followers is a very conservative estimate of political influence for several reasons. First, most politician Twitter feeds are public, which means tweets are available to anyone with or without a Twitter account. Additionally, many politicians often link their Twitter accounts to other social media or official websites. Being a follower of a politician is just one way of accessing tweets. Second, there is also the possibility of a "two-step flow"; followers increase the reception of a tweet by retweeting, sharing it via other social media or through offline political discussions (Gainous and Wagner 2014). This potentially has more impact because it comes from a more credible source—a friend. The ability of a politician's message to be amplified depends on the number of followers.

Table 11.3 outlines the number of followers for the leaders and the parties including followers at the beginning and the end of the campaign period and the percentage of increase for each party and leader and overall for each category. More than 342,000 accounts followed a party or leader.[5] While this is an extremely small portion of eligible voters, Twitter users are a desirable group of citizens—they tend to be politically engaged. American research has found that individuals who use social networking sites for politics are more active in traditional areas of political participation (Smith et al. 2009). And Canadian research shows that online and offline political engagement are deeply intertwined in Canada (Bastien et al. 2015). The election campaign generated some excitement with all leaders and parties gaining new followers over the 38-day campaign. Some 96,000 people began following one of the three main party leaders during the campaign while just over 5,000 people began following a party. However, the main takeaway from Table 11.3 is that like offline Canadian politics, party leaders are the superstars of the Twitterverse. On Election Day, 96 percent of all partisan Twitter followers followed a party leader. The party–leader follower ratio is 1:17.[6] That is, on average, for every one person that followed a party account, 17 followed a party leader. Overall, when people choose to follow party politics on Twitter, they do so through the lens of the party leaders (see Small 2010). This can be interpreted as another instance of behavioral personalization, with citizens choosing to pay attention to leaders instead of parties. This means that potential personalize political communication by party leaders could impact a considerable number of citizens.

Tweeting about Leaders and Parties in the 2011 Federal Election

We begin by assessing how leaders and parties used Twitter during the campaign. As noted in Table 11.1, the three party leaders tweeted a total of 293 times over the 38-day campaign. Even though Twitter is seen to encourage

182 Tamara A. Small

TABLE 11.4 Twitter personalization in the 2011 federal election

Leader	Individualization	Privatization	Partization
@pmharper	18.9%	8.4%	72.6%
@M_Ignatieff	59.3%	6.8%	33.9%
@jacklayton	69.4%	5.6%	25.0%
Total	45.6%	7.1%	47.3%
@liberal_party	67.3%	0.0%	32.7%
@NDP_ElectionHQ	39.9%	0.0%	60.1%
Total	43.0%	0.0%	57.0%

Note: The tweets coded as "Other" are removed from this table. As noted in Table 11.2, tweets such as @replies and retweets were considered other. Twenty-three percent of leader tweets were coded and 20 percent of party tweets (all from @liberal_party).

frequent posting because the limit is only 140 characters, the three leaders tweeted an average of two or three tweets (2.6) each day of the campaign. Whether this is a sufficient use of Twitter is difficult to know. However, it is less likely that leader tweets would overwhelm the accounts of followers and thus making them more likely to be read. Previous research on the 2011 federal elections shows that Canadian party leaders mainly use Twitter for broadcasting campaign information (Small 2014). The broadcast tweets of the leaders are a mix of event announcements, policy statements, and status updates from the leaders' tour. Social tweets, in the form of @replies or retweeting occurred less than 20 percent of the time.

Table 11.4 provides the results of the content analysis; both leaders and party mattered in the tweeting strategies of party leaders. Leaders tweeted about themselves and their activities, but they also often tweeted about party policy. Indeed, a small majority of leader tweets were personalized (53 percent) compared to those focused on the party (47 percent). While there are differences among the three leaders, one area where there is some consensus is with regards to online privatization. The data show that the three leaders rarely used their tweets to present a non-political persona during the 2011 campaign. Less than 8 percent of tweets provided a sense of the person behind the leader. These results mirror those of Zamora Medina and Zurutuza Muñoz (2014), who found that Spanish leaders focus much more on campaigning than showing a personal persona to voters on Twitter. Almost three-quarters of tweets by the Canadian leaders focused on politics or the election campaign.

When party leaders do bring attention to themselves in their tweets, it was in the form of individualization. Forty-six percent of tweets by the leaders personified party and campaign information by using or implying a personal pronoun. The level of individualization varied from leader to leader. NDP leader Jack Layton had the

Parties, Leaders, Online Personalization **183**

greatest number of individualized tweets at nearly 70 percent. This is in part because many of Layton's tweets were about the promotion of campaign events. For instance,

> jacklayton: Toronto: join me tomorrow for an important #NDP election rally: http://ndp.ca/hhu5V #Cdnpoli #elxn41

Layton's tweets also personalized the party's election platform:

> jacklayton: Unlike @pmharper, I'll give small businesses a break – & create Cdn jobs. Watch the ad: http://ndp.ca/hhuni #Cdnpoli #NDP #elxn41

Here it is not that an NDP government would give a tax break, which under Canada's cabinet government is technically true. Rather the proposal is something Layton would personally accomplish. The highly personalized nature of Layton's tweets may not be surprising, given how important Layton was to the NDP's success in that campaign. The NDP became the official opposition for the first time in history in 2011, with overwhelming success in the province of Québec. Many attribute this success to Layton's personal popularity; he was the only leader who was perceived positively in 2011 (Fournier et al. 2013). Like Layton, Ignatieff's tweets were very much focused on the day-to-day life on the leaders' tour—where the leader was and what the leader said. One example of this is:

> M_Ignatieff: This morning in Hamilton, I'll make clear, firm commitments on health care.

The tweets of Liberal leader Michael Ignatieff were also considerably individualized at almost 60 percent.

Conservative leader and prime minister Stephen Harper approached Twitter very differently than his rivals; less than 20 percent of his tweets were individualized during the election. The following tweets are typical of the prime minister:

> pmharper: We will ensure that people living in rural Canada will have access to the services that they need most. http://ow.ly/4tHvb

> pmharper: A Conservative Government will ensure that there are enough volunteer firefighters in rural Canada. http://ow.ly/4tB7u

The terms "we" and "Conservative Government" are used often in Harper's tweets rather than personal pronouns, as was the case with Layton and Ignatieff. Even though the activities of the leaders' tour were central topics of the feed, Harper was not the star of his own tweets. There may be several reasons for this; first, since the party only operated a single account, unlike the Liberals and NDP, it is plausible that account served primarily as the party's account despite being named

184 Tamara A. Small

after the leader. Second, disciplined communication has long been a part of the Conservative strategy under Harper. A former Conservative campaign manager has pointed out that the leader should never improvise, candidates should never speak about personal beliefs, and electronic communication must be "careful and dignified" (Flanagan 2009, p. 284). These rules are evident in Harper's tweeting. It is also possible that Harper's personal popularity was waning. Leader evaluations of Harper "slightly but significantly" decreased between the previous election in 2008 and 2011 (Fournier et al. 2013, p. 889). While Harper's tweets differed from the other leaders, partization was common among all three leaders. One-third of Ignatieff's tweets and one-quarter of Layton's made no reference to the leader and were completely focused on the party. Overall, the leader tweets are overwhelmingly focused on politics and the campaign presented in a mix between personalized and party-oriented style.

Interestingly, the same conclusion exists for the party feeds—both the party and the leader are given attention in the tweets. The two parties tweeted a total of 555 times during the campaign, although more than 90 percent of them were by the Liberals. It is not evidently clear why there is such a disparity between the two parties and the parties and the leaders. As Table 11.4 shows that the content on @NDP_ElectionHQ was highly personalized. Indeed, the NDP feeds were more about Jack Layton than the party organization. Like Layton's feed, the NDP feed was also focused on campaign events. As such, there was actually very little difference between the two feeds.

> jacklayton: I'm about to launch the 2011 #NDP election campaign. Watch it live: http://ndp.ca/hhuXX #Cdnpoli

> NDP_ElectionHQ: Watch live right now: @JackLayton launches the 2011 #NDP election campaign. Be a part of it: http://ndp.ca/hhuXX #Cdnpoli

Both feeds essentially inform voters of Layton's event schedule. This again may speak to the popularity of Layton and that the leader was a strategic asset in the party's communication strategy. Or it could be that the NDP merely conceived of Twitter as an event calendar to encourage on- and offline mobilization of followers. The Liberals produced more party-oriented tweets compared to the NDP, but Ignatieff also figured prominently on the @liberal_party at 40 percent. For instance, during the English-language televised debate, the Liberal's live-tweeted comments made by Ignatieff. Almost 100 debate tweets were produced in real-time. The feed also retweeted from @M_Ignatieff. In this way, the Liberal leader's own words were an important part of the party feed. In the case of both party feeds, other candidates running for election were rarely mentioned in tweets unless they were at a campaign event with the leader. Despite the presence of 307 other candidates, the party feeds were very centralized, focusing on the generic party organization or the leader.

Conclusions

There were great expectations around the use of Twitter by Canadian political parties in the 2011 federal election. By the end of the campaign, many believe it did not live up to the hype. As one commentator put it

> While all the major parties opened their eyes and arms to social media, it's not quite the inspiring story that the Obama victory was … In fact, it was everyone but the politicians who managed to leverage social media successfully during the campaign.
>
> (ComputerWorld Canada 2011)

Nevertheless, considerable content was tweeted by the parties and leaders and several thousand people followed them over the 38-day campaign.

Offline Canadian politics is highly personalized in institutional, media, and behavioral capacity. And it appears that this personalization has moved into digital politics as witnessed through the Canadian partisan Twitterverse in the 2011 federal election. This analysis has highlighted both behavioral and media personalization on Twitter. In other countries, party leaders created personalized websites, but Canadian leaders did not. By establishing their own Twitter feeds, Canadian party leaders engaged in online behavior that did not exist prior to social media. Leaders are considerably more popular on Twitter than the parties. In terms of citizen behavior, followers chose to become involved in the Twitter campaign through the accounts of the party leaders.

Nevertheless, it is not clear how much any of this mattered. As the analysis indicates, the difference between the party and leader feeds with regards to media personalization was rather unremarkable. First, both sets of feeds focused on politics and the campaign. While this makes sense for the party, it is less so for the leaders. Previous research had suggested that Twitter as a personalized media could provide benefits by creating more intimate and face-to-face-like connections with voters. Nevertheless, privatization barely figured into the tweeting strategies of the Canadian leaders during this campaign. Next, both sets of feeds focused on both the leader and the party. The leaders tweeted often about their activities and announcements as they crisscrossed the country on the leaders' tour. But they also tweeted about general party announcements and aspects of the platform. And the parties basically did the same—tweeting about the party and tweeting about what the leaders were up to. Indeed, the content of the two sets of feeds was quite similar.

The similarity between the two sets of feeds is likely related to the nature of the Canadian campaigning. Compared to American campaigns, which can begin a year so in advance, Canadian federal elections are very short. As such the campaign is intensely focused around the leaders' tour; "the imperative of the leader's tour is driven by the party platform and ballot question the

186 Tamara A. Small

party is trying to establish" (Bélanger et al. 2003, 440). Earlier examinations of online campaigning in Canada have noted how tied the parties' use of digital technologies are with the tour. On Canadian campaign websites, the event calendars, campaign diaries, photo galleries, and news stories are all focused on the activities and pronouncements of the leaders (Small 2007). As discussed earlier, both party and leader Twitter feeds provided a lot of leaders' tour information including campaign events and daily policy announcements. It appears that Canadian parties conceive of Twitter as a way to tweet the leaders' tour as it happens. The individualization of tweets is a function of the fact that the leader tour is highly individualized. To be sure, there has been a personalization of Twitter politics in Canada in the sense that there was considerable attention paid to the party leaders. At the same time, however, the party organization cannot be said to have been diminished in Twitter communication in this campaign.

Notes

1 It is worth noting that studies on online personalization on legislative websites also exist (see Stanyer 2008; Koop and Marland 2012).
2 Even though the Bloc Québécois (BQ) had seats in the House of Commons, they are excluded from this analysis. The BQ run candidates in only the French-speaking provinces of Québec.
3 A writ is a formal written order from the chief electoral officer instructing the returning officer in each electoral district to hold an election to elect an MP. The writ is dropped after the governor-general, on the request of the prime minister, has dissolved the legislature.
4 The tweets were collected daily during the election by hand by a research assistant.
5 To be sure, it is likely that an account followed more than one party or leader. Therefore, this number tells us little about the number of individual people following the partisan Twitterverse in Canada.
6 The party–leader follower ratio uses averages rather than totals, as there are more leaders than parties.

References

Adam, S. and M. Maier. 2010. Personalization of Politics: A Critical Review and Agenda for Research. In C. Salmon (ed.), *Communication Yearbook 34*. London: Routledge, pp. 213–57.
Bastien, F., D. Dumouchel, H. Jansen, T. Giasson, R. Koop, and T.A. Small. 2015. *Towards New Patterns of Political Engagement? Canadians' Participation in the Digital Era*. Paper presented to the Annual Meeting of the Canadian Political Science Association, Ottawa, Ontario, June 2–4.
Bédard, M. and J.R. Robertson. 2008. *Political Parties and Parliament Recognition*. Ottawa: Library of Parliament.
Bélanger, P., R.K. Carty, and M. Eagles. 2003. The Geography of Canadian Parties' Electoral Campaigns: Leaders' Tours and Constituency Election Results. *Political Geography* 22(4): 439–55.

Parties, Leaders, Online Personalization **187**

Benoit, W.L. 2011. Content Analysis in Political Communication. In E.P. Bucy and R.L. Holbert (eds.), *Sourcebook for Political Communication Research: Methods, Measures, and Analytical Techniques*. Abingdon: Taylor & Francis, pp. 268–79.

Bentivegna, S. 2008. Italy: The Evolution of E-campaigning 1996–2006. In S. Ward, D. Owen, R. Davis, and D. Taras (eds.), *Making a Difference: A Comparative View of the Role of the Internet in Election Politics*. Lanham, MD: Lexington Press, pp. 217–34.

Canadian Press. 2011. Social Media Takes Off in First Week of Campaign. *CTV.com*, www.ctv.ca/servlet/ArticleNews/story/CTVNews/20110402/social-media-election-11040 2/20110402?s_name=election2011.

Clarke, H.D., J. Jenson, L. LeDuc, and J.H. Pammett. 1991. *Absent Mandate: Interpreting Change in Canadian Politics*. Toronto: Gage Educational Publishing.

ComputerWorld Canada. 2011. Canada's First Social Media Election Missed the Mark, www.itworldcanada.com/article/canadas-first-social-media-election-missed-the-mark/43657#ixzz3e0QNZWCX.

Cross, W. 2004. *Political Parties*. Vancouver: UBC Press.

Cross, W., J. Malloy, T.A. Small, and L. Stephenson. 2015. *Fighting for Votes: Parties, the Media and Voters in the 2011 Ontario Election*. Vancouver: UBC Press.

Davis, R., D. Owen, D. Taras, and S. Ward. 2008. Conclusion. In S. Ward, D. Owen, R. Davis, and D. Taras (eds.), *Making a Difference: A Comparative View of the Role of the Internet in Election Politics*. Lanham, MD: Lexington Press, pp. 257–69.

Effing, R., J. van Hillegersberg, and T. Huibers. 2011. Social Media and Political Participation: Are Facebook, Twitter and YouTube Democratizing Our Political Systems? In E. Tambouris, A. Macintosh, and H. de Bruijn (eds.), *Electronic Participation: Third IFIP WG 8.5 International Conference, ePart 2011*. Delft: Springer.

Flanagan, T. 2009. *Harper's Team: Behind the Scenes in the Conservative Rise to Power*, 2nd edn. Montreal-Kingston: McGill-Queen's Press.

Fournier, Patrick, Fred Cutler, Stuart Soroka, Dietlind Stolle, and Éric Bélanger. 2013. "Riding the Orange Wave." *Canadian Journal of Political Science* 46 (4).

Gainous, J. and K.M. Wagner. 2014. *Tweeting to Power: The Social Media Revolution in American Politics*. Oxford University Press.

Giasson, T. and T.A. Small. 2014. *#elections: The Use of Twitter by Provincial Political Parties in Canada*. Paper presented at the British Association of Canadian Studies. London, April 25.

Giasson, T., G. Le Bars, F. Bastien, and M. Verville. 2013. Qc2012: l'utilisation de Twitter par les partis. In É. Bélanger, F. Bastien, and F. Gélineau (eds.), *Les Québécois aux urnes. Les partis, les médias et les citoyens en campagne*. Montreal: Les Presses de l'Université de Montréal, pp. 133–46.

Gidengil, E., N. Nevitte, A. Blais, J. Everitt, and P. Fournier. 2012. *Dominance and Decline: Making Sense of Recent Canadian Elections*. University of Toronto Press.

Hermans, L. and M. Vergeer. 2012. Personalization in e-Campaigning: A Cross-National Comparison of Personalization Strategies Used on Candidate Websites of 17 Countries in EP Elections 2009. *New Media & Society*: 7292.

Hooghe, M. and S. Vissers. 2008. Websites as a Campaign Tool for Belgian Political Parties: A Comparison between the 2000 and 2006 Local Election Campaigns. In S. Ward, D. Owen, R. Davis, and D. Taras (eds.), *Making a Difference: A Comparative View of the Role of the Internet in Election Politics*. Lanham, MD: Lexington Press.

Jansen, H., F. Bastien, T. Giasson, R. Koop, and T.A. Small. 2014. *The Digital Divide Meets the Democratic Divide: The Internet and Democratic Citizenship in Canada*. Paper presented to the 23rd World Congress of Political Science, International Political Science Association, Montréal, Québec, July 19–24.

Koop, R. and A. Marland. 2012. Insiders and Outsiders: Presentation of Self on Canadian Parliamentary Websites and Newsletters. *Policy & Internet* 4(3–4): 112–35.

Kruikemeier, S. 2014. How Political Candidates Use Twitter and the Impact on Votes. *Computers in Human Behavior* 34: 131–9.

Kruikemeier, S., G. van Noort, R. Vliegenthart, and C.H. de Vreese. 2013. Getting Closer: The Effects of Personalized and Interactive Online Political Communication. *European Journal of Communication* 28(1): 53–66.

Lalancette, M., A. Drouin, and C. Lemarier-Saulnier. 2014. Playing Along New Rules: Personalized Politics in the 24/7 Mediated World. In A. Marland, T. Giasson and T.A. Small, *Political Communication in Canada: Meet the Press and Tweet the Rest.* Vancouver: UBC Press, pp. 144–59.

Lee, E.-J. and S.Y. Oh. 2012. To Personalize or Depersonalize? When and How Politicians' Personalized Tweets Affect the Public's Reactions. *Journal of Communication* 62(6): 932–49.

McAllister, I. 2007. The Personalization of Politics. In R.J. Dalton and H.-D. Klingemann (eds.), *The Oxford Handbook of Political Behavior.* Oxford University Press, pp. 571–88.

Parmelee, J.H. and S.L. Bichard. 2011. *Politics and the Twitter Revolution: How Tweets Influence the Relationship between Political Leaders and the Public.* Lanham, MD: Lexington Books.

Rahat, G. and T. Sheafer. 2007. The Personalization(s) of Politics: Israel, 1949–2003. *Political Communication* 24(1): 65–80.

Schweitzer, E.J. 2008. Germany: Online Campaign Professionalization in the 2002 and 2005 National Elections. In S. Ward, D. Owen, R. Davis, and D. Taras (eds.), *Making a Difference: A Comparative View of the Role of the Internet in Election Politics.* Lanham, MD: Lexington Press, pp. 235–55.

Small, T.A. 2007. Canadian Cyberparties: Reflections on Internet-Based Campaigning and Party Systems. *Canadian Journal of Political Science* 40(3): 639–57.

Small, T.A. 2010. Canadian Politics in 140 characters: Party Politics in the Twitterverse. *Canadian Parliamentary Review* 33(3): 39–45.

Small, T.A. 2014. The Not-So Social Network: The Use of Twitter by Canada's Party Leaders. In A. Marland, T. Giasson, and T.A. Small (eds.), *Political Communication in Canada: Meet the Press and Tweet the Rest.* Vancouver: UBC Presss.

Smith, A.W., K.L. Schlozman, S.Verba, and H. Brady. 2009. *The Internet and Civic Engagement.* Washington, DC: Pew Internet & American Life Project.

Stanyer, J. 2008. Elected Representatives, Online Self-Presentation and the Personal Vote: Party, Personality and Webstyles in the United States and United Kingdom. *Information, Communication & Society* 11(3): 414–32.

Trimble, L., A. Wagner, S. Sampert, D. Raphael, and B. Gerrits. 2013. Is It Personal? Gendered Mediation in Newspaper Coverage of Canadian National Party Leadership Contests, 1975–2012. *The International Journal of Press/Politics* 18(4): 462–81.

Van Aelst, P., T. Sheafer, and J. Stanyer. 2012. The Personalization of Mediated Political Communication: A Review of Concepts, Operationalizations and Key Findings. *Journalism* 13(2): 203–20.

Van Santen, R. and L. Van Zoonen. 2010. The Personal in Political Television Biographies. *Biography* 33(1): 46–67.

Voerman, G. and M. Boogers. 2008. The Netherlands: Digital Campaigning in the 2002 and 2003 Parliamentary Elections. In S. Ward, D. Owen, R. Davis and D. Taras (eds.),

Making a Difference: A Comparative View of the Role of the Internet in Election Politics. Lanham, MD: Lexington Press, pp. 197–215.

Zamora Medina, R. and C. Zurutuza Muñoz. 2014. Campaigning on Twitter: Towards the "Personal Style" Campaign to Activate the Political Engagement During the 2011 Spanish General Elections. *Comunicación y sociedad/Communication & Society* 27(1): 83–106.

12

SOCIAL MEDIA COMING OF AGE

Developing Patterns of Congressional Twitter Use, 2007–14

David S. Lassen and Leticia Bode

One of the defining features of modern elections is the abundance of easily accessible information available to voters. Although individuals have long been the recipients of direct mail, phone calls, visits, and television advertisements from campaigns, the continued development and widespread use of online communication methods during elections has made a vast amount of information about candidates available to voters at their discretion. The increasingly widespread use of websites, blogs, and social media like Twitter has deposited an enormous amount of information about candidates and their views in publicly accessible archives. To an unprecedented level, citizens in recent elections have therefore been able to actively search for and obtain detailed information about a candidate's issue positions, personal characteristics, and relationships.

Existing research suggests that this sea of available information can significantly mold individuals' decisions about whether to participate in politics and the form that action should take (Alvarez 1998; Lupia and McCubbins 1998; Wattenberg et al. 2000; Mutz 2006). Yet a picture of the extent to and manner in which candidates use new, online communication methods is still developing, including among incumbent members of Congress. Those who succeed in gaining a seat in Washington are often inherently cautious about changing the communication styles and tools that accompanied their earlier victories. Thus, Congressional adoption of and adaptation to tools such as Twitter has occurred gradually. In this manner, as Twitter use has become more common and expected among members, stable, enduring patterns of elite tweeting may be emerging, allowing us to better identify and draw meaning from deviations from such expectations. Future candidates for Congress may anticipate and plan for their use of online tools such as Twitter in much the same way that previous generations of candidates needed to create strategies for newly popular televised campaign advertisements or websites.

Social Media Coming of Age **191**

Twitter's essential costlessness, direct distribution to the mass public, and propensity for amplification, both internally and by traditional media outlets (Lipinski and Neddenriep 2004; Arceneaux and Weiss 2010), provide strong incentives for members to both use the service as well as refine their strategic approach to it. Similarly, the same features may make Twitter an unusually useful site for scholars of Congressional behavior as members quickly, publicly, and often personally respond to events and arguments. Yet questions of whether or how much elite users have altered their communication habits because of Twitter's features or audience remain open. A growing group of studies has examined members' Twitter use, but few have sought to systematically understand how such content has changed over time. As a result, we currently do not have a thorough, baseline account of Congressional Twitter use. In this chapter we provide just such an account.

Using a variety of existing features of candidate tweets including their frequency and the nature of the language used in each, we perform an initial examination of the frequency and type of tweets produced by members of Congress during 2007–9 and 2011–14. Studying these tools has important implications for democratic outcomes including political knowledge, vote choice, political trust, and democratic representation.

Theory

As suggested above, constituent communication is an important area of research given the large effects it may have on important democratic norms and behaviors. Research has long concluded that constituent communication and campaign communication more broadly can increase turnout, an important democratic outcome (Lau and Pomper 2001; Goldstein and Freedman 2002; Freedman et al. 2004; for exceptions see Ashworth and Clinton 2007 Ansolabehere et al. 1999). Member communication also tends to increase public understanding of issue positions and stimulate political knowledge more generally (Cover and Brumberg 1982; Lipinski 2004; Lau et al. 2007). Changes in political knowledge, in turn, can affect collective preferences (Althaus 1998; Kuklinski et al. 2000; Gilens 2001), as well as the decision to turn out and for whom (Wattenberg et al. 2000; McMurray 2013), thereby affecting the representational style of members of Congress (Grimmer 2013b). Communication with constituents, whether direct or mediated, also has the ability to affect political trust (Patterson 1993) as well as political efficacy (Lau et al. 2007).

A rich history of scholarship has therefore focused on the content as well as the importance of member communication with constituents, potential voters, and the public at large. Classic works on the topic by Mayhew (1974) and Fenno (1978) painted an enduring portrait of members of Congress as strategic speakers focused on re-election. Specifically, these authors highlight the centrality of direct constituent communication for electorally minded elites. Whether in

192 David S. Lassen and Leticia Bode

person, franked mail, traditional media, or new media, members of Congress are eager to interact with the public.

More recent research on Congressional communication has considered specific circumstances in which communication is most frequent and valuable (see, for example, Druckman et al. 2009; Grimmer 2013a, 2013b). Members who are electorally vulnerable or newly elected most actively communicate with constituents (Cover 1980), for example, which often leads to greater support in public opinion and electoral margins (Ridout et al. 2004). More broadly, member–constituent communication differs between incumbents and challengers—reflecting their "varying attitudes toward risk" (Druckman et al. 2009, p. 343)—and between members of the majority and minority parties (Lipinski 2004). At all times, members are strategic communicators, conveying information to others in order to accomplish specific goals.

As new forms of communication have been developed in recent years, most members of Congress (and their campaign staffs) have included these in their campaign toolbox in some manner. Many members now maintain a social media presence on sites such as Facebook, Twitter, YouTube, Instagram, and more. Depending on the length of their time in Congress and the associated trust they have developed in their previous communication efforts, members may more or less quickly adopt new communication technologies or practices. Early adopters are often young members seeking to establish and define themselves among constituents and institutional peers (D'Alessio 1997, 2000). Adaptation appears quickest when members see examples of both successful implementation by other elites as well as increased relevance among the public (Evans and Oleszek 2003). This transition to new media has occurred relatively rapidly, with early evidence that most members adopt new technologies within three to four election cycles after their initial campaign use (Foot and Schneider 2006; Gulati and Williams 2010).

Over time, as adoption expands, the content that members post using new technologies also often becomes more similar. Members are close observers of one another and are quick to note the relative success of their peers' communication strategies. Within a few years of the launch of the first Congressional websites, for example, "certain content and functionality or tools [had become] standard features" on the vast majority of member sites (Williams and Gulati 2009). Similarly, members often hesitate to fully engage with particularly interactive media such as websites and blogs (Stromer-Galley 2000; Druckman et al. 2007, 2014; Williams and Gulati 2012). Wary of allowing others to influence their message, the Congressional elite appear to often use new media in a somewhat narrow way, to disseminate information to constituents and potential voters in a top-down communication model (Taylor and Kent 2004).

Why Twitter?

We may therefore expect members of Congress to embrace new communication technologies in relatively short and uniform order. Yet Twitter is an unusually

Social Media Coming of Age **193**

restrictive tool, offering its users precious little room for expression. Tweets are limited to just 140 characters and are designed to be conversational and easy to directly respond to. Because of its structure, Twitter may therefore seem an odd choice for elected officials interested in producing clear, contextualized, controlled messages. It is therefore unclear if we should expect most members of Congress to become regular and enduring Twitter users. It is similarly unclear if member tweeters have produced unique content on the service. Some Congressional users may simply tweet pre-existing messaging strategies or even non-political, personal information. In July 2015, for example, Jason Chaffetz (R-UT; @jasoninthehouse) posted a childhood photo of himself and his younger brother at the beach, a message with seemingly limited political value but fitting with the common Twitter theme "Throwback Thursday." To date, no comprehensive measures of such activity have been published.

Importantly, however, Twitter is different from many other communication outlets available to members of Congress in that it allows direct, inexpensive, unmediated contact with constituents and potential voters. Distributing a tweet is essentially costless and can be done by a member or her staff in a matter of moments without requiring additional online structure (as for a website) or use of scarce resources. Any member may therefore tweet as often as he or she likes, without concern for cash on hand, available air time, or physical constraints like those associated with traditional mail. Further, tweets can include links to other information and may therefore act as a marketing tool, directing larger audiences to longer-form content such as campaign websites, news articles, or other social media outlets. Tweets also offer members an instantaneous outlet for their thoughts and feelings. When responding to breaking news events, members may turn first to the accessible immediacy offered by Twitter. During Barack Obama's 2014 65-minute State of the Union address, for example, members of Congress and their staffs posted more than 1,000 tweets (Roston and Willis 2015).

These features also make Twitter an attractive communication method for researchers. In addition to the public, readily accessible nature of its content, Twitter provides a constant, readily accessible tool to members of Congress as well. Never more than a smartphone away, it is likely that members' tweets represent a less filtered, more real time window into their perceptions and strategic calculations. On Twitter members need not wait for an ad buy, graphics team, or voice actor to construct a public message. Instead, they may be entirely unfiltered in a manner hitherto rivaled only by the brief moments in which they were interviewed on live television—and then only in part given the presence of a journalist. Additionally, the structure of Twitter has been influential in other settings as well, with tweet features such as hashtags (general topic markers), retweeting (quoting or sharing another user's post), and @mentions (linking directly to another user's Twitter feed) beginning to appear in other media.

A number of studies from disparate fields also argue that part of the adaptive process among members is likely due to the nature of Twitter. These authors

194 David S. Lassen and Leticia Bode

contend that communication technologies themselves help to shape, in part, the form and language involved in the content distributed on them (Herring 2004). The features and user interface of each technology make some content easier to create and, therefore, more likely. Further, as linguistic and communication practices become institutionalized on a given medium, new users become more likely to follow suit. Thus, a set of norms, expectations, and revealed potentials are developed as users begin to communicate via a new technology. A robust literature (see Van Dijk 2012; Lewis and Fabos 2005) provides evidence in support of this phenomenon in online communication, especially using social media, but it may be especially prevalent among strategic, public communicators such as members of Congress. Constantly seeking to appeal to constituents, incumbent representatives and senators are likely to pay close attention (either themselves or through staffers and consultants) to the nature of the communication landscape they operate in.

Scholarship that directly considers member use of Twitter is growing rapidly. Several studies have outlined portions of early patterns of member adoption (Lassen and Brown 2011; Williams and Gulati 2012), and a basic understanding of content of member tweets is also beginning to emerge (Bode et al. 2011; Golbeck et al. 2010; Parmalee and Bichard 2011; Gainous and Wagner 2014). Yet important questions remain, particularly about the content of each tweet. What drives Twitter use? What do member tweets look like? Do they focus on politics or policy? What Twitter tools (hyperlinks, @mentions, etc.) do they employ in order to reach out to others in this medium? This study seeks to answer many of these questions. Equally important, Twitter is still a new and evolving medium. By studying it now, we document how a new media technology was employed by members in its first years, allowing us to then observe how use of the technology changes over time. We also hope that studying Twitter may elucidate broader communication goals of members of Congress.

Research Questions

We therefore expect that member Twitter activity during the three campaigns differed in some ways while remaining consistent in others. As members of Congress became more familiar with Twitter, their tweet behavior may have substantially changed, yet their ultimate goals of securing re-election, institutional power, and preferred policy did not. Thus, while members may have begun to use Twitter more frequently in recent elections, the nature of that usage is less clear. In this chapter we therefore examine how three aspects of Twitter use by Congressional elites have changed over time.

First, we consider the individual and collective volume of use and ask:

> *RQ1: Do members of Congress individually and as a group today use Twitter more often than they did in the past?*

Second, we account for each member's use of Twitter's structural features such as retweets, hashtags, and mentions of other Twitter users. We anticipate that by 2014 members' had a greater level of comfort with the day-to-day use of Twitter than when the first Congressional accounts were created in 2007. Therefore we ask:

> *RQ2: Did use of Twitter in terms of unique features such as retweets, hashtags, or mentions of other Twitter users, change over time?*

Third, comfort with Twitter may also mean members are willing to use it in different ways in terms of the content they post. Specifically, we consider the extent to which members employ four types of language over time, giving rise to our final research questions:

> *RQ3: Has use of Twitter for non-political purposes changed over time?*
> *RQ4: Have references to political parties changed over time?*
> *RQ5: Have references to political issues changed over time?*
> *RQ6: Have appeals to constituents or calls for action changed over time?*

Data and Methods

To examine these potential patterns in member online activity we compared the Twitter behavior of all incumbent members of Congress in the years 2007–9 and 2011–14. In order to focus our data on members facing similar incentives and demands, we define incumbent members as sitting members who appear on the ballot in the next general election for which they are eligible. Thus, our data does not include members who retired, lost a primary election, ran for another office, or otherwise vacated their position for any reason other than being defeated at the ballot box at the end of a given cycle. Restricting our data in this manner also increases the likelihood that the members in our data shared similar goals. Finally, this group of members is often of most interest to scholars. Our final sample includes 478 candidates in 2007–8, 464 in 2009, 457 in 2011–12, and 459 in 2013–14.

We next collected all the tweets posted by any Twitter account associated with each sampled member.[1] To ensure the completeness of our data, one author has collected all Congressional tweets at least once each year since 2008.[2] Although many members maintain a single, principal Twitter handle for official Congressional business, many also create one or more additional accounts for use in each electoral cycle. While representative Timothy Bishop regularly tweets using the handle @TimBishopNY, for example, he also distributed content using @TimBishop2014 during the 2014 election and @TimBishop2012 during the 2012 election. A full representation of a candidate's Twitter activity thus must include content from each relevant account as we do.

We constructed our training set of tweets by hand-coding 1,000 tweets from each election cycle in our data.[3] Tweets from each cycle were selected using a random sample stratified by chamber and party. Thus, in each set of years we drew 250 tweets at random from House Republicans, 250 from House Democrats, 250 from Senate Republicans, and 250 from Senate Democrats. We determined individual party membership by the party with which each member caucuses. We then hand-coded each tweet for the presence of a number of content features as follows.[4] The first category for which we coded was what we think of as sophisticated Twitter use. This is use of the medium that goes beyond simply reporting text, and includes either a hyperlink to more information, an @mention (@user) to tag or talk to another user, a hashtag linking the tweet to similar tweets, or a direct reply, which is simply a tweet directed at another user (indicated by an @ mention starting the tweet). Because of their universal availability and the manner in which they can shape a tweet, we refer to these aspects as the *structural features* of a tweet. We identified these features by noting the presence and placement of unique character strings (e.g., the "#" symbol for hashtags) associated with each.

The second categories of language we identified center on more traditional political concepts that we refer to as the *content features* of a tweet. The first thing we identified, somewhat counterintuitively given our sample, is the presence of non-political language. Some tweets may reflect personal information, in an effort to seem down-to-earth and reach constituents on a personal level (Slaby 2014). We also coded for mentions of specific policies. It might be expected that politicians avoid such mentions, in an effort to avoid alienating anyone who might disagree with them. On the other hand, they also might see Twitter as an important means of reaching out to voters and constituents and explaining their positions, and taking credit for what they have done in the policy arena (Mayhew 1974). We also coded for partisan language, which includes all references to major political parties. Thus, all uses of GOP, Republican, or Democrat are represented here. We also coded subtler references to partisan politics under this heading. Hashtags urging voters to "turnNCblue," for example, are treated as references to the Democratic Party and are included here. We also coded references to the media, as this represents an important element of using Twitter—trying to disseminate information and reach a broader audience (Gainous and Wagner 2014). This includes any reference to a candidate being covered in the media, as well as links to media. Appeals to take action were also coded, including appeals to read or learn more, come to an event, volunteer, vote, or donate money. Finally, we coded for events, including those that had already taken place, those that were ongoing, and future events.

To identify the frequency of each content feature in our broader sample, we next trained a collection of three algorithms (support vector machine, glmnet, and maximum entropy; Jurka et al. 2012) to automatically identify the presence of our selected content categories. Classifiers of this type are known as "bag of words" tools because they assign codes based on a comparison of the relative

Social Media Coming of Age **197**

frequency of all words in each text. In doing so they separate and trim each word down to its essential form and discard information about the words' relative order. Although this means abandoning some information about the texts, as Grimmer and Stewart (2013) note, tools of this type are sufficiently powerful for the vast majority of text analytic tasks in political science, including those of interest here. Classifiers of this type have been used for a variety of text analytic purposes with consistent success across a variety of disciplines, including political science (e.g., Grimmer and Stewart 2013; Grimmer 2013b).

Using the completed training tweets we then trained our three classifiers. We tested each classifier using fivefold cross validation by randomly withholding 20 percent of coded training tweets, training each algorithm with the remaining 80 percent, and then testing the success with which each classifier identified the features of interest in the previously hand-coded, withheld portion of the training set. Individually, no classifier consistently achieved more than 75 percent success in identifying distinct content features. Taken together, however, the three methods—when in agreement—accurately applied each code in 90 to 96 percent of tweets. Instances of disagreement between the classifiers were resolved by hand-coding.

Results

We begin by reviewing patterns of the volume of member Twitter usage. Table 12.1 reports the total number of tweets posted by members in our sample during each of the seven years for which we have data. Unsurprisingly, members of Congress posted few messages using Twitter in 2007, a time when the service was still in its infancy and had relatively few users in general. Member use quickly expanded, however, increasing nearly tenfold in each of the next two years. The volume of member use continued to expand from 2011 to 2014, with members in our data posting nearly 300,000 tweets during the 2014 calendar year. Although the year-to-year increase has become less volcanic, it has nonetheless remained steady, even as the proportion of sitting legislators using the service has reached saturation. The large, steady volume of content collectively disseminated by members via Twitter is evidence, we argue, that the practice of distributing a large number of brief messages that can be produced quickly is appealing to members of Congress and thereby has become a reasonably permanent, increasingly predictable feature of modern service in elective office.

Twitter's popularity in the halls of Congress is also evident in the number of offices it has reached. Table 12.2 reports the total number of members in our sample who posted at least one tweet in the years we examine. In its earliest years, Twitter was little more than a novelty with fewer than 10 percent of members in either chamber disseminating even one tweet in 2007 and 2008. By the end of 2009, however, nearly four in ten members maintained at least one active account

198 David S. Lassen and Leticia Bode

TABLE 12.1 Total tweets posted by year

	Tweets
2007	224
2008	4,233
2009	40,230
2011	73,391
2012	205,911
2013	222,310
2014	296,304

TABLE 12.2 Member users by year

	Senate	*House*	*Republicans*	*Democrats*	*Total*
2007	3	7	8	2	10
	(0.033)	(0.018)	(0.038)	(0.007)	(0.021)
2008	11	34	32	13	45
	(0.120)	(0.088)	(0.154)	(0.048)	(0.094)
2009	32	148	119	61	180
	(0.400)	(0.385)	(0.633)	(0.221)	(0.388)
2011	60	283	209	134	343
	(0.698)	(0.763)	(0.820)	(0.663)	(0.751)
2012	86	347	243	190	433
	(1.0)	(0.935)	(0.953)	(0.941)	(0.947)
2013	82	352	224	210	434
	(0.932)	(0.949)	(0.961)	(0.929)	(0.946)
2014	86	368	235	219	454
	(0.978)	(0.992)	(1.0)	(0.969)	(0.989)

Proportion of incumbents with given characteristic reported in parentheses.

and by 2012, usage was essentially ubiquitous. Early party and chamber differences also disappeared by 2012 when nearly 95 percent of members in our sample were active Twitter users, with most maintaining at least two accounts (one for official business and one for campaign activities). Usage rates remained exceptionally high in 2013 and 2014, again suggesting the current and future importance of Twitter and other social media in understanding Congressional communication.

In Table 12.3 we next turn to the same over time usage patterns, but now examine them at the level of individual members. Similar to the aggregate numbers, the median Twitter user in Congress has also steadily increased his or her usage since 2007, although in less dramatic fashion as individual use increased

Social Media Coming of Age   199

TABLE 12.3 Total tweets by member and year

	Median	Mean	Max
2007	13	22	62
2008	28	94	1,551
2009	146	224	1,505
2011	149	210	1,559
2012	339	469	3,069
2013	467	512	2,117
2014	489	648	3,971

about half as rapidly as collective totals did before 2010. Instead, much of the steep increase in overall usage appears to have been driven by an expanded pool of users and some members becoming especially prolific tweeters. Indeed, it was not unusual for the most prolific users in 2013–14 to post five to seven tweets a day, approximately five times the daily total of most other users. This gap between the bulk of social media users in Congress and the most enthusiastic elite has persisted with a small handful of members continuing to post several thousand tweets a year, while the vast majority of incumbents have posted no more than a few hundred in any given year.

Differences in tweet volume, however, can tell only part of the story. Twitter offers more than a platform from which to implement an existing message strategy. It also provides space and incentives to innovate. Twitter is a networked environment with a range of internally specific heuristic practices and tools such as hashtags and @mentions, designed to quickly convey meaning and connect content and users. In such a setting, members can benefit from using Twitter's unique features, thereby both improving other users' perceptions of them and providing more readily available content to elite audiences such as journalists, activists, voters, party leaders, and other government officials. In this manner, members can effectively increase both the range and influence of their messages. We therefore also examined the *structural features* of member-produced content. Table 12.4 reports the frequency with which members used four such features not available in traditional, offline forms of outreach: the provision of hyperlinks, referencing another Twitter user by their account handle (an "@mention"), the inclusion of one or more hashtags (often used as a quick topic marker), and directly replying to another user.

The results in Table 12.4 indicate that members' use of unique Twitter features has grown over time in a manner similar to overall usage rates. The one exception to this pattern is hyperlinks, which members have routinely included in half or more of their tweets since 2009. Over time, a growing number of member tweets have included other features we tracked, with more than half of all member tweets posted in 2014 including at least one @mention and a similar amount including

200 David S. Lassen and Leticia Bode

TABLE 12.4 Structural features of member tweets

	Hyperlink	@mention	Hashtag	Direct reply
2007	0.48	0	0	0
2008	0.20	0.01	0	0
2009	0.54	0.06	0.05	0.01
2011	0.67	0.27	0.34	0.01
2012	0.66	0.34	0.43	0.02
2013	0.62	0.45	0.49	0.01
2014	0.68	0.50	0.52	0.01

Cells report proportion of median incumbent's tweets with given feature.

at least one hashtag. Because such content and networking signals of this kind are unavailable in traditional modes of communication such as television advertisements and stump speeches, the increasing popularity of these elements suggest that members may not view Twitter as simply an additional avenue to broadcast pre-existing messages, but may be tailoring the content they send to the public via Twitter. At the least, it signals that the approach taken by members and their staff to online social media as communication and networking platforms has changed over time.

Note too that these changes among elites have taken place during a period in which the broader Twitter community has developed behavioral norms and expectations. Regular Twitter users (including journalists) now often expect members of Congress to abide by these conventions when tweeting. Legislators and the president alike have been publicly evaluated and at times taken to task over their Twitter habits. For a time, senator Chuck Grassley (R-IA) drew frequent public criticism for his then esoteric and idiosyncratic style of tweeting (e.g., Biddle 2011). Grassley eventually changed and professionalized his accounts, citing the criticism of other users and the press as a main motivation for doing so (Stanton 2015).

Finally, we also examined a variety of *content features* in order to consider the nature of the messages members distribute via Twitter. Table 12.5 reports the proportion of the tweets posted by the median member in our data that include references to specific types of content. Four things immediately stand out in this table. First, the proportion of tweets members post with non-political content has increased to a significant 13 percent of the median member's tweets in 2014. At the same time, the increase has slowed substantially and this total is far less than some feared at the onset of officials' use of the service. Instead, members appear to have consistently and overwhelmingly used Twitter to distribute political messages. Second, there are clear election effects here. Policy messages diminish in 2008, 2012, and 2014 when compared with the immediately preceding and following years (but show no clear upward or downward trends

Social Media Coming of Age 201

TABLE 12.5 Content features of member tweets

	Non-political	Policy	Party	Media	Appeal for action	Announce event
2007	0.00	0.32	0.13	0.06	0.08	0.18
2008	0.03	0.28	0.04	0.07	0.15	0.19
2009	0.05	0.45	0.06	0.11	0.17	0.28
2011	0.09	0.41	0.06	0.08	0.17	0.21
2012	0.11	0.35	0.05	0.06	0.16	0.20
2013	0.12	0.44	0.04	0.06	0.16	0.22
2014	0.13	0.38	0.03	0.05	0.15	0.21

Cells report proportion of median incumbent's tweets that reference each feature.

apart from this). Third, the relative infrequency of direct engagement with and appeals to the public (including direct replies in the previous table, appeal for action in this table, and announce event in this table) suggest that members still primarily utilize Twitter as a broadcast medium, similar to the messaging strategies they used in the past. Although there are some key differences here with traditional modes of communication (13 percent non-political content is still a significant amount), there are a lot of similarities in content as well. Finally, there seems to be a learning effect with regard to mentions of political parties. Party mentions have decreased significantly over time. This might suggest member tweets are less negative than they used to be (referencing the opposing party), or that members are using Twitter more for their own purposes and less for toeing the party line.

Discussion

Our data consistently support the idea that members of Congress are not only using Twitter far more today than in previous elections, but also that they are doing so in an evolving manner. Although in some ways members appear to be shaping their tweeted content to better comply with the norms of the Twitter community, in other ways they may be importing previously developed patterns of constituent communication by decreasing their mention of political parties, offering more links, more hashtags, more @mentions, and more calls to action, and by including more non-political information in their tweets. It is also worth noting that many Twitter communication elements have settled into consistent patterns, changing little over the period of time we consider. These include references to policy, references to the media, direct replies to other users, and event announcements. In either case, members appear to be investing more resources and interest in Twitter as the service continues to play an important role in American online communication.[5]

Ultimately, however, it is difficult to be entirely satisfied with any measure of current Twitter activity or to confidently identify enduring patterns of elite Twitter use. As a company, Twitter is still less than eight years old and has experienced dramatic changes in features, user interface, and device availability. The relative youth of Twitter as a communication tool combined with the shifting sands of online communication in general suggest that patterns of elite tweeting may still be subject to change in the future. For the present, therefore, we principally argue only that members are tending toward a set of stable Twitter behaviors but may not have yet settled into institutionalized patterns.

Even as Twitter use among political elites continues to evolve, however, it may play an important role in the American political system for at least three reasons. First, by providing a large amount of diverse information potentially directly from a member, tweeted material may shape patterns of mass political behavior. As individuals acquire more information about candidates they often feel more confident in their own decision-making and therefore become more willing to engage in political action (Wattenberg et al. 2000; Marcus and MacKuen 1993). Second, the type of information provided by member tweets is often unique. Because of the instantaneous nature of Twitter and the secondary importance many members appear to ascribe to it, member tweets often include more frank, personal information than is available elsewhere. Although some members use staff and other institutional resources to construct and manage their Twitter presence, others seem to continue to find great satisfaction in frequently tweeting their personal thoughts and experiences. Although Chuck Grassley now does so more rarely, for example, he will still at times use Twitter to call for the History Channel to change its name or report on dead deer he or his staff have hit with a car (Sanchez 2015). It is difficult to imagine any member including content of this type in a prepared policy speech or campaign mailer. Snatches of thought of this kind are radically new bits of member-created content (and our data show they are more common as time goes on) and their effect remains uncertain. Such messages provide a momentary insight into a member's mind of the kind previously unattainable for the vast majority of the public. It is possible that consuming such apolitical content may help some individuals feel a connection with a candidate and therefore come out to vote (Slaby 2014).

Third, member Twitter use may also provide an important signal among political elites. Although many assume that members use Twitter in an effort to engage with the voting public, members may tweet as a signal to party leaders or other elites (including journalists) of their digital acumen, campaign skill, or policy positions. The increased use of @mentions over time may also represent more engagement between political elites within Twitter. Future research should expand on this possibility to better understand how members are making use of new media.

Overall, however, these data provide new evidence of the fluid nature of Congressional Twitter use and suggest that though the ultimate goal and impact of members' tweets remain underspecified, the unique nature of tweeted material

Social Media Coming of Age **203**

may carve out an important place for it in the modern political system. Our data provide a valuable baseline that can be used in future studies to compare and contrast subsets of Twitter activity. Twitter use provides us with a much more sensitive and rapid window into member preferences, perceptions, and strategizing. Because Twitter is so low-cost and easy to produce, members seem more likely to post about a person, issue, or topic—even a non-political topic—with a tweet than any other media, thus providing insight into their perceptions and goals. Studying Twitter is therefore invaluable to understanding the broader political communication motivations of members of Congress, over and above the tweets themselves.

Notes

1   At the time of collection a small number of tweets were inaccessible, either because Twitter had restricted access to the related account or the user had deleted the post. These tweets are therefore not included in our dataset. The total number of accounts affected is small, however, representing less than 2 percent of the total number of sampled accounts and it is unlikely that their omission significantly affected our findings. Our data therefore includes more than 98 percent of all sampled member content posted during our sampled years.
2   Due to an unforeseen technical problem with the code used for collection, however, the data for 2010 was corrupted and is therefore not included here.
3   We include tweets posted in 2009 in our data for the 2008 election cycle.
4   A complete codebook is available upon request.
5   Twitter use among the general public is quickly rising. In late 2010 approximately 8 percent of Internet users reported being Twitter users. By early 2013 that number had doubled to 16 percent for all Internet users, with 27 percent of Internet users aged 18–29 also reporting Twitter activity (Duggan and Brenner 2013).

References

Althaus, S. 1998. Information Effects in Collective Preferences. *American Political Science Review* 92(3): 545–58.

Alvarez, R.M. 1998. *Information and Elections.* Ann Arbor: University of Michigan Press.

Ansolabehere, S.D., S. Iyengar, and A. Simon. 1999. Replicating Experiments Using Aggregate and Survey Data: The Case of Negative Advertising and Turnout. *American Political Science Review* 93(4): 901–9.

Arceneaux, N. and A.S. Weiss. 2010. Seems Stupid Until You Try It: Press Coverage of Twitter, 2006–09. *New Media & Society* 12(8): 1262–79.

Ashworth, S. and J.D. Clinton. 2007. Does Advertising Exposure Affect Turnout? *Quarterly Journal of Political Science* 2(1): 27–41.

Biddle, S. 2011. Senator Chuck Grassley is the Worst Twitter User in the United States of America. *Gizmodo.com*, http://gizmodo.com/5796338/senator-chuck-grassley-is-the-worst-twitter-user-in-the-united-states-of-america.

Bode, L., D. Lassen, Y.M. Kim, B. Sayre, D.V. Shah, E.F. Fowler, T. Ridout, and M. Franz. Forthcoming. *Politics as Usual? Campaign Broadcast and Social Messaging.* Online Information Review.

Cover, A.D. 1980. Contacting Congressional Constituents: Some Patterns of Perquisite Use. *American Journal of Political Science* 24(1):125–35.

Cover, A.D. and B.S. Brumberg. 1982. Baby Books and Ballots: The Impact of Congressional Mail on Constituent Opinion. *American Political Science Review* 76(2): 347–59.

D'Alessio, D. 1997. Use of the World Wide Web in the 1996 US Election. *Electoral Studies* 16(4): 489–500.

D'Alessio, D. 2000. Adoption of the World Wide Web by American Political Candidates, 1996–1998. *Journal of Broadcasting & Electronic Media* 44(4): 556–68.

Druckman, J.N., M.J. Kifer, and M. Parkin. 2007. The Technological Development of Congressional Candidate Web Sites: How and Why Candidates Use Web Innovations. *Social Science Computer Review* 25(4): 425–42.

Druckman, J.N., M.J. Kifer, and M. Parkin. 2009. Campaign Communications in US Congressional Elections. *American Political Science Review* 103(3): 343–66.

Druckman, J.N., M.J. Kifer, and M. Parkin. 2014. US Congressional Campaign Communications in an Internet Age. *Journal of Elections, Public Opinion, and Parties* 24(1): 20–44.

Duggan, M. and J. Brenner. 2013. The Demographics of Social Media Users—2012, http://pewinternet.org/Reports/2013/Social-media-users.aspx.

Evans, C.L. and W.J. Oleszek. 2003. The Internet Institutional Change. In J.A. Thurber and C.C. Campbell (eds.), *Congress and the Internet*. New York: Prentice Hall, pp. 99–123.

Fenno, R. 1978. *Home Style: House Members in Their Districts*. New York: Pearson.

Foot, K.A. and S.M. Schneider. 2006. *Web Campaigning*. Cambridge, MA: MIT Press.

Freedman, P., M. Franz, and K. Goldstein. 2004. Campaign Advertising and Democratic Citizenship. *American Journal of Political Science* 48(4): 723–41.

Gainous, J. and K.M. Wagner. 2014. *Tweeting to Power: The Social Media Revolution in American Politics*. New York: Oxford University Press.

Gilens, M. 2001. Political Ignorance and Collective Policy Preferences. *American Political Science Review* 95(2): 379–96.

Golbeck, J., J. Grimes, and A. Rogers. 2010. Twitter Use by the US Congress. *Journal of the American Society for Information Science and Technology* 61(8): 1612–21.

Goldstein, K. and P. Freedman. 2002. Campaign Advertising and Voter Turnout: New Evidence for a Stimulation Effect. *Journal of Politics* 64(3): 721–40.

Grimmer, J. 2013a. Appropriators Not Position Takers: The Distorting Effects of Electoral Incentives on Congressional Representation. *American Journal of Political Science* 57(3): 624–42.

Grimmer, J. 2013b. *Representational Style in Congress: What Legislators Say and Why It Matters*. New York: Cambridge University Press.

Grimmer, J. and B.M. Stewart. 2013. Text as Data: The Promise and Pitfalls of Content Analysis Methods for Political Texts. *Political Analysis* 21(3): 267–92.

Gulati, G.J. and C.B. Williams. 2010. *Communicating with Constituents in 140 Characters or Less: Twitter and the Diffusion of Technology Innovation in the United States Congress*. Paper presented at the Annual Meeting of the Midwest Political Science Association, Chicago, IL, April 22–25.

Herring, S.C. 2004. Slouching Toward the Ordinary: Current Trends in Computer-Mediated Communication. *New Media & Society* 6(1): 26–36.

Jurka, T.P., L. Collingwood, A.E. Boydstun, E. Grossman, and W. van Atteveldt. 2012. RTextTools: Automatic Text Classification via Supervised Learning. R package version 1.3.9, http://CRAN.R-project.org/package=RTextTools.

Kuklinski, J.H., P.J. Quirk, J. Jerit, D. Schweider, and R.F. Rich. 2000. Misinformation and the Currency of Democratic Citizenship. *Journal of Politics* 62(3): 790–816.

Lau, R.R. and G.M. Pomper. 2001. Effects of Negative Campaigning on Turnout in US Senate Elections, 1988–1998. *Journal of Politics* 63(3): 804–19.

Lau, R.R., L. Sigelman, and I.B. Rovner. 2007. The Effects of Negative Political Campaigns: A Meta-Analytic Reassessment. *Journal of Politics* 69(4): 1176–209.

Lassen, D. and A.R. Brown. 2011. Twitter: The Electoral Connection? *Social Science Computer Review* 29(4): 419–36.

Lewis, C. and B. Fabos. 2005. Instant Messaging, Literacies, and Social Identities. *Reading Research Quarterly* 40(4): 470–501.

Lipinski, D. 2004. *Congressional Communication: Content and Consequences.* Ann Arbor: University of Michigan Press.

Lipinski, D. and G. Neddenriep. 2004. Using "New" Media to Get "Old" Media Coverage: How Members of Congress Utilize Their Web Sites to Court Journalists. *The Harvard International Journal of Press/Politics* 9(1): 7–21.

Lupia, A. and M.D. McCubbins. 1998. *The Democratic Dilemma: Can Citizens Learn What They Need to Know?* New York: Cambridge University Press.

Marcus, G.E. and M.B. MacKuen. 1993. Anxiety, Enthusiasm, and the Vote: The Emotional Underpinnings of Learning and Involvement During Presidential Campaigns. *American Political Science Review* 87(3): 672–85.

Mayhew, D. 1974. *Congress: The Electoral Connection.* New Haven, CT: Yale University Press.

McMurray, J.C. 2013. Aggregating Information by Voting: The Wisdom of the Experts versus the Wisdom of the Masses. *Review of Economic Studies* 80 (1): 277–312.

Mutz, D. 2006. *Hearing the Other Side: Deliberative Versus Participatory Democracy.* New York: Cambridge University Press.

Parmalee, J.H. and S.L. Bichard. 2011. *Politics and the Twitter Revolution: How Tweets Influence the Relationship between Political Leaders and the Public.* Lanham, MD: Lexington Books.

Patterson, Thomas. 1993. *Out of Order.* New York: Knopf.

Ridout, T., D.V. Shah, K. Goldstein, and M. Franz. 2004. Evaluating Measures of Campaign Advertising Exposure on Political Learning. *Political Behavior* 26(3): 201–25.

Roston, M. and D. Willis. 2015. The State of Our Union: Tweeted. *New York Times,* January 21.

Sanchez, H. 2015. Chuck Grassley Talks Twitter Secrets. *Roll Call,* http://hoh.rollcall.com/chuck-grassley-keeps-killing-it-140-characters-at-a-time.

Slaby, M. 2014. *Digital Campaigning: 2012 and Beyond.* Talk given at Digital Divides, Washington, DC, https://smpa.gwu.edu/digital-campaigning-2012-and-beyond.

Stanton, J. 2015. How Twitter Ruined Twitter for Chuck Grassley. *BuzzFeed,* www.buzzfeed.com/johnstanton/how-twitter-ruined-twitter-for-chuck-grassley#.yapO8ym6qG.

Stromer-Galley, J. 2000. Online Interaction and Why Candidates Avoid It. *Journal of Communication* 50(4): 111–32.

Taylor, M. and M.L. Kent. 2004. Congressional Web Sites and Their Potential for Public Dialogue. *Atlantic Journal of Communication* 12(2): 59–76.

Van Dijk, J. 2012. *The Network Society.* New York: Sage.

Wattenberg, M.P., I. McAllister, and A. Salvanto. 2000. How Voting Is Like Taking an SAT Test: An Analysis of American Voter Rolloff. *American Politics Research* 28(2): 234–50.

Williams, C. and G.J. Gulati. 2009. Closing Gaps, Moving Hurdles: Candidate Web Site Communication in the 2006 Campaigns for Congress. In C. Panagopoulos (ed.), *Politicking Online: The Transformation of Election Campaign Communications*. New Brunswick, New Jersey: Rutgers University Press.

Williams, C. and G.J. Gulati. 2012. Social Networks in Political Campaigns: Facebook and the Congressional Elections of 2006 and 2008. *New Media & Society* 15(1): 52–71.

13

FROM A TWEET TO A SEAT

Twitter, Media Visibility, and Electoral Support

Reimar Zeh

The microblogging service Twitter has gained a certain notoriety in political communication. Partially inspired by its alleged role in 2012 presidential elections in the United States and Europe, and partially due to the scholarly attention it attracts. In regards to the overall use of Twitter, its importance might not seem fully justified (yet) since in terms of reach it is still a niche or elite media in most countries. Nevertheless, Twitter has certain advantages over other social media platforms such as Facebook. Communication on Twitter is public (Vaccari and Valeriani 2015, p. 1026), whereas on Facebook it is often restricted to defined subgroups of friends or followers (Vargo et al. 2014, p. 297). It is easy to use and for that matter easy to research. However, more importantly, research shows that actors involved in political communication prefer Twitter to Facebook (Parmelee 2014; Parmelee and Bichard 2012).

When politicians use Twitter, quickly the question is raised whether it does them any good. Yet measuring the impact or success of this new channel of communication is not an easy task. First, since its reach is limited, it might be argued, that there is no impact on the public at all. Second, there are different ways in operationalizing the impact. Some of the indicators are provided by Twitter itself, the number of followers, the number of favorited single tweets, or the amount or retweets or citations a single tweets accumulates. However, the number of followers, mentions or replies does not always translate into overall influence as Cha et al. (2010) have pointed out. Alternatively, one might look for indicators outside Twitter, such as visibility in the press or even the number of votes a party or politician receives in an election.

Media visibility is a key factor to electoral success (Hopmann et al. 2010). Parties and candidates direct a lot of their campaign efforts on generating (favorable) media coverage. The priming theory helps to explain how amount and nature

208   Reimar Zeh

of coverage influence the attitudes of the voters and therefore lay out how the coverage contributes to electoral success (Iyengar and Kinder 1987). Due to the complexity of modern democracies, it seems to be nearly impossible to systematically link specific media coverage to electoral support—there are too many media outlets and too many candidates or parties. Still, to get some insight how old and new media are related to each other in the context of an election, it is worth the effort. Small societies offer the advantage to study these relationships to a higher level of detail. This chapter sets out to examine the role of Twitter and other media outlets in the last national election of 2013 in the grand duchy of Luxembourg. Several features of the country make it an ideal petri dish for the analysis of specific aspects of political communication in a campaign context: First, the media system is comparably frugal with a limited number of newspapers and only one commercial television provider. Second, there is only a small number of candidates competing for (only) 60 seats in the national parliament. The electoral law is highly personalized, allowing voters to distribute their vote to individual candidates across party lists.

To analyze the role of old and new media on electoral support, this chapter draws on several data sources: The results of the last national election, the activity on Twitter of each candidate, his presence in a nationwide newspaper and the number of Google-hits each candidate name produced prior to the Election Day. The different data sources are amalgamated into a dataset that allows studying the impact of the different media outlets while controlling for structural factors such as incumbency and party affiliation.

Media Visibility in Election Campaigns

The effect on mere media visibility on voter choice has seldom been studied. In an experiment during the British General Election of 1997, Norris et al. (1999, pp. 141–2) found no significant evidence that media visibility altered the attitudes of the voters. On the other hand, there is scarce evidence for visibility effects in field studies. Semetko and Schönbach (1994) found in the German election of 1990 that media presence—regardless of its tone towards a party—fosters electoral support. Comparing Dutch and German data, Kleinnijenhuis et al. (2001, p. 356) argued that news coverage on the top party candidate increases the odds of that party winning, although party identifications remained the best predictor of individual voting intentions. Especially among undecided voters, mere media visibility effects on voting seem to occur (Hopmann et al. 2010, p. 400). These studies all have in common, that ideology or party orientation plays a crucial role in the electoral decision. In the Luxembourgish case, voters, already decided on a party can still choose between candidates on the ballot paper. In such a setting, media visibility might become an important cue in the decision-making process.

Early studies on the impact of newer media on voting behavior show that web presence is a significant predictor of electoral support (D'Alessio 1997; Gibson and McAllister 2006). Yet others argue, that websites reach mainly supporters of the parties or candidates that are already engaged. These seemingly contradictory findings can be reconciled: While websites and social media still "preach to the converted" (Norris 2003) at a first step, these converted preach to their peers, as Vissers (2009) suggested. Thus new media might initiate a two-step flow of communication. Political actors who refrain to use these new channels of communication do not activate this potential. Web-active candidates raise more funds, they attract more attention of the classic media, which in turn generates more favorable coverage and political fans and followers are actively persuading through interpersonal communication. The link between web activity and electoral support is usually measured on an aggregate level, on the level of candidates or parties. The use of these channels usually is studied on individual survey data. The seemingly contradictory results from the different levels mainly teach us to be cautious when interpreting correlations of aggregated data. Similar results are known from agenda-setting research where strong correlations of aggregated agendas are not always reproduced on the individual level of personal assessments issue priorities (Rössler 1997).

Newer research provides not uncontested evidence that content of social media sites (Boyd and Ellison 2007) allows the predicting of election results. Williams and Gulati (2008) demonstrated that the number of Facebook followers was a strong predictor of the state-wise share of vote in the presidential primaries in 2008, even if campaign spending and the presence in traditional media were controlled. Tumasjan et al. (2011) revealed that references to the six parties in parliament and their top candidates on Twitter before the national election in Germany in 2009 were a precise indicator for the election outcome. Franch (2012) predicted the outcome of the 2010 general election in the UK with a very narrow margin using aggregated social media data.

If social media, regardless of their sometimes limited proliferation in society reflect or even allow to forecast public opinion, we might assume, that presence or visibility in social media services is favorable to actors struggling for public support.

Vaccari (2015, p. 1038) pointed out that "[t]he number of users who followed politicians did not correlate with their levels of electoral support." On the other hand, Kruikemeier, Noort, and Vliegenthart (2013) demonstrated that even after multivariate controls, Twitter activity is related to electoral support. While at first these findings appear contradictory, they result from the different possibilities that the electoral systems provide. Italians vote for party lists while the Dutch system allows to give votes to actual candidates. The results from Kruikemeier et al. (2013) replicate Gibson and McAllister's (2006) results for Twitter activity. Nevertheless, party affiliation or incumbency proved to be more influential on the number of votes the candidates received than Twitter activity. Furthermore, the visibility in classic media had a stronger impact than the number of followers on Twitter (Kruikemeier et al. 2013, p. 13).

Users of online political information are especially keen on forms of two-way communication. Farnsworth and Owen (2004) highlighted the important role of email contact as a motive to use candidate websites. The same holds true for Twitter users, the possibility of two-way communication seems to be its major asset (Parmelee and Bichard 2012, p. 65). Again Kruikemeier et al. (2013, p. 13) show that interactivity is rewarded by the voters. While politicians seldom engage into two-way interactions with their voters, Congressional representatives used Twitter to mainly disseminate information about themselves and their policies, only in about 7 percent of the posts on Twitter did they respond to other users (Golbeck et al. 2010, p. 1617). German parties and top candidates used Twitter in the 2013 election campaign likewise more as an additional channel to spread information rather than to interact (Dusch et al. 2014). Burgess and Bruns (2012) pointed out that Twitter is especially useful to spread information that is not found on mainstream media. With regard to the media environment of Luxembourg, this feature should especially attract the non-established parties or candidates outside the party establishment.

Luxembourg—A Special Place?

Apart from its size, Luxembourg has some very distinct characteristics. To begin with, the media system is unique. Luxembourg is one of the only countries with no public television. Instead, the privately owned commercial station RTL is obliged to provide a basic public service of information and cultural programming; in turn, the station is freed form licensing fees (Barth and Hemmen 2008). Not surprisingly, the station enjoys an audience share of nearly 50 percent among Luxembourgers (IP Network 2014). Yet, since the 1990s, a public service FM-radio station was introduced with a clear mission to promote socio-cultural aspects of Luxembourgish life. Nevertheless a rich bouquet of international television broadcasters from the neighboring countries Belgium, France, and Germany and other EU member states are accessible to Luxembourg households through cable or satellite.

The absence on direct competition on the television market is in contrast to a diverse press landscape given the small size of the country. Furthermore, the press shows a high degree of political parallelism. Six daily newspapers are currently published on the Luxembourg market, four of them having clear leanings to political parties. The market leader, *Luxemburger Wort* is co-owned by the archdiocese and therefore close to the Conservative Party CSV. The *Tageblatt* is co-owned by trade unions with a clearly leaning to the workers' party. The *Journal* leans to the Liberal Party whereas the Communist Party owns the *Zeitung vum letzebuerger Vollek*. Articles are usually published in all three official languages, Luxembourgish,

French and German, with a certain dominance of German. Adding to that, the state heavily subsidizes the press either through tax breaks or through direct transfer. These transfers are justified by the importance of the press for democracy. All newspapers that freely distribute and employ more than five journalists receive this state aid. Compared to larger countries, journalists have multiple ties to the political and economic elite of the country. In that sense they could be considered as part of the political-economical elite (Barth and Hemmen 2008, p. 215).

Media use and attitudes towards media reflect the uniqueness of the Luxembourgish situation. In 2009, respondents to a national opinion poll named the press the most important source of information (30 percent) followed by television (27 percent), while the Internet was named only by 4 percent (Dumont et al. 2011, p. 100). Needless to say that newer surveys report a rising importance of the Internet as a source of political information. The latest Eurobarometer survey measuring media use reports high levels of usage for all media channels for respondents from Luxembourg. Likewise, trust in classic media is comparably high (European Commission 2013). These studies reflect the dominance of the press in the country. The internet in general and social media specifically are, more than elsewhere, an additional path for basically the same information. In a media environment that is characterized by a high degree of political parallelism, the desire of political actors to bypass the journalistic gatekeepers might be smaller compared to countries with a more independent press.

Additionally, the political system bears some exceptional features. Since the Second World War coalition governments always ruled the country. Besides the legislative period from 1974 to 1979, the Christian Democrats provided the prime minister, teaming up either with either the liberal or the social-democratic party. The necessity to form coalitions is associated with low ideological distance between the three main parties. Therefore, and due to the economic prosperity, extremist parties had little room to develop, characterizing Luxembourg as a "consensus-democracy" (Dumont et al. 2008, p. 155). The three parties still receive about 73 percent of the popular vote.

The electoral system provides an additional hurdle for small parties. Furthermore, it weakens the role of the parties by leaving it to the voters which candidates from a party list actually get seats in the parliament. The country is divided into four constituencies: North, East, Center (around the capital), and the South. In each constituency, a number of seats are elected according to the relative population size. The system technically disadvantages small parties especially in the smaller constituencies (North and East) with only nine and seven seats respectively on the ballot.

Preferential vote allows voting for candidates from different parties (panachage). Since every Luxembourger between 18 and 75 resident in the country is required to vote, the turnout is very high, only a small number of blank or invalid ballots are cast. A growing portion of votes are cast individually, meaning that that the voters actually assign personalized votes even across parties lists. In 20 years, from 1989 to 2009 the percentage of voters who simply voted for one party list dropped significantly from 68 percent to 52 percent in 2009. Likewise, the proportion of votes split between different parties rose from 18 percent to 37 percent (Dumont et al. 2008, p. 159, 2011, p. 168). In other words, in 2009 48 percent of the voters directly and actively chose specific candidates from the ballot list. While the results for split ballot voting have not been published yet for 2013, there is reason to believe, that the importance of the candidates did not diminish. To some extent the tendency to cast personalized votes can be explained by the small distance between voters and candidates. Second, developments such as de-alignment and growing personalized campaigning magnify the change. Adding to that, the party list on the ballot does not reflect the party hierarchy, but simply lists the candidates in alphabetical order, except for the candidate who heads the party list in his/her district.

Data and Research Questions

The dataset for this study was melded from four different sources, where the single candidate constituted the unit of analysis. The data for the electoral support was collected from a government website (www.elections.public.lu). The ballot results for each candidate were collected by district. The official results report how many votes each candidate received. Second, for each party in a district, the number of total votes, votes for the party list and personalized votes are reported. When a voter just selects a list, each candidate from that party gets one vote. The number of personalized votes (*suffrages nominatifs*) can be easily calculated as a rough indicator for the individual electoral support of a candidate. Since the parties have regional strongholds, the district serves as an additional control variable. For example, the socialist party is traditionally strong in the south of Luxembourg, which was once a European center of mining and steel-industry. Except for the front-runners, the candidates are listed in alphabetical order. Still, list-effects might also occur, and therefore the position on the list serves as a further control together with the party, gender, and incumbency in the previous legislative session.

   To test the impact of old and new media on electoral support, three different sources were tapped for data. First all candidates were looked up in a Nexis-like press database for one leading daily newspaper—the *Tageblatt*. The number of articles for each candidate published prior to Election Day entered the dataset as a proxy for media visibility, since other newspapers, including the market leader *Luxemburger Wort*, offered no archive of the printed content. Second, all candidate names with the corresponding party name were searched on Google. The search was restricted to hosts from ".lu" and for the timespan of the previous legislative session. This was done so that that Luxembourgish politicians who are highly visible on the European level—like the former prime minister Jean-Claude Juncker or minister of foreign affairs Jean Asselborn—would not distort the results. Third, for all 540 candidates, the Twitter site was checked to see whether or not they had

From a Tweet to a Seat **213**

an account before October 20, 2013—Election Day. In the case of ambiguous names, the account was further scrutinized for references to the candidate's party or to Luxembourg politics in general. Twitter accounts that had no connection to politics were not registered. For each account, we added the metadata, which the analysis-platform Twitonomy usually provides, to the dataset. Again, the cutoff date was October 20, 2013.

The data allow us to answer the following research questions:

RQ1: Does media visibility translate to electoral support? Adding to that, we will analyze which channel press, Internet, or social media have the highest impact on the vote.

RQ2: Given the different access to traditional media, are there differences between the parties concerning the impact of internet visibility and Twitter presence?

RQ3: Since Twitter is potentially an interactive medium, does interactivity foster electoral support? Are there certain communicative styles that can be measured through the metadata that help to gain votes?

Results

The general election in 2013 was a snap election after Juncker, prime minister since 1995, lost a vote of no confidence caused by a scandal concerning the intelligence service. Only for the second time in post-war history, the election pushed the ruling Christian democrats (CSV) out of the government. Prime minister Juncker was replaced by the Liberal Party leader Xavier Bettel, who now heads a three-party coalition of liberals (DP), Social democrats (LSAP), and Greens. Of the competing nine parties, six managed to win seats in the parliament. Table 13.1 summarizes the outcome of the election in study and reports the Twitter activity among the candidates. Only four parties had candidates using Twitter substantially.

While an average of 10 percent of the candidates had Twitter accounts, the actual use varied even more. Politicians from the Green Party and from the Pirate Party used Twitter extensively, while other politicians only sporadically tweeted.

Clearly, the "younger" parties use Twitter more frequently, as Table 13.2 demonstrates: The internet-savvy Pirates and the Greens not only tweet more often, but they also adopt a dialogue-oriented style by mentioning other users more frequently or even replying to tweets of other users. Adding to that, hashtags and links are often used to ease the access of the tweets and to provide additional information that exceeds the 140-character limit.

In order to find answers to RQ1, we calculated a general linear model to estimate the number of personalized votes (weighted by the size of the district) for each candidate. Gender, region, party-affiliation, incumbency and the place on the list are entered as controls into the model. Media visibility, number of hits in Google and Twitter activity constitute the explanatory variables.

214 Reimar Zeh

TABLE 13.1 Election result and dataset

Party name	Description	Seats gained	Popular vote in %	Female candidates in %	Candidates with Twitter accounts in %	N of candidates
ADR	Conservative Protest Party	3	6.6	38	5	60
CSV	Christian Democratic Party	23	33.7	32	10	60
DP	Liberal Party	13	18.3	25	17	60
Déi Gréng	Green Party	6	10.1	43	25	60
KPL	Communist Party	0	1.6	33	0	60
Déi Lénk	Left Party	2	4.9	47	5	60
LSAP	Social Democrat Party	13	20.3	27	27	60
PID	Split-off of the ADR	0	1.5	40	7	60
Piratepartei	Pirate Party	0	2.9	23	28	60

Source of election results: Gouvernement du Grand-Duché de Luxembourg (2014).

TABLE 13.2 Twitter activity by party affiliation

Party	Tweets	Followers	Mentions	Replies	Links	Hashtags	N of candidates
ADR	19.7	52.7	0.7	9.0	1.0	0.7	3
CSV	46.0	443.2	8.2	34.2	2.7	2.0	6
DP	201.9	1363.7	113.3	20.3	25.7	72.3	9
Déi Gréng	725.3	656.3	489.0	96.8	174.8	261.1	15
KPL	—	—	—	—	—	—	n/a
Déi Lénk	236.7	238.3	105.7	168.3	3.0	54.3	3
LSAP	134.7	425.1	63.2	40.1	10.9	32.9	16
PID	29.0	13.7	10.7	15.3	0.0	1.3	3
Piratepartei	1112.9	347.3	670.3	108.1	128.2	361.0	17

Table 13.3 summarizes the results for the first model. The control variables account for a considerable amount of the variance. Although we adjusted the dependent variable for the varying size of the districts, the region remains a significant predictor. Regional differences in party support are substantial. Most importantly, and as expected, the party of the candidate is the most important cue for the voting decision. Holding a seat in parliament or the government also helps to accumulate votes. A high place on the list also increases the number of votes, which mainly mirrors that the top candidates head the list. Men receive slightly more votes than women do, but the gender effect disappears in

TABLE 13.3 Generalized linear model: Explaining electoral support for parliamentary candidates

	F	$Part.\ \eta^2$	B	
Circumscription of the candidate[§]	32.1	0.16***		
Party of the candidate[§]	41.9	0.39***		
Incumbency	59.2	0.10	139.8***	
pos. on List	38.4	0.07	−98.5***	
Gender	1.4	0.00	11.5	n.s.
Google hits	32.5	0.06	0.1***	
Media visibility	170.1	0.25	0.8***	
Twitter activity	2.7	0.01	23.2	n.s.
N	540			
Adj. R^2	0.78***			

§ Factors

*** $p < 0.001$.

a multivariate model. Above all, being mentioned in the press as well as presence in the (Luxembourgish) Internet—as measured through hits in a Google search—increased votes. Candidates who maintain a Twitter account receive twice as many votes, as those who do not (t = 2.94; p = 0.003; n = 540), yet the effect fails to be significant after applying multivariate controls. While the impact of media prominence is plausible, the finding for the Google hits need some additional explanation. Candidates for the Luxembourgish parliament often hold offices in their parish or in the party organization. They therefore appear on party websites and websites of the cities and local councils. Given the small if not invisible blogosphere and the limited number of online news outlets, Google hits may reflect the importance of the candidate in the political system, maybe even more than the visibility in the press, since the newspapers do not cover the proceedings of every local council in great detail.

The explanatory power of media prominence also reflects the easy access the traditional parties have to the press. Newer and smaller parties cannot rely as much on "automatic" coverage for their candidates and might therefore look for alternative pathways that, in Luxembourg as well as elsewhere, are offered by the Internet and social media. We therefore calculated the models again, but separately for the parties. In the view of the low Twitter activity of some parties, we constrain the analysis to parties in which at least 6 of the 60 (10 percent) candidates use Twitter. By estimating the sources of electoral support separately for each party, we exclude the influence of party preference from the model. Thus, the models show the influence on voting behavior that come after the choice for an ideological position has been made.

216 Reimar Zeh

TABLE 13.4 Generalized linear model: Electoral support by parties

	CSV	DP	Gréng	LSAP	Pirate
	Part. η^2	Part. η^2	Part. η^2	Part. η^2	Part. η^2
Circumscription[§]	0.59★★★	0.46★★★	0.32★★★	0.23★★	0.26★★
Incumbency	0.16★★	n.s.	0.18★★	n.s.	n.a.
Pos. on list	0.19★★	0.09★	0.07★	0.15★★	0.36★★★
Gender	n.s.	n.s.		n.s.	
Google hits	0.13★	n.s.	n.s.	n.s.	n.s.
Media visibility	n.s.	0.35★★★	n.s.	0.19★★	0.46★★★
Twitter activity	n.s.	n.s.	0.08★	n.s.	0.12★★
N	60	60	60	60	60
Adj. R^2	0.79★★★	0.77★★★	0.72★★★	0.63★★★	0.66★★★

§ Factors

★★★ $p < 0.001$; ★★ $p < 0.01$; ★ $p < 0.05$.

Turning to RQ2, the models reveal differences for the candidates from different parties. The model calculated for the Christian Democratic Party (CSV) has the best fit, which mainly comes from structural influences. In contrast to our expectations, Google—but not media visibility—yields additional explanatory power. Since the CSV in its long years in power has gained nearly hegemonic status (Dumont et al. 2008), probably all 60 candidates enjoy regular coverage, leading to little variance in this independent variable. The electoral support for candidates from the other two traditional parties (DP and LSAP) is chiefly explained by presence in the traditional media, while candidates from the Greens and the Pirates gain votes from Twitter activity after rigorous multivariate control. Table 13.4 also shows that for four of the five parties in question, online visibility has no independent influence on the candidate results. The number of Google hits and the number of newspaper articles for each candidate is correlated. Multicollinearity is not an issue for the model of the entire sample but it reaches problematic levels (VIF > 2) in the split-models for the CSV and the Green candidates.

The high impact of press coverage for the Pirate Party demands further explanation. Most of their candidates were not covered by the press, but a few raised their voices (and were heard) in the context of the NSA scandal revealed by Edward Snowden. Their assumed expertise in the field of IT security in the context of a snap election called because of the domestic intelligence scandal gave them news value. This newsworthiness helped specific Pirate candidates who received media coverage, but did not increase the total votes that the party accumulated.

It seems to be common knowledge that those candidates who engage in two-way communications profit (more) from their Internet appearance or social media commitment. In RQ3, we ask whether this is corroborated in the Luxembourgish case under study. Again, we limit the scope to the candidates

From a Tweet to a Seat **217**

from the five parties with significant Twitter activity. Indicators that reflect to a certain extent communicative styles are now included in the models: The overall number of published tweets, the frequency of "mentions" and "replies" measure to a limited degree the interactivity on Twitter. Although we do not know with whom they engage in dialogue—voters or other politicians. Using hashtags and links are proxies for the provision of information in tweets. Hashtags are used to organize discussions on Twitter. A tweet that uses a certain, established hashtag is accessible to those following the discussion. Links in Twitter often provide additional information from other websites.

As Table 13.5 demonstrates, communicative style matters for candidates more active on Twitter. We do not find effects for the two former coalition partners CSV and LSAP. Our data shows that candidates from these parties are highly visible and do not have much to gain from tweeting. In this regard, the Liberals seem to be more modern than the other established parties. Their voters embrace additional information through Twitter. Giving them links brings the Liberals some additional votes. The same holds true for candidates from the Green Party, except that the impact of tweets with links is much stronger. Their voters reward the usage of links. Green voters as well as voters of the Pirate Party welcome the use of hashtags, which makes it easier to follow discussions around a certain topic or issue.

Table 13.5 also suggests that the Pirates make the most of Twitter by engaging in two-way communication. Their reply rate reaches only an average of 10 percent similar to the reply rate for the Green candidates. Given that replies exert an independent influence on their votes, this indicates that Pirates are actually talking to their voters, whereas discussion (measured by replies and mentions) by Greens and Liberals are not rewarded. One explanation for this difference may be that the dialogue of older parties stays in the elite sphere among other politicians or journalists rather than engaging the voters themselves.

Conclusion and Discussion

Our data connects voter behavior, candidate activity and journalistic output. Although aggregated on the level of the single candidate, the results are based on actual votes and not voting intentions as most survey-based studies are. Problems of surveys research like social desirability, false opinions or non-responses do not distort our results. Having said that, aggregate data allows limited inferences about individual behavior. The risk of falling for an ecological fallacy is apparent. The unique setup provided by the specific situation found in the Luxembourg case allows us to gain valuable insights on the role of media and new media in elections. The Luxembourgish voting system enables us to look at cues relevant for voting decisions. In particular, it enables us to look at these cues separately from issues and political ideology.

218 Reimar Zeh

TABLE 13.5 Generalized linear model: Electoral support through communicative styles

	CSV	DP	Gréng	LSAP	Pirate
	Part. η^2	Part. η^2	Part. η^2	Part. η^2	Part. η^2
Circumscription[§]	0.28★★	0.57★★★	0.39★★★	0.22★★	0.30★★★
Incumbency	0.32★★★	0.55★★★	0.53★★★	0.34★★★	n/a
Pos. on list	0.14★★	0.20★★	0.10★	0.16★★	0.33★★★
Gender	n.s.	n.s.	n.s.	n.s.	n.s.
Mentions	n.s.	n.s.	n.s.	n.s.	n.s.
Replies	n.s.	n.s.	n.s.	n.s.	0.37★★★
Links	n.s.	0.07★	0.32★★★	n.s.	n.s.
Hashtags	n.s.	n.s.	0.08★	n.s.	0.17★★
N	60	60	60	60	60
Adj. R^2	0.47★★★	0.90★★★	0.75★★★	0.48★★★	0.70★★★

§ Factors

★★★ $p < 0.001$; ★★ $p < 0.01$; ★ $p < 0.05$.

First, our results show that media matters for choosing which candidate to vote for on a party list, when the order of the list is not a sufficient cue. The equation is simple—candidates more visible in the media (i.e., in the newspaper we analyzed) and with a bigger presence in the Luxembourgish cyberspace receive more votes. Presumably the effect occurs because voters look for names they know on the ballot list and do not simply follow alphabetical order. We have to admit, there is a hitch to this result. We were only able to analyze the aggregated candidate presence in one newspaper, which is the second largest in terms of circulation. Adding to that, the daily press shows a high degree of partisanship. We argue that this will affect the tone but not the quantity of the coverage and therefore this shortcoming poses just a small threat to our argument.

The influence of the Internet visibility on voting might be more particular to the Luxembourgish case. As mentioned earlier, websites with the country domain ".lu" are mostly official websites of state or political institutions as well as the websites of the few media outlets. Therefore, the number of Google hits a candidate name attracts simply reflects his or her local prominence—something that is not easy to generalize across borders.

Second, our data shows that the activity of Luxembourgish parliamentary candidates on Twitter paid off in terms of electoral support. While the three established parties—CSV, LSAP, DP—and the Communist Party enjoy the partisanship of the daily press, Greens and Pirates lack this support. Subsequently they developed more activity on social media and especially on Twitter. The voters rewarded that. This effect was most pronounced for the most active party on Twitter—the Pirates.

From a Tweet to a Seat **219**

Third, the communicative style that the Pirate Party candidates employed paid off in votes. Those candidates engaging more actively in two-way communication or, put simpler, those who replied to tweets more often, gained more electoral support. Nevertheless, this did not translate to seats in the parliament, which might be a broad hint that the political structures still matter in electoral success.

We tacitly assumed a direct link between Twitter activity and electoral support in this chapter. But our data does not fully justify this assumption. Things might be a bit more complicated. We have no resilient data on Twitter use among the Luxembourgish population. While we can well assume a high penetration of the Internet in this society in general, Twitter might still be a niche media for the elite. Thus these findings need further explanation. If Twitter is not widely used among the electorate, how can it have such an effect on the election outcome? First, we might assume an indirect effect: Journalists use Twitter extensively and cover tweeting politicians more and with a more positive tone. Second, and more importantly, Twitter is understood as an integral part of professional political communication. It is a proxy for good campaigning and therefore journalists measure the degree to which a candidate does it well.

While this might seem plausible for the traditional and established parties and to a certain extent for the Green Party, this line of thinking fails to explain the results for the Pirates. They have limited access to the mainstream media and are able to connect to their voters over the internet and Twitter. By engaging in a dialogue, they mobilize their supporters.

While one might argue that these results are not particularly novel, they corroborate the findings of Kruikemeier, Noort, and Vliegenthart (2013) in a different and unique media environment. The high degree of political parallelism in Luxembourg serves as a bigger obstacle for new parties than the neglect by more unaffiliated mainstream journalists in larger societies. Twitter has put a big dent in that obstacle.

This study adds support to the notion that media presence and especially presence in social media translates into votes. More evidence from different political systems is needed to strengthen this conclusion. Furthermore, future research should not only focus on studying the relevance of the proliferating different social media channels, but it should also focus on shedding more light on the reasons for the apparent influence of mere visibility in social media on voting behavior and political attitudes.

References

Barth, C. and M. Hemmen. 2008. Medien und Medienpolitik. In W. Lorig and M. Hirsch (eds.), *Das Politische System Luxemburgs: Eine Einführung*. Wiesbaden: VS Verl. für Sozialwiss. 208–28.

Boyd, D.M. and N.B. Ellison. 2007. Social Network Sites: Definition, History, and Scholarship. *Journal of Computer-Mediated Communication* 13: 210–30.

220 Reimar Zeh

Burgess, J.E. and A. Bruns. 2012. (Not) the Twitter Election: The Dynamics of the #ausvotes Conversation in Relation to the Australian Media Ecology. *Journalism Practice* 6: 384–402.

Cha, M., H. Haddadi, F. Benevenuto, and K.P. Gummadi. 2010. *Measuring User Influence in Twitter: The Million Follower Fallacy*. Paper presented at the Proceedings of the Fourth International AAAI Conference on Weblogs and Social Media, Washington, DC, May 23–26, www.aaai.org/ocs/index.php/ICWSM/ICWSM10 SM/ICWSM10/paper/view/1538.

D'Alessio, D. 1997. Use of the World Wide Web in the 1996 US Election. *Electoral Studies* 16: 489–500.

Dumont, P., F. Fehlen, and P. Poirier. 2008. Parteiensystem, politische Parteien und Wahlen. In W. Lorig and M. Hirsch (eds.), *Das politische System Luxemburgs*. Wiesbaden: VS Verlag für Sozialwiss. 155–89.

Dumont, P., R. Kies, A.P. Spreitzer, M. Bozinis, and P. Poirier. 2011. *Les élections législatives et européennes de 2009 au Grand-Duché de Luxembourg. Rapport élaboré pour la Chambre des Députés*. Luxembourg: Service Central des Imprimés de l'Etat.

Dusch, A., S. Gerbig, M. Lake, S. Lorenz, F. Pfaffenberger, and U. Schulze. 2014. Post, Reply, Retweet—Einsatz und Resonanz von Twitter im Bundestagswahlkampf 2013. In C. Holtz-Bacha (ed.), *Die Massenmedien im Wahlkampf*. Wiesbaden: Springer Fachmedien, 275–94.

European Commission. 2013. *Die Mediennutzung in der Europäischen Union*. Standard Eurobarometer 80. Brussels: European Commission.

Farnsworth, S. J., and D. Owen. 2004. "Internet Use and the 2000 Presidential Election." *Electoral Studies* 23: 415–29.

Franch, F. 2012. (Wisdom of the Crowds)^2: 2010 UK Election Prediction with Social Media. *Journal of Information Technology & Politics* 10(1): 57–71.

Gibson, R.K. and I. McAllister. 2006. Does Cyber-campaigning Win Votes? Online Communication in the 2004 Australian Election. *Journal of Elections, Public Opinion and Parties* 16:243–63.

Golbeck, J., J.M. Grimes, and A. Rogers. 2010. Twitter Use by the US Congress. *Journal of the American Society for Information Science and Technology* 61: 1612–21.

Gouvernement du Grand-Duché de Luxembourg. 2014. Elections législatives 2013, www.elections.public.lu/fr/elections-legislatives/2013/index.html.

Hopmann, D.N., R. Vliegenthart, C. de Vreese, and E. Albæk. 2010. Effects of Election News Coverage: How Visibility and Tone Influence Party Choice. *Political Communication* 27: 389–405.

IP Network. 2014. *Television International Key Facts 2014*. Luxembourg: RTL-Group.

Iyengar, S. and D.R. Kinder. 1987. *News that Matters. Television and American Opinion*. University of Chicago Press.

Kleinnijenhuis, J., M. Maurer, H.M. Kepplinger, and D. Oegema. 2001. Issues and Personalities in German and Dutch Television News. *European Journal of Communication* 16: 337–59.

Kruikemeier, S., G.V. Noort, and R. Vliegenthart. 2013. *The Relationship Between Campaigning on Twitter and Electoral Support: Present or Absent?* Paper presented at the Annual Conference of the International Communication Association, London, June 17–21.

Norris, P. 2003. Preaching to the Converted? Pluralism, Participation and Party Websites. *Party Politics* 9: 21–45.

Norris, P., J. Curtice, D. Sanders, M. Scammell, and H.A. Semetko. 1999. *On Message: Communicating the Campaign*. London: Sage.

Parmelee, J.H. 2014. The Agenda-Building Function of Political Tweets. *New Media & Society* 16: 434–50.

Parmelee, J.H. and S.L. Bichard. 2012. *Politics and the Twitter Revolution: How Tweets Influence the Relationship between Political Leaders and the Public*. Lanham, MD: Lexington Books.

Rössler, P. 1997. *Agenda-Setting. Theoretische Annahmen und empirische Evidenzen einer Medienwirkungshypothese*. Opladen: Westdeutscher Verlag.

Semetko, H.A. and K. Schönbach. 1994. *Germany's "Unity Election": Voters and the Media*. Cresskill, NJ: Hampton Press.

Tumasjan, A., R.O. Sprenger, P.G. Sandner, and I.M. Welpe. 2011. Election Forecasts with Twitter: How 140 Characters Reflect the Political Landscape. *Social Science Computer Review* 29: 402–18.

Vaccari, C., and A. Valeriani. 2015. Follow the Leader! Direct and Indirect Flows of Political Communication during the 2013 Italian General Election Campaign. *New Media & Society*: 1025–43.

Vargo, C.J., L. Guo, M. McCombs, and D.L. Shaw. 2014. Network Issue Agendas on Twitter during the 2012 US Presidential Election. *Journal of Communication* 64: 296–316.

Vissers, S. 2009. *From Preaching to the Converted to Preaching through the Converted*. Paper presented at the ECPR Joint Sessions of Workshops, Lisbon, April 14–19.

Williams, C. and J. Gulati. 2008. *What Is a Social Network Worth? Facebook and Vote Share in the 2008 Presidential Primaries*. Paper presented at the Annual meeting of the American Political Science Association, Boston, MA, August 28–31.

CONCLUSION

Richard Davis

Even though but a decade old, Twitter already has become an important electoral communication tool between candidates/parties and their specific constituencies. As this volume has explained, Twitter now affects various facets of electoral campaigns. And it has done so on a global scale encompassing a panoply of political and media systems.

This book has demonstrated that Twitter matters in elections. Across the globe, elections are being impacted by this new form of communication between electoral players—candidate organizations, political parties, journalists, and voters. Players are adapting to Twitter in order to facilitate communication with other players and, in the case of candidates and party organizations, seeking ultimately to affect electoral outcomes. Let's review these various effects of Twitter.

Journalists, Traditional Media, and Twitter

Traditional journalists (newspapers, radio, and television) held the established role in mass electoral communication through the twentieth century. However, journalists are adapting to a digital age, including Twitter's entrance into the realm of candidate communication. As we learned from Peter Hamby (Chapter 1) as well as Logan Molyneux et al. (Chapter 3), journalists covering elections in the United States are increasingly using Twitter to keep abreast of campaign developments. Yet, the adoption of Twitter as a journalistic tool also affects journalism itself. Twitter is impacting the newsgathering and reporting processes. It is accelerating the pace of news generation (since tweets can be nearly instantaneous), leading journalists to skirt the boundaries of objectivity with retweets and commentary that emphasize analysis and offer opportunities for partisanship, and creating a

Conclusion **223**

personal brand for journalists with audiences that gives the impression of breaking down the wall between journalists and audiences.

Yet, journalists are resisting the elements of Twitter's style that would overturn journalistic standards. Journalists are holding on to their long-held practices of shunning partisanship. Of course, that effort becomes more difficult on a platform that thrives on partisanship. Journalists strive to maintain the image of objectivity by avoiding partisan tweets or even judgments about what they retweet. And they are retaining a distance from audiences by not being transparent about their views and only rarely retweeting the views of the general public.

Journalists also are not surrendering control over their own content. Twitter is not setting media agendas. That may be a surprise given the extent of journalistic usage of Twitter. However, as Christina Holtz-Bacha and Reimar Zeh point out in Chapter 2, Twitter simply is not having the impact on the traditional media agenda that might be predicted.

Does that mean Twitter possesses only a limited effect on media? According to Evelien D'heer and Pieter Verdegem's study of Belgium's European Union elections in Chapter 4, Twitter may be contributing to a current trend in European media. They analyzed a transnational media environment in Belgium where the media system is both fragmented by region and language and set in the midst of a European media context. They found that, while Belgium's traditional media adhered to the nation's specific regional and language divides, Twitter did not necessarily do so. Hence, they conclude that Twitter holds the potential to contribute to the further "Europeanization" of political communication through election coverage that transcends cultural/regional/linguistic boundaries.

Mass Participation

One of the promises for the Internet, and each communication platform connected to it, has been the potential for facilitating greater mass political participation. The extent to which that promise has been fulfilled, or may yet be fulfilled, has been the subject of intense debate (Margolis et al. 1997; Davis 1998; Bimber 1999; Elin and Davis 2002; Zukin et al. 2006; Papacharissi 2010). The emergence of Twitter's role poses that same question today (Parmelee and Bichard 2012; Park 2013; Gainous and Wagner 2014; Bode and Dalrymple 2014).

Does Twitter actually stimulate political participation? Our book does not answer that question directly, but we do ask whether those using Twitter actually attempt to do so. Chapter 5 by Heather Evans addressed whether Twitter content is intended to motivate political involvement. She found that candidates for US Congress sometimes do use Twitter to encourage civic engagement by tweet recipients. And, not surprisingly, competitiveness increases the volume of messages about participation as candidates seek to mobilize supporters to affect electoral

224 Richard Davis

outcomes in their favor. However, Evans concluded that such messages were not as frequent as they might be, suggesting that candidates could do more to facilitate electoral participation via Twitter.

Candidate and Party Use of Twitter

Several chapters have demonstrated Twitter's usage by candidates and political parties seeking to incorporate this new communication venue into their electoral strategies. David Lassen and Leticia Bode (Chapter 12) established that members of the US Congress are gradually including Twitter into their electoral toolboxes. They do so because Twitter is a relatively inexpensive form of communication that allows them to disseminate their messages readily to followers. In doing so, they are accepting Twitter's particularities, but they are still utilizing Twitter in a form similar to other types of constituent communication. That suggests that the purpose of candidate communication is not simply to move to a new platform for novelty or to signal technological adaptability. Instead, they are seeking another venue for the unidirectional communication they need in order to achieve re-election goals. In other words, regardless of the form of the medium, it is still employed for a basic purpose—communication to effect electoral victory.

Even though Twitter is a new tool for electioneering, candidates are still exploring how best to use the medium for their own purposes. Part of that challenge is integrating Twitter into other media messages. A cohesive media strategy is designed to reinforce campaign messages across platforms rather than communicate disparate messages depending on the type of media. Nevertheless, the actual implementation of this tactic is not easy. Kate Kenski and Bethany Conway (Chapter 7) showed that even presidential campaigns are finding it difficult to impose message discipline through Twitter. The repetition of a message, which is a critical component of advertising, was missing from the two presidential campaigns. While the Obama campaign was more consistent in its messaging, neither campaign was as disciplined in its Twitter messaging as might be expected from a presidential campaign.

Blogs, Facebook, Twitter, and other social media forums emphasize the personal because they are created primarily by individuals and are expected to reflect individual approaches. In systems dominated by candidate-centered campaigns, such personalization fits neatly into the existing political system emphases. But what about party-centered systems? Is Twitter largely unused or differently used in such settings? Or does Twitter reorient the party emphasis towards individual candidates? In Chaper 11, Tamara Small examined Canada, which is a party-oriented electoral system where Twitter has been actively used in electoral settings. She found that Canadian party leaders did establish their own presence on Twitter, which would suggest the influence of personalization common in candidate-centered systems. However, she also discovered little difference between

Conclusion **225**

the party feeds and the leader feeds, suggesting that there was little personalization separate from the party message. In other words, in a party-based system, the existence of Twitter had not displaced the parties or undermined the party system.

Of course, the bottom line for Twitter use by candidates and parties is the effect on electoral outcomes. Does Twitter actually affect who wins? Reimar Zeh (Chapter 13) found that, in Luxembourg, the Pirate Party, through its use of Twitter, was able to overcome the partisan support granted other major parties in traditional media. Although shunned by the traditional media, the party won votes through a Twitter-oriented campaign. His research should prompt more studies of the actual impact of candidate and party Twitter use on electoral outcomes.

Another promise of the Internet, and then social media, was a reduction of the emotional distance between candidates and voters. With the Internet, so some predicted, candidates and voters could and would interact directly, leading to new levels of personal engagement. Finally, the unidirectional nature of mediated campaign communication would be replaced by greater interactivity.

However, from the study by Sara Bentivegna and Rita Marchetti (Chapter 8), we learn such a promise remains empty. They concluded that Italian candidates in the European elections preferred the broadcast model of communications, i.e., the traditional mode of unidirection, rather than interactivity. However, newer parties were more likely to challenge the traditional communication modes and seek to communicate more personally with voters. Similarly, Tamara Small (Chapter 11) learned that, in Canada, the broadcast model also prevailed in party tweets.

Nor did interactivity necessarily translate into political power. Reimar Zeh's study of Luxembourg parties found that, even though the small and new Pirate Party gained votes through its social media-oriented campaign, it did not gain seats in parliament. In other words, political structures still matter.

That doesn't mean that the Twitter audience is necessarily passive in electoral campaigning. However, that activity may not be in the form of interaction with a candidate. In the United States, some Twitter users are acting to upset Twitter campaigns by elites, particularly candidate campaigns. As Joel Penney (Chapter 10) found, Twitter has allowed for some form of participatory politics. It may not be in the form of interactivity with a candidate. But it can occur through "meme warriors" or individuals who participate independently in promoting a candidate online. One means for doing so is appropriating a candidate's intended Twitter image and message for their own purposes. Whether candidates or parties of the future can control such independent efforts is questionable. However, the existence of bashtagging does suggest that, unlike broadcast or print media, power to shape messages is not subject to the elite control. Therefore, candidate and party electioneering on Twitter must recognize that this medium is not like traditional media and ultimately should not be treated as such.

Another interesting finding about the Twitter audience is the correlation between their emphases and those of the general public, as Jisue Lee et al.

226 Richard Davis

(Chapter 6) discovered. Retweets about candidates in South Korea's presidential elections paralleled the public's interest in those same candidates.

One of the earliest questions concerning the role of the Internet in politics had to do with the effect of gender on who participates and how they did so (Bimber 2000; Ono and Zovodny 2003). This question was particularly important given the initial dominance of men in the Internet generally, as well as the blogosphere and the Twitterverse particularly. However, over time, that gender imbalance has shifted both in the online audience as well as in politics generally. In the United States, the number of women using Twitter now outnumbers men and the number of female candidates and officeholders has dramatically increased.

Marion Just, Ann Crigler, and Rose Owen (Chapter 9) examined how gender affects candidate use of Twitter in US elections. They find some significant differences attributable to gender. Female candidates who are trailing their opponents are less likely to attack those opponents than are male candidates in the same electoral situation. Also, tweets from women were more likely to be retweeted than tweets from men and to be "favorited" by others. And, female candidate tweets demonstrated more diversity in the photos sent by tweets. In sum, there are some important distinctions in the way male and female candidates approach Twitter, as well as in the way their supporters interact with them via Twitter.

Conclusions about the Role of Twitter in Elections

This unique volume has brought together a diverse group of scholars who study the electoral role of Twitter in a variety of contexts and settings and from distinctive angles. The comparative perspective included herein has broadened this volume by allowing readers to examine Twitter's influence on parties, candidates, campaigns, and elections across diverse systems. No extant book does so.

As a result, we can see that Twitter is impacting electoral players and, in some cases, reshaping campaigns. Candidate campaigns and party organizations are utilizing Twitter for communication with at least some subsets of voters. Twitter is affecting journalistic news routines and approaches to news reporting. This new medium also is affecting ordinary citizens since, as Penney showed, it has become a medium for the expression of opinion through bashtagging that can distort a candidate's message.

At the same, Twitter may not be as influential as some expect. It may not be setting the media agenda, overturning journalistic objectivity, stimulating interactivity, or shaping electoral outcomes. Campaigns are still primarily unidirectional. Candidates and parties still view any campaign communication as their opportunity to broadcast rather than as an obligation to interact. And electoral structures have not been overthrown by this new medium. Instead, Twitter must operate within system contexts that may constrain or enhance its role.

Conclusion **227**

At the end of our analysis about Twitter, there are still critical questions about elections that we have raised through the presentation of these studies. One is the basic question of Twitter's future. Is it a novelty that will fade with 8-track tapes and mood lamps? Or has Twitter acquired a niche that promises a long future as a communications forum?

Another regards political engagement. Does Twitter increase electoral participation? Does it increase awareness of candidates, political knowledge, or voter turnout? Can it become a tool for greater civic engagement? Or does the political Twitter audience already hold high levels of civic engagement? Can a Twitter message of increased political involvement reach Twitter users who do not typically use Twitter for political purposes?

Will Twitter remain primarily a unidirectional medium that fosters candidate communication with voters, but limits voter communication with candidates? Under what circumstances could Twitter become a more interactive medium, particularly for major parties and candidates?

Still another concerns the role of journalists in covering campaigns and elections. Is Twitter gradually eroding the traditional model of journalistic objectivity? Will journalists seek to adapt their Twitter uses to conform to traditional journalistic roles or will they be overwhelmed by the expectations of Twitter in terms of opinion expression and alter those roles? If the latter, what will journalism become?

Yet another is the power of system context. Do certain political structures constrain Twitter's electoral role? For example, are parliamentary, party-based systems less susceptible to Twitter's influence than presidential, candidate-based systems with more emphasis on personal campaigning?

Can Twitter affect electoral outcomes? This is not an easy question to answer, particularly given the limited reach of Twitter among the electorate generally and the even smaller reach of the political Twitterverse. But, like Zeh, scholars should seek to determine the extent to which Twitter can affect conversion, reinforcement, and mobilization of voters.

Or, at a lower level, can Twitter at least become a major element in campaign strategy? Given its niche appeal, is Twitter capable of becoming important in a campaign seeking to reach large numbers of voters, particularly undecided ones, or is it confined to roles in communication with journalists and supporters?

There is no dearth of research questions for future researchers seeking to understand the role of Twitter in elections. We have sought to answer some of them and to raise more. We have attempted to highlight new research that is pushing the boundaries of our knowledge about Twitter, as well as to introduce scholars across the globe who are studying Twitter's political effects. In that sense, no academic book is really complete. But if we have stimulated others to continue our efforts, we are satisfied.

References

Bimber, B. 1999. The Internet and Citizen Communication With Government: Does the Medium Matter? *Political Communication* 16: 409–28.

Bimber, B. 2000. Measuring the Gender Gap on the Internet. *Social Science Quarterly* 81: 868–76.

Bode, L. and K.E. Dalrymple. 2014. Politics in 140 Characters or Less: Campaign Communication, Network Interaction, and Political Participation on Twitter. *Journal of Political Marketing*. Published online before print.

Davis, R. 1998. *The Web of Politics: The Internet's Impact on the American Political System*. New York: Oxford University Press.

Elin, L. and S. Davis. 2002. *Click-on Democracy: The Internet's Power to Change Political Apathy into Civic Action*. Boulder, CO: Westview Press.

Gainous, J. and K.M. Wagner. 2014. *Tweeting to Power: The Social Media Revolution in American Politics*. New York: Oxford University Press.

Margolis, M., D. Resnick, and C. Tu. 1997. Campaigning on the Internet: Parties and Candidates on the World Wide Web in the 1996 Primary Season. *The International Journal of Press/Politics* 2: 59–78.

Ono, H. and M. Zavodny. 2003. Gender and the Internet. *Social Science Quarterly* 84: 111–21.

Papacharissi, Z.A. 2010. *A Private Sphere: Democracy in a Digital Age*. Cambridge: Polity Press.

Park, C. 2013. Does Twitter Motivate Involvement in Politics? Tweeting, Opinion Leadership, and Political Engagement. *Computers in Human Behavior* 29: 1641–8.

Parmelee, J.H. and S.L. Bichard. 2012. *Politics and the Twitter Revolution: How Tweets Influence the Relationship Between Political Leaders and the Public*. Lanham, MD: Lexington Books.

Zukin, C., S. Keeter, and M. Andolina. 2006. *A New Engagement? Political Participation, Civic Life, and the Changing American Citizen*. New York: Oxford University Press.

INDEX

#AreYouBetterOff 161–2, 164–70
@mention 193, 196, 199, 201–2; *see also* @ user
@name 62; *see also* @user
@replies 175, 182
@reply 130; *see also* @replies
@user 3, 5, 92, 196
@username 114; *see also* @user
2012 (US) election 49, 52, 75–9, 162, 165, 168, 195; *see also* 2012 (US) presidential election
2012 (US) presidential election 45–6, 117, 159, 169, 207
2013 German parliamentary election campaign 27, 30
2014 election 64, 75, 78, 86, 126, 139
2014 European Elections 59; in Belgium 58, 60, 63, 223; in Italy 126–8, 132–4, 137–9

Adbusters 165, 167, 169
Agence Europe (European Union press agency) 63, 66
Ahn, Chul-soo 94, 98–102
ALDE 65–6
Americans for Prosperity 162
Annemans, Gerolf 68
API 32, 45, 62, 94, 117, 128
application programming interface (API) 45, 62; *see also* API
Axelrod, David 18, 21, 22, 25, 117, 120

Bak, Geun-hye 94, 98–103
Bak, Jung-hee 98

bashtagging 7, 159–62, 164–9, 225–6
BBC 59, 65
Belgian candidates 58, 60–9; Dutch-speaking 60–2, 65–9; Flemish 65–9; French-speaking 60–2, 65–9
Belgium 6, 57–69, 178, 210, 223; Brussels 60, 64; Flanders 58, 60–6, 69–70; Wallonia 58, 60–9
Bentivegna, Sara 7, 126, 225
Berliner Zeitung 32, 38; *see also* newspapers, German
Bettel, Xavier 213
Bishop, Timothy 195
Bloc Québécois 175
Bode, Leticia 6, 190, 224
Brauchli, Marcus 20
broadcast communication model 133, 138
Brüderle, Rainer 33
Buzzfeed 13, 14, 18–19, 45, 162

Canada 173–86, 224–5; elections 174–86
Canada Elections Act 176
Center for Information and Research on Civic Learning and Engagement (CIRCLE) 76–7, 79, 86
Center on Congress at Indiana University 76
challengers 78, 81–2, 84–7, 192
Chicago 13, 19, 25
Christian Democratic Party of Luxembourg (CVS) 211, 213, 216
Christian Democrats Union (CDU) 30–1, 33–7, 40

230 Index

Christian Social Union (CSU) 30–1, 33–7, 39–40
Citizens United decision 165
civic engagement 6, 75–81, 83–7, 223, 227
Clinton, Hillary 2
CNN 13, 16, 20
Coddington, Mark 6, 43
coding 5, 32, 62–3, 95–8, 145, 196–7
communication, political: in Canada 173–4, 177, 181; in Congress 203; in Europe 57–8, 63, 69, 223; in retweets 106; in SNS 106, 163–4; in South Korea 91, 93; in Twitter 7, 50, 52, 93, 203, 207–8, 219
communication: campaign 4, 62, 111, 142–3, 191, 225–6; candidate 222, 224, 227; constituent 191–2, 201, 224; interpersonal 92, 209; member 191–2; online 27, 145, 177, 190, 194, 201–2; two-way 210, 216–7, 219; unidirectional 115, 224–7; *see also* communication, political
Communist Party 210, 218
competitiveness 79, 82–3, 86, 144, 223
Congress: and Civic Engagement 76–8; Twitter use 6, 75–6, 115, 143–4, 190–5, 197–203, 210, 223–4
Conservative Party: in Canada 175, 179, 183–4; in Luxembourg 210
Conway, Bethany A. 7, 111, 224
Costello, Dick 43
Crigler, Ann N. 7, 141, 226
CSV 210, 213, 216–8
Culture Jam 167–8
culture jamming 159–60, 164–9

Davis, Richard 1, 222
Democrat 147, 152, 154, 196; Christian Democrat 30, 33, 211, 213, 216; civic engagement and tweets 76–82, 84–7; Social Democrats 30, 36, 213
Democratic National Committee (DNC) 112, 116–22
Democratic National Convention 162
Democratic Party (DP) 111, 116, 118, 126, 196; Christian Democratic Party 216; Free Democratic Party 30; New Democratic Party 175; *see also* Democrats
Der Spiegel 32
detournement 164
D'heer, Evelien 6, 57, 223
die tageszeitung 32, 38; *see also* newspapers, German

Die Welt 32, 38; *see also* newspapers, German
DOI (diffusion of innovation) 91–2
Dorsey, Jack 13

Eisenhower, General Dwight D. 111
electoral support 207–9, 212–16, 218–19
emotionalization 133–5, 139
Euranet 63, 66
Euronews 63
Europe (EU) 57–61, 63–66, 68–9, 126, 130, 135, 207; Europeanization 57–8, 69, 223
Europe Decides 58
European (EU) Commission 59, 61, 62, 65
European (EU) elections 57–63, 68, 126–8, 132, 135, 137, 178, 225; European elections in Belgium 58–69; *see also* 2014 European Elections
European Council 126
Europeanization 57–8, 69, 223
Evans, Heather 6, 75, 223

Facebook 62, 95, 209; compared to Twitter 1, 4, 30, 52, 90, 207
fact-checking 30, 46–8, 50
Fehrnstrom, Eric 17, 24, 117, 120
female (women) candidates 7, 78, 142–7, 150, 155, 226
Fenno, Richard 141–3, 154, 157
Five Stars Movement (M5S) 126–7, 129, 132–7, 139
Forza Italia (FI) 126
France 66, 210
Frankfurt School 163
Frankfurter Rundschau 32, 38; *see also* newspapers, German
Free Democratic Party (FDP) 30–1, 33, 36

gatekeeping 43, 49–50, 53
gender: and party 79, 141–7, 152–7, 212–4; and social media 142–5, 226; and Twitter/tweets 7, 82–3, 142–3, 146–50, 152, 154–5, 157, 226
Germany 27–32, 35, 40–1, 90, 93, 178, 208–10
Google 208, 212–13, 215–16, 218
Göring-Eckardt, Katrin 31, 33
Grassley, Chuck 200, 202
grassroots intermediaries 160–1, 170
Green Party (Greens): in Canada 175; in Germany 30–40; in Italy 135; in Luxembourg 213, 216–19

Gröhe, Hermann 31, 33
Gysi, Gregor 31, 33

Hamburger Abendblatt 32, 38; *see also* newspapers, German
Hamby, Peter 6, 13, 222
Hamilton, Lee 76–7
Harper, Stephen 179, 183–4
hashtags 3–5, 97, 131, 199–201, 213; hashtag debate 17, 59, 69; keywords 5, 92, 94; party use 131–2, 164, 168–9, 170, 195–6, 201, 217; promotional 135, 159–62, 164–8
Holtz-Bacha, Christina 1, 6, 27, 223
House of Commons 175–6
House, US 75–83, 86–7, 143–4, 196
hyperlinks 115, 196, 199; *see also* links
hypermedia campaigning 58

Ignatieff, Michael 179, 183–4
images, Twitter 3, 5, 51–3, 131, 145, 150–2
incumbency 78–9, 82–3, 86–7, 142, 208–9, 212–3
incumbents 78–87, 143, 190, 192, 194–5, 199; *see also* incumbency
individualization 177, 179, 182, 186
innovation 78, 131, 134, 173; diffusion of innovation (DOI) 91–3; tradition and 128, 137–9
Instagram 192
Internet: campaign use 5, 19, 22, 27–9, 40, 129, 215–16, 218, 225–6; public use 4–5, 167, 219, 223; and social media 57, 61, 211, 213, 215–16, 225
Italy 126–30, 135, 137, 178

Journal 210
journalism 13, 16, 22, 46, 50; Twitter 23, 43, 222
journalism, political 16, 44–6; humor 47–8; objectivity 46–9; Twitter's future in
Journalists, Twitter use 43–53; personal branding 49; gatekeeping 41, 49–50; *see also* journalism; journalism, political
Juncker, Jean-Claude 212–13
Just, Marion R. 1, 7, 141, 226

Kenski, Kate 7, 111, 224
Korean Gallup 98

LaBolt, Ben 18–19
Lassen, David 6, 190, 224
Layton, Jack 179, 182–4
Lee, Jisue 6, 90, 225

Liberal Party (Liberals) 175, 179, 183–4, 210, 213, 217
links 3, 49, 115, 131, 193, 213, 217; *see also* hyperlinks
Luxembourg 7, 208, 210–19, 225
Luxemburger Wort 210, 212

Marchetti, Rita 7, 126, 225
mass autocommunication 133
meme 52, 167–8
"meme warriors" 160, 167–9, 225
MEP 59, 62, 65, 66–8
Merk, Beate 31, 36
Merkel, Angela 31, 33, 35, 37–9
microblogging 1, 28–9, 43–4, 58, 91, 114, 207
Mitteldeutsche Zeitung 32, 38; *see also* newspapers, German
mobilization 40, 75, 112, 115, 133–4, 139, 157, 184
Molyneux, Logan 6, 43
Mon, Lorrie 6, 90
Moon, Jae-in, 94, 98–103
Mourão, Rachel R. 6, 43

National Election Commission in South Korea 91
NBC News 18, 21, 25
Netherlands 90, 93, 178
New Democratic Party (NDP) 175, 179, 182–4
New York Times 13–14, 18–22, 25–6
newspapers 19–21, 29, 64–5, 208, 210–12, 215–16, 218
newspapers, German 29, 30–5, 38
normalization 45, 53
Nürnberger Nachrichten 32, 38; *see also* newspapers, German

Obama, Barack: campaign 14, 19, 40, 90, 111–12, 115–22, 142; and Romney 17–20, 117–22, 154, 159, 162; on Twitter 1, 26, 40, 90, 115–22, 193, 224
Owen, Rose A. 7, 141, 226

Park, Sung Jae 6, 90
Parker, Ashley 13, 25
parliament 30, 35, 128, 175–6, 211, 213–14; Belgian 64–5, 68; Dutch 168; European 6, 58–9, 64, 68–9; German 27, 30; Luxembourgish 215, 218–19, 225; Moldovan 2; national 28, 208–9
participation, political 159, 181, 223
partisanship 16, 76, 80–7, 218, 222–3

232 Index

Penney, Joel 7, 159, 225–6
personalization 7, 135, 173–82, 185–6, 224–5
Pew Research Center 21, 143
Pew's Project for Excellence in Journalism 20
Pirate Party (Pirates) 5, 18, 20, 43, 213, 216–19, 225
Politico 13, 15–16, 45
privatization 177, 179, 182, 185
Promoted Trends 159–62, 164, 166, 169
public opinion polling 90–1, 93–4, 97–106
Python Twitter API 94

Québec 175, 183

Reeves, Rosser 111
Renzi, Matteo 126
repetition 111–22, 224; campaigning 111, 120–1; candidate use 116–22; consistency 112–13, 120–2; duplication 116–17, 120–2; satiation effect 112; social media 116–17; tedium effect 113; tweets 117–22
Republican 17, 162, 196; candidates 146–7, 152, 156; civic engagement and tweets 78–87
Republican National Committee (RNC) 16, 112, 116, 118–20, 161, 166
Republican Party 111, 116, 118, 156, 159
retweeting (RT) 5, 23, 36–8, 47–9, 181; in South Korea 90–100, 102–3, 106; in 2012 and 2014 US general election 116–19, 145, 147–8, 152–6
Rheinische Post 32, 38; *see also* newspapers, German
Romney, Mitt: campaign 13–14, 19–20, 24–5, 112, 118, 122, 159, 161–2, 165–6; and Obama 14, 17–20, 111–12, 116, 122, 154; on Twitter 24, 116–22, 161–2, 165–6
Rösler, Philipp 31, 33, 36
RTL 66, 68, 210
Rubio, Marco 2
Rucker, Philip 13–14
Ryu, Hohyon 6, 90

Sächsische Zeitung 32, 38; *see also* newspapers, German
Saenuri Party 98, 101
Sanders, Bernie 2
Schulz, Martin 59
screenshorting 52
Seibert, Steffen 31

Senate, US 75–6, 78, 83–7, 141–8, 154–6, 196
Situationists, French 165
Small, Tamara 7, 173, 225
Smith, Ben 14, 18
snark 24, 44, 48
Social Democratic Party (SPD) 30–40, 211, 213
social networking sites (SNS) 27–30, 90–1, 93, 113–15, 143, 150, 181
social system 92–3
South Korea 3, 98, 226; April 2012 general election 90–4, 106
Spiegel Online 32, 38–9; *see also Der Spiegel*
Staes, Bart 68
State of the Union address 21, 193
Steinbrück, Peer 33–40
Stevenson, Richard 22, 26
Stuttgarter Zeitung 32, 38; *see also* newspapers, German
"Super PAC" 162, 165
Supreme Court 21, 165

Tageblatt 210, 212
Tea Party 156
The Left (Die Linke) 30–1, 37–8
Thyssen, Marianne 68
Times 19, 25
Trittin, Jürgen 31, 33
Trump, Donald 2
tweeting, live 4, 50, 184
Twitter handle 62, 195; *see also* @user
Twitter presence: Impression Management 128, 134–8; Personal Marketing 128, 134–8; Re-intermediation 128, 134–8
Twitter Revolution 2

United MinJoo 98
University of Texas at Austin 43

Van Brempt, Kathleen 68
Van Overtveldt, Johan 67
Verdegem, Pieter 6, 57, 223
Verhofstadt, Guy 65–7
volunteerism 82, 84, 87
VRT 58, 65

Washington 14–16, 20, 25–6, 190
Washington Post, The 13, 15, 20, 165

YouTube 90, 142, 143, 192

Zeh, Reimar 6, 7, 27, 207, 223, 225, 227
Zeitung vum letzebuerger Vollek 210